STUDIES IN LABOUR
AND SOCIAL LAW

GENERAL EDITORS

BOB HEPPLE

Professor of English Law in the University of London, at University College

PAUL O'HIGGINS

Professor of Law in the University of London, at King's College; Fellow of Christ's College, Cambridge; and Member of the Royal Irish Academy

Partial Unemployment

The Regulation of Short-time Working in Britain

ERIKA M. SZYSZCZAK

MANSELL

LONDON AND NEW YORK

First published 1990 by Mansell Publishing Limited
A Cassell imprint
Villiers House, 41/47 Strand, London WC2N 5JE, England
125 East 23rd Street, Suite 300, New York 10010, USA

© Erika M. Szyszczak 1990. The Statutory Instruments reproduced in Appendix C
are British Crown Copyright.

British Library Cataloguing in Publication Data

Szyszczak, Erika M.
  Partial unemployment: the regulation of short-time
  working in Britain. – (Studies in labour and social law.)
  1. Great Britain. Personnel. Lay-offs & Short time
  working
  I. Title   II. Series
  344.10412596

  ISBN 0–7201–2067–5
  ISBN 0–7201–2068–3 Pbk

Library of Congress Cataloging-in-Publication Data

Szyszczak, Erika M.
    Partial unemployment: the regulation of short-time working in
  Britain/Erika M. Szyszczak.
        p.   cm. – (Studies in labour and social law)
    Includes bibliographical references.
    ISBN 0–7201–2067–5 ISBN 0–7201–2068–3 (pbk.)
    1. Layoff systems – Law and legislation – Great Britain.   2. Part-
  time employment – Law and legislation – Great Britain.   3. Insurance,
  Unemployment – Law and legislation – Great Britain.   I. Title.
  II. Series.
  KD3110.S99   1990
  344.41′01137 – dc20
  [344.1041137]   90–30363
                                                               CIP

Set in 10/12 pt Linotron Baskerville
by Fakenham Photosetting Limited, Fakenham, Norfolk
Printed and bound in Great Britain by Biddles Ltd, Guildford and King's Lynn

CONTENTS

For Lorna
and the memory of Peter

Preface

Yosser: Gizza job . . .
Malloy: I haven't got any jobs. There are no jobs here any more. For one
reason or another. I laid off fourteen men yesterday. I grew up with some
of them.

Alan Bleasdale, *Boys from the Blackstuff*, 1983.

The recession of the 1970s and 1980s focused the attention of a generation of
politicians, policy makers and academics, as well as our popular culture, on
the nature and significance of work shortages. Much debate and comment has
passed and been exchanged on the question of how to reduce unemployment,
whether by stimulating economic growth or by reducing working time so that
available work can be shared around. In particular the question arises of how
to reduce the rate of redundancies and ameliorate the impact of redundancies
and lay-offs and yet allow sufficient flexibility in the labour market.

Less attention has been given, however, to one particular economic and
social problem which constantly recurs in examining moves between employment and unemployment. It is the specific problem addressed in this book, of
how to regulate and compensate for partial unemployment caused by short-
time working and lay-offs. The media regularly report these occurrences[1] but
the legal response to these situations is not so easy to define, report or comment
upon. Yet short-time working and lay-offs are not new phenomena. Economic
boom and depression has accompanied the development of industrialized
countries for more than a century and the cyclicality of employment has
always given rise to such problems.[2] Furthermore, partial unemployment may
arise at any time as a result of natural disasters, mechanical failure or strike
action which cause temporary stoppages of work.

Partial unemployment is not a familiar term in British legal or social policy
language.[3] It is a title adopted from the Continental classification of the
subject. An alternative title would be 'Compensation for Short-time Working',
the term used in the United Kingdom and the United States. But this is rather
a narrow description of the complex issues which arise out of the regulation of
short-time working and lay-offs. Compensation both for job loss on the
termination of the contract of employment arising out of an unfair dismissal or a
redundancy situation and also for a reduction of earnings while the contract of
employment *subsists* has become a prominent feature of modern statutory

employment rights. Partial unemployment, on the other hand, raises wider issues and may be seen as a discrete legal and social concept. The term 'Compensation for Short-time Working' fails to capture the problems arising from a temporary suspension of the employment relationship and does not tackle the more fundamental questions of whether an employer has the *legal* right to reduce working time and how far working time can be reduced without destroying the employment relationship.

Given the wide range of causes of work shortages and the differences in duration, form and effects, one would expect different and flexible responses to be taken by policy makers to the various situations. Indeed, much of the legal response has been *ad hoc*, state intervention being conditioned by short-term responses to immediate problems such as economic recession, with little consideration of the interaction of the different forms of legal regulation of the long-term policy implications of the responses.

This book begins with an overview of the central policy questions which dominate the regulation of partial unemployment. In particular Chapter 1 addresses the issue of why the common law approach cannot survive in a modern industrial setting and why there is a need for employers to compensate for partial unemployment as part of a wider employment strategy of minimizing long-run labour costs. This chapter also examines some of the factors which give rise to the recognition by the state of the need to intervene in the labour market and provide welfare provision during times of economic and political crisis.

The role of the contract of employment plays a central part in the book. In Chapters 2 and 3 it is argued that contractual principles provide the historical link and the continuity in the legal regulation of partial unemployment. These chapters explain how the central role ascribed to contract provides some flexibility, allowing employers to adapt to work shortages, but fails to provide the necessary legal and financial protection to workers. It also considers why the state was obliged to assume a more directive role in the regulation of partial unemployment. In particular the growth of statutory employment protection rights dependent upon minimum periods of continuous employment has placed greater emphasis upon the desirability of maintaining the employment relationship at the *formal* level. Since the consequences of partial unemployment are closely related to many of the employment protection rights (such as statutory guarantee payments, redundancy payments and unfair dismissal, sex and race discrimination compensation) partial unemployment has assumed a new and technical meaning. The statutory guarantees have not provided an effective remedy, however, partly because the Conservative governments since 1979 have not built upon the 'floor of rights' protection but have sought to dismantle that floor as part of their 'deregulatory' policies[4] and partly because the legal and social issues arising from partial unemployment were not addressed in either a rational or efficient way in the 1960s and 1970s.

Chapter 3 thus ends with a discussion of the retreat to the common law forced on employees. They have had to utilize contractual and equitable remedies in order to challenge deductions from pay, reductions in working time and the variation of contractual terms which may occur as a result of partial unemployment.

Chapters 4 and 5 trace what is still a continued tension, between the state's desire to maintain an abstentionist role in employment law and its obligation to assume an interventionist role during times of political crisis (such as the two world war periods) or economic crisis (such as the recession experienced in the 1970s and early 1980s). A second purpose of these chapters is to highlight three areas of employment law normally regarded as marginal. Thus detailed attention is given to the operation of the statutory guarantee payment provisions, the redundancy lay-off payments provisions and Special Employment Measures.

Most of the research was carried out between 1983 and 1985 at a time when one Special Employment Measure, the Temporary Short-time Working Compensation Scheme (TSTWCS), dominated compensation for short-time working, particularly in the manufacturing sector of industry. The TSTWCS was a big scheme: it is estimated that over one million jobs threatened by redundancy were covered by the TSTWCS and that over three million people were placed upon short-time working in order to avoid redundancies.[5] The sheer size of the scheme eclipsed other forms of compensation for short-time working and therefore the main focus of the project was to monitor the application of this scheme. Empirical research was conducted through interviews and our own surveys on the operation of TSTWCS within individual firms. In addition, the administration of the scheme by the Department of Employment was studied as well as the general impact of the scheme upon collective bargaining, individual employment rights and its impact upon the labour market in the light of its declared aim of *averting* redundancies.

In fact it proved difficult to monitor the day-to-day workings of the TSTWCS. The Department of Employment would not divulge the names of individual firms in receipt of the subsidy since it regarded the recipients as 'clients'. Equally it was impossible to gain access to the internal rules and regulations which governed the more precise administration of the scheme.[6] Hardly any 'legal' issues emerged over the application of the scheme other than a few complaints to the Parliamentary Commissioner for Administration. Indeed there was little 'legal' material for the lawyer to get her hands on. Although the TSTWCS would seem to have added even more complexity to the web of regulatory measures governing partial unemployment the scheme was welcomed as a simple replacement of these complex measures providing a single and financially advantageous scheme to compensate short-time working. Since we were obliged to search for recipients of the subsidy we were able to draw parallels with firms in similar situations who were not receiving the subsidy, and one factor which emerged was the lack of legal standing for competitors who were not in a position to declare redundancies but felt aggrieved that similar firms were receiving the subsidy. While most trade unions interviewed within the firms receiving the subsidy were happy to go along with TSTWCS application since it represented a 'last ditch' attempt to save ailing sectors of industry, the consequences of suspending guaranteed week agreements were not fully comprehended during the consultations over implementing short-time working. In terms of the impact of the TSTWCS on collective bargaining this may have had significant consequences, particularly over the development of collective bargaining after the scheme ended. This seems particularly important in the light of our empirical work revealing that the scheme did not fulfil its aim of averting redundancies; it merely postponed them.[7]

Although very few 'traditional' legal issues arose during the operation of the scheme this does not mean that legal rights or interests were unaffected. The scheme itself did not provide any legal means whereby aggrieved applicants or competitors or trade unions could air their grievances. Chapter 5 suggests some ways in which research in the area of Public Law might be utilized in order to subject 'leaflet law' to more detailed legal scrutiny. Although Special Employment Measures have been reduced by the Conservative government, 'leaflet law' is still used in areas which affect the size and composition of the labour market, particularly in the areas of training and 'ameliorative' social security measures. And although these schemes will create their own set of legal problems, the study of the TSTWCS provides some insights into the nature of the legal problems and rights which may require legal scrutiny. What does emerge is that the traditional focus of labour law may need to be widened to encompass economic measures which regulate the labour market and the interaction of labour law and social security law.

As this book was nearing completion the Department of Employment issued a Consultative Document announcing the abolition of the National Dock Labour Scheme.[8] This scheme had its origins in the Second World War, marking the end of casual labour in the docks and providing one of the most comprehensive industry-wide forms of protection against the consequences of partial unemployment. The abolition of the National Dock Labour Scheme in the Dock Work Act 1989 might lead one to question whether the idea of protection against partial unemployment is out-dated and at odds with the current government's attitude towards the (de)regulation of the labour market. Today the buzz words are 'flexibility', 'privatization' of social security risks and the 'enterprise economy'. An important factor which emerges from a historical study of partial unemployment, however, is that work shortages will always occur whatever form of political and economic philosophy governs the operation of the labour market. While large-scale economic depressions exacerbate the problems of partial unemployment, for some industries prone to strike action or sensitive to production or market changes or climatic conditions[9] partial unemployment is a fact of life. Chapter 6 therefore examines the different ways in which partial unemployment is regulated in other industrialized countries. These responses range from the use of general social security schemes to finance the compensation for short-time working to the use of special funds to cover this particular social risk. Chapter 6 also examines the concept of worksharing, in its historical context and also in its modern civil rights context. These two themes show how worksharing may help to cope with work shortages and can also be a means of restructuring employment rights and introducing the principle of non-discrimination in the allocation of available work. The chapter ends with a discussion of the present government's attitudes towards the restructuring of the labour market: the policies and politics of 'deregulation' and 'flexibility'.

Drawing upon these policy proposals and the EC Commission's labour market initiatives, as well as the comparative material, the final chapter suggests ways in which the regulation of partial unemployment in Britain could be rationalized. The conclusions from the book are that the duplication of finance and the complexities found in the present regulation of partial unemployment result in inefficiencies and inequities, leaving many workers unprotected. To remedy this situation it is proposed that partial unemployment should be located as one of the employment protection risks covered during the *subsistence* of the contract of employment. The present myriad of compensation mechanisms should be streamlined by the creation of a special Short-time Working Fund, mirroring the system whereby other reasons for a reduction in earnings are compensated, namely statutory sick pay and maternity pay, by the payment and administration of short-time working compensation by employers, the payments being reimbursed through the National Insurance system. Short-time working creates more complex issues than the statutory sick pay and maternity pay schemes and therefore various exemptions and safeguards would be necessary in order to administer the scheme effectively.

NOTES

1. Although 'lay-offs' are often taken to mean redundancies or dismissals in the popular understanding of the term.

2. See Beveridge, W.H., *Unemployment: A Problem of Industry*, (London, Longmans, Green and Co., 1909).

3. Cf. the use made of the term in Chapter 3 of Ogus, A. and Barendt, E. *The Law of Social Security*, (London, Butterworths, 1988).

4. The financial aspects of partial unemployment have also been affected by the twin policy of cutting back in the area of public expenditure on social security provision.

5. Richards, J. and Szyszczak, E., 'Short-time Working in Great Britain: Historical Developments and the Decline of Unemployment Benefit for Short-time Compensation', Short-time Working Project, Working Paper No. 15, Canterbury, University of Kent (1985).

6. Details were provided in DE Leaflet PL 692. See also Freedland, M.R. 'Leaflet Law: The Temporary Short-time Working Compensation Scheme', 9 *Industrial Law Journal*, pp. 254–8 (1980).

7. See Metcalf, D. and Richards, J., 'Subsidised Worksharing, Redundancies and Employment Adjustment: A Study of the Temporary Short-time Working Compensation Scheme', Short-time Working Project, Working Paper No. 22, Canterbury, University of Kent, 1985; Metcalf, D. 'Employment subsidies and Redundancy', in Blundell, R. and Walker, I. (eds) *Unemployment, Search and Labour Supply*, (Cambridge, Cambridge University Press, 1986).

8. *Employment in the Ports: The Dock Labour Scheme*, Cm 664 (1989).

9. Although inclement weather is usually a reason for partial unemployment, favourable weather conditions may also affect production or create changes in market conditions. For example, while we were researching the ESRC project the mild winter weather of 1984/5 was blamed for the decision to put 200 workers on a three-day week in January 1985 and to lengthen the Christmas holiday at the Heinz baked beans factory in Norfolk (*The Times*, 20 December 1984).

Acknowledgements

The initial research for this book was carried out on a project commissioned by the Economic and Social Research Council Monitoring of Labour Law Panel. I am grateful to Professor David Metcalf, Professor of Industrial Relations at the London School of Economics, and Dr John Richards (now at Bedford Modern School) for allowing me to use economic and statistical data derived from the project in this book. A research grant from the British Academy enabled me to update some of the initial data for publication. Many people provided advice and information on the original research project and on a draft of this book. In particular Professor Bob Hepple and Bob Simpson were extremely generous with the time they spent reading the draft and providing new ideas and insights which have been incorporated into the text. While they have improved the final version of the work they are not responsible for its inadequacies or for the ideas expressed. Finally, thanks are extended to Richard Disney, for his intellectual stimulation, criticisms and, above all, his own commitment to domestic worksharing.

Abbreviations

ACAS	Advisory Conciliation and Arbitration Service
AEU	Amalgamated Engineering Union
ASTMS	Association of Scientific, Technical, and Managerial Staffs
ASWDKW	Amalgamated Society of Wire Drawers and Kindred Workers
AUEW	Amalgamated Union of Engineering Workers
CHDE	Coppersmiths, Heating and Domestic Engineers
CSEU	Confederation of Shipbuilding and Engineering Union
CSMTS	Card Setting Machine Tenters' Society
EDTP	Employment Development and Training Programme
EEF	Engineering Employers' Federation
EETPU	Electrical, Electronic, Telecommunications and Plumbing Union
FTATU	Furniture, Timber and Allied Trades Union
GMBATU	General and Municipal Boilermakers and Allied Trades Union
GMWU	General and Municipal Workers' Union
NALGO	National and Local Government Officers Association
NJCMVRRI	National Joint Council for the Motor Vehicle Retail and Repair Industry
NUFLAT	National Union of Footwear, Leather and Allied Trades
NUGMW	National Union of General and Municipal Workers
NUSMW	National Union of Sheet Metal Workers
SOGAT	Society of Graphical and Allied Trades
TGWU	Transport and General Workers' Union
TSTWCS	Temporary Short-time Working Compensation Scheme
UCATT	Union of Construction, Allied Trades and Technicians
USDAW	Union of Shop Distributive and Allied Workers

1

Introduction

THE ISSUES

Partial unemployment is the situation where an employer and employee are bound by a contract of employment but there is either a total absence of work available and the employees are 'laid off' or there is a shortage of work and the employees are working less than normal hours. The work shortage may arise as a result of many factors and may take different forms across different industries. There may be cyclical trade depressions in either the economy as a whole or in particular industries. There may be seasonal slack periods of work; a temporary market failure, or a temporary dislocation in production may arise as a result of inclement weather, a mechanical failure or industrial action. These incidents may occur within the firm or they may arise outside the firm but have a direct bearing upon the operations of the firm.

In the United States, the term 'lay-off' usually connotes an ending of the employment relationship with the prospect of re-hiring if the situation improves. The legal and conceptual issues are complicated in British law. While termination of the contract of employment with re-engagement does occur[1] other forms of lay-off and short-time working are utilized where the contract of employment is technically still subsisting and the question arises as to what rights and obligations arise in the continuing employment relationship.

In contrast to some industrialized states Britain has not adopted a coherent policy towards the regulation of partial unemployment arising as a result of lay-offs and short-time working.[2] Instead, partial unemployment has been addressed in an *ad hoc* way. This is surprising since partial unemployment is not new and the Ford dispute of 1988 showed that with the increasing interdependence of manufacturing, controlled by multinational companies, a dislocation in production may have repercussions across a wide range of different but interlocking production units both at home and abroad.[3] The focus of this book is to explain how such a complex system of handling partial unemployment came about, interpreting the policy issues underlying the various forms of regulation as well as commenting upon alternative ways of regulating and compensating for partial unemployment.

The issue of partial unemployment raises four central policy questions. First, should employers have the right to impose a lay-off or reduce the working week and, if so, in what circumstances and on what terms? Secondly, should partial unemployment be compensated? If so, the third question is, by whom? Should the state provide comprehensive social insurance; is there a duty upon employers or trade unions to shoulder some or all of the burden; or should individual workers bear the consequences? The fourth question is of more recent origin and has wider policy implications: which employees should bear the incidence of short-time working?

The Right to Lay-off Workers or Impose Short-time Working

The state has intervened in modern times in order to regulate the termination of the employment relationship. However, the right to lay-off workers or vary the contract of employment still rests within the domain of contract law rather than statutory regulation. Chapter 2 traces the historical evolution of the right to lay-off workers. Of particular concern is the way the common law adapted the simple 'wage–work' bargain to accommodate a wider duty of reciprocity by obliging the employer to provide work or wages in order to maintain the employment relationship. Chapter 3 goes on to analyse modern developments to the contract of employment, in particular the interrelationship of common law principles with the statutory employment protection rights relating to the termination of the employment relationship. As we shall see, while the contract of employment remains a highly individualistic affair, the employer no longer retains total control over the right to lay-off or impose short-time working since the *consequences* of such work reductions are within the ambit of statutory regulation.

Should Partial Unemployment Be Compensated?

Originally the common law found difficulty in accommodating the idea of paying wages to an employee when there was no work available. Indeed, right into this century some people continued to express their abhorrence to the idea of paying a worker 'for doing nothing': the worker should take the good times with the bad.[4] It was recognized that if an employer was to retain an interest in skilled labour she would have to undertake a legal duty to maintain the employment relationship by providing either work or wages. This idea of a guaranteed wage found its way into collective bargaining, particularly in the post-1945 period, when the state actively encouraged such agreements. However, partial unemployment has not been adequately regulated by the use of contract or collective rights and the state has openly recognized the need to compensate partial unemployment by more public measures. The major state contribution was the development of a comprehensive system of social security and this scheme was used regularly in the inter-war years as a means of compensating short-time working. In more recent years the state has imposed mandatory duties upon employers to provide compensation for partial unemployment by providing a redundancy payment for certain instances of prolonged lay-off and short-time working and secondly through the use of statutory guarantee payments. Finally, the 1970s saw open acknowledgment of the need to compensate short-time working through the use of employment subsidies such as the Temporary Short-time Working Compensation Scheme. Thus for most of this century there has been recognition that partial unemployment should be compensated. This leads us to ask why this should be so and why should the state encourage employers to develop more than a minimal employment relationship?

Compensation for partial unemployment arising from a statutory guarantee payment, a redundancy payment or compensation for unfair dismissal are relatively new forms of statutory employment protection arising from the 'floor of rights' package introduced by successive governments in the sixties and seventies. These rights comprise compensation for job loss, as well as introducing a measure of security of earnings while the contract of employment subsists. Various explanations have been put forward for the reasons and the content of the modern statutory employment rights. For some commentators the rights are an acknowledgment of the weakness of collective bargaining as a means of ensuring a consistently high standard of protection for all workers.[5] Others see the rights as an acknowledgment of property rights in a job; or alternatively as an overall trend towards corporatist control.[6] Even before the introduction of these statutory guarantees, however, employers had recognized the need to offer more than the simple wage–work bargain to employees if efficient wage bargains were to be struck. Indeed, as we shall see in Chapter 2, even the common law acknowledged the right of workers paid by results to be given the opportunity to work in order to receive wages, and the post-1945 period saw the acceptance by employers of collective bargaining over guaranteed wage agreements.

Labour economics offers us some theories as to why sophisticated contracts of employment emerge.[7] The recognition of the need to compensate for partial unemployment is part of the wider employment strategy of minimizing long-run labour costs. Although varying labour input with demand appears to maximize profits in the short run, under certain circumstances a strategy of partial unemployment may reduce turnover costs and maintain higher worker productivity. Laying-off workers or replacing workers who have left the firm involves many costs to the employer: in particular, costs involved in hiring, training and administration. Some firms are able to rely upon a high turnover of casual labour to carry out all or certain tasks and so do not need to enhance the wage–work bargain. These firms hire and fire at will. Usually this kind of work will be unskilled and require little or no training. It may often be seasonal work and will often be carried out by young people. These job characteristics are not always present in such circumstances: weak employment contracts may also be found in skilled occupations and occupations which are relatively well paid. Such occupations are to be found in the construction, vehicle manufacturing and the old 'Fleet Street' style printing industries. In this kind of occupation, workers can develop an attachment to a particular local industry rather than just one employer. Okun argues that four factors are usually necessary for this situation to occur.[8] First, there must be several local firms in the industry. Secondly, the firms must have extremely variable demands for labour. Thirdly, the workers' skill must be general, in the sense that it is easily transferable across firms within the industry. Fourthly, the individual worker's skill must be recognized either through agreements developed by employer or unions in the industry or perhaps by state recognition procedures; for example, the provision of training courses or the granting of professional qualifications.

Not all firms or industries are able to rely upon weak employment contracts in this way. Competition within the labour market leads to a situation where theoretically workers and employers are constantly searching to improve their position. To reduce the risk of losing workers or failing to attract enough skilled workers, employers find it worthwhile to enter into what labour economists define as 'explicit contracts'. This is where employers assume binding contracts for a specified period of time about some aspects of the employment package. Compensation for partial unemployment may be one of these aspects. This explains why many firms guarantee an annual salary and why collective bargaining over guaranteed week agreements is found in skilled occupations prone to temporary fluctuations in demand.

It is perhaps easier to envisage the process as a game of bluff. The employer has to gauge the minimum amount of insurance and protection she should offer a worker in order to retain the worker's skills while allowing the firm to remain competitive in the labour market. If we accept the idea that most workers are 'risk averse' and cannot easily obtain social insurance protection, they will opt for an employer who can satisfy their chosen trade-off of wage protection against average wage level and will be prepared to stay with the employer rather than chance their luck by constantly moving to where work is better paid but perhaps without the wider guarantees. Firms, on the other hand, are able to offer this insurance so long as they are not 'risk averse' and have access to the capital markets in order to provide the necessary insurance guarantees to workers. Firms are in competition with one another and therefore they must strike the most efficient wage bargain in order not only to remain viable but also to maximize profits. This explains why limitations are put upon the length and amount of employment guarantees and why some absences from work are compensated and others are not. The use of 'explicit contracts' creates rigidities in the labour market and may lead to an immediate short-term increase in costs to the firm.

In addition to 'explicit contracts', labour economists also identify the use of 'implicit contracts'. These may be found in conjunction with 'explicit contracts' or may be used by some firms instead of 'explicit contracts'. 'Implicit contracts' are used where the firm does not want to commit itself too explicitly to future guarantees of work or wages. Thus the firm attempts to recruit workers and encourages them to stay with the firm by making statements about the future nature of employment that are not binding. By making such statements, however, the firm is risking its reputation as a viable employer and attractor and retainer of skilled workers if the statements do in fact turn out to be wrong.

Theories of 'explicit' and 'implicit' contracts together with changing political and social expectations help provide some explanations as to why employers have come to accept that partial unemployment should be compensated. What then of the state? Why should it also assume responsibility for compensating partial unemployment? Throughout this century the state has openly acknowledged its responsibility to provide public social insurance for a wide variety of social risks and most prominently for unemployment, particularly for those workers who have been in work and have paid National Insurance contributions. From fairly early on in the development of the social security scheme a distinction emerged between partial unemployment and long-term unemployment and this distinction is still prevalent.[9] The recognition of the need to compensate partial unemployment is also seen in the state's intervention in the labour market in the 1970s and early 1980s in the form of employment subsidies. One of the reasons for this intervention was to control the unemployment statistics, to prevent temporary lay-offs and large-scale redundancies from swelling the number of people registering as unemployed. In addition, the state recognized the need to keep firms viable, to conserve training and skills and to prevent the knock-on effects that large-scale plant closures would have in local communities. Thus we can conclude that the recognition of the need to compensate for partial unemployment is not altogether motivated by altruistic concerns of the employer or the state over workers' welfare but forms part of a wider goal of revising expectations in the labour market.

On Whom Should the Cost of Partial Unemployment Fall?

At common law, until the Court of Appeal ruling in *Devonald* v. *Rosser and Sons*,[10] the burden of partial unemployment was borne by individual workers.

There is evidence of worksharing occurring within particular trades; work-sharing bringing with it the idea that work shortages might be borne by the local community as a whole rather than specific individuals.[11] The late nineteenth century saw Friendly Societies and trade unions developing systems of private unemployment insurance in trades prone to cyclical unemployment. The unemployment benefit was financed from workers' insurance contributions. The reasons why the state intervened to introduce a system of public social security are complex. Classical economic theory would argue that such interventions arise as a result of market failure. However, we find that the state social security scheme tended to substitute for, rather than complement, the private social security schemes. Indeed some occupations such as cotton spinning opposed the introduction of the state scheme[12] and private occupational schemes funded by a mixture of employer and employee contributions are still in evidence long after the state scheme was established.[13] Alternative theories have suggested that a comprehensive system of state social security was introduced to bring into state control the insurance contributions from workers and employers to enable the state to raise revenue.[14]

The widespread use and perceived abuse of social security to finance partial unemployment during the inter-war years motivated the state to shift some of the financial burden of partial unemployment on to individual employers. Several reasons were put forward for this change in policy: to prevent the distortion of unemployment statistics, to reduce public expenditure and to prevent cross-subsidization of the financing of partial unemployment. These issues are discussed and analysed in Chapter 4.

Paradoxically, in the recent recession threats of high and long-term unemployment led to the state once again subsidizing compensation for partial unemployment through employment subsidies. This happened against a general policy of attempting to reduce public expenditure and brought criticisms of unfair competition from other European Community states and firms not eligible for the subsidy. This policy received criticism also from the House of Commons Public Accounts Committee which questioned the rationale and efficacy of such schemes.[15]

In addition to the state subsidy of compensation for partial unemployment employers may bear the costs of providing such compensation. In the case of collectively agreed guaranteed week agreements these are often limited in time and amount of guaranteed pay. The statutory scheme of guaranteed payments is also of a limited amount and duration. Employers do not necessarily bear the full costs of these payments since they may be offset against profits or tax liability or passed on to the consumer. For some time the state partially reimbursed redundancy payments through the Redundancy Fund. Such claims on the fund were not 'experience-rated'; that is, employers were not penalized for drawing upon the fund, and the same objections to cross-subsidization raised against the use of the social security scheme to finance partial unemployment compensation were raised against the use of the Redundancy Fund. Subsequently section 27 of the Wages Act 1986 abolished redundancy rebates for employers employing more than ten people, and section 7 of the Employment Act 1989 totally abolishes redundancy rebates.

Which Employees Should Bear the Incidence of Work Shortages?

This question may be put in different ways. Is there a duty upon the employer to minimize work shortages? If so, to whom is the duty owed? To individual workers, to trade unions, the state, society in general? Is it a substantive legal right, or merely a procedural right, or only a moral obligation to avoid work shortages where possible? Or is there a duty to allocate the available work among some or all of the workforce? Added to this is a supplementary question. Should the risk of partial unemployment lie where it falls or should certain categories of workers be protected from full or partial unemployment because they have particular skills or long-service records with the firm which should be rewarded? There is historical evidence of accepted worksharing patterns[16] and the use of employment subsidies in recent years has also facilitated worksharing. It would seem, however, that employers have no special duty to minimize work shortages or to implement worksharing.[17] The question of worksharing has assumed significance in debates emerging from the United States where blacks, other ethnic minority groups and women have entered the labour market in increasing numbers and have sought to use the law to challenge the discriminatory impact of established industrial relations practice. Central issues have been questions such as whether workers with greater seniority should be protected against lay-off and job loss or whether the dismissal of part-time or temporary workers before the application of the customary 'last in first out' procedure amounts to an act of discrimination. Such questions are also being asked in the legal forum in Britain[18] and in Europe[19] although the amount of litigation and debate is by no means as extensive as that of the United States.[20]

Linked to the question of worksharing is a wider question not specifically addressed in the limited and individualistic discourse of British employment law.[21] This is the issue of whether there is a wider duty upon the state to encourage worksharing by allowing people *without* work access to the available work.[22] Most of the Western European states have considered the possibility of legislated structural changes in working time as one way of dealing with high unemployment rates and the European Community has been at the forefront of a labour market policy aimed at making what is presently viewed as marginal or vulnerable work more attractive. The hope is that people will then move from full-time secure positions into such positions as part-time work, thus introducing some flexibility into the labour market. These initiatives have not had a warm reception from the member states of the European Community who have continued to follow conservative and orthodox economic policies. The United Kingdom government in particular has consistently opposed undertaking such a duty.[23] Instead, the move in Britain has been towards promoting an 'enterprise culture' with attempts to deregulate the employment relationship by restricting some of the employment protection rights in order to introduce flexibility into the labour market. The issue of whether this move towards 'flexibility' is a new phenomenon has generated some debate. Pollert, for example, argues against the conventional wisdom by pointing out that issues of flexibility in the workforce and attempts to segregate the labour market should be seen as part of a longer historical process of maintaining managerial discretion and prerogative in organizing the labour market.[24] These issues are discussed in greater detail in Chapter 6.

NOTES

1. See *Fitzgerald* v. *Hall Russell and Co. Ltd.* [1969] 3 All ER 1140; Freedland, M.R. *The Contract of Employment*, (Oxford, Clarendon Press, 1976) at p. 96 ff.

2. See Best, F. and Mattesich, J., 'Short-time Compensation Systems in California and Europe', 103 *Monthly Labor Review*, No. 7 pp. 13–22 (1980); Industrial Relations Services, 'International Short-time and Lay-offs', *European Industrial Relations Review and Report No. 111*, pp. 15–19 (April 1983); MaCoy, R. and Morand, M.J., *Short-time Compensation: A Formula for Work Sharing*, (New York, Pergamon Press, 1984); Emerson, M., 'Regulation or Deregulation of the Labour Market', 32 *European Economic Review*, pp. 775–817 (1988).

3. See *The Independent*, 'Ford UK Strike Casts Shadow over Europe', 9 February 1988 and 'Integration of Ford Plants Speeds Lay-offs in Europe', 12 February 1988.

4. See the discussion of *Browning* v. *Crumlin Valley Collieries Ltd.* [1926] 1 KB 522 in Chapters 2 and 3 and the views of Sachs, E., *The Law of Employment: A Summary of the Rights of Employers and Employees*, (London, Pitman, 1947) at p. 22.

5. See Szyszczak, E., 'Employment Protection and Social Security' in Lewis, R. (ed) *Labour Law in Britain*, (Oxford, Basil Blackwell, 1986). Contrast the view of Dickens, L., 'Falling through the Net: Employment Change and Worker Protection', 19 *Industrial Relations Journal*, pp. 139–53 (1988), where she criticizes the role played by the legislative framework of upholding the preference for collective bargaining and thereby relegating the role of legal regulation. Cf. Hakim, C., 'Employment Rights: A Comparison of Part-time and Full-time Employees', 18 *Industrial Law Journal*, pp. 69–83 (1989); Disney, R. and Szyszczak, E.M., 'Part-Time Work: Reply to Catherine Hakim', 18 *Industrial Law Journal*, pp. 223–8 (1989).

6. See *inter alia*: Clark, J. and Wedderburn, Lord, 'Modern Labour Law: Problems, Functions and Policies', in Wedderburn, Lord, Lewis, R. and Clark, J. (eds) *Labour Law and Industrial Relations: Building on Kahn-Freund* (Oxford, Clarendon Press, 1983); Lewis, R. 'Collective Labour Law', in Bain, G.S. (ed) *Industrial Relations in Britain*, (Oxford, Basil Blackwell, 1983); Hepple, B., 'Individual Labour Law', *ibid.*; Collins, H., 'Capitalist Discipline and Corporatist Law', 11 *Industrial Law Journal*, pp. 78–93 and 170–7 (1982).

7. For a clear account of these issues see Hamermesh, D.S. and Rees, A.R., *The Economics of Work and Pay*, (New York, Harper and Row, 4th edn, 1988).

8. Okun, A.M., *Prices and Quantities*, (Oxford, Basil Blackwell, 1981) at p. 82.

9. Beveridge, W.H., *Unemployment: A Problem of Industry*, (London, Longmans, Green and Co., 1909); Harris, J., *Unemployment and Politics*, (Oxford, Oxford University Press, 1972).

10. (1906) 2 KB 728.

11. See Whiteside, N., 'Welfare Legislation and the Unions during the First World War', 23 *Historical Journal*, pp. 857–74 (1980); Turner, H.A., *Trade Union Growth, Structure and Policy*, (London, Allen and Unwin, 1962).

12. See Whiteside, N. *ibid.*

13. Gilson, M.B. and Riches, E.J., 'Employers' Additional Unemployment Benefit Schemes in Great Britain', 21 *International Labour Review*, pp. 348–94 (1930).

14. See Disney, R., 'Unemployment Insurance in Britain', in Creedy, J. (ed) *The Economics of Unemployment in Britain*, (London, Butterworths, 1981); 'Theorising the Welfare State: The Case of Unemployment Insurance in Britain', 11 *Journal of Social Policy*, pp. 33–57 (1982); Deacon, A., 'Systems of Interwar Unemployment Relief', in Glynn, S. and Booth, A. (eds) *The Road to Full Employment*, (London, Allen and Unwin, 1987).

15. House of Commons, Fourth Report from the Committee of Public Accounts Session 1983–4, Department of Employment Manpower Services Commission Special Employment Measures, 7 November 1983 (HC 1982–3 235-i and 235-ii), (London, HMSO).

16. See Bakke, E.W., *Insurance or Dole? The Adjustment of Unemployment Insurance to Economic and Social Facts in Great Britain*, (New Haven, Yale University Press, 1935); Turner, H.A., *Trade Union Growth, Structure and Policy*, (London, Allen and Unwin, 1962).

17. This issue was the subject of wide debate in the United States, see *inter alia*: Blumrosen, A.W. and Blumrosen, R.G., 'The Duty to Plan for Fair Employment Revisited: Work Sharing in Hard Times', 28 *Rutgers Law Review*, pp. 1082–1106 (1975); Summers, C.W. and Love, M.C., 'Work Sharing as an Alternative to Lay-offs by Seniority: Title VII Remedies in Recession', 124 *University of Pennsylvania Law Review*, pp. 893–941 (1976). Under British law the employer retains a wide prerogative to declare redundancies (see *Moon* v. *Homeworthy Furniture (Northern) Ltd.* [1977] ICR 177 (EAT) and may avoid unfair dismissal liability when jobs are lost through reorganization of working time and conditions (see *Hollister* v. *National Farmers' Union* [1979] ICR 542 (CA)). Cf. the recent developments in the litigation under Council Directive 77/187/EEC (OJ 1977 L61/26) and The Transfer of Undertakings (Employment Protection) Regulations 1981 (SI 1981/1794) in Szyszczak, E., 'Employment Protection on the Transfer of an Undertaking', 52 *Modern Law Review*, pp. 691–703 (1989).

18. See *Clarke and Powell* v. *Eley (IMI) Kynoch Ltd.* [1982] IRLR 482; *Kidd* v. *DRG* [1985] IRLR 190.

19. See the Bakaert-Cockerill litigation in Belgium, Centre for Research on European Women, *Crew Reports*, Vol. IV, No. 12 (December 1984).

20. Blumrosen, R.G., 'Work Sharing, STC, and Affirmative Action', in MaCoy, R. and Morand, M.J. (eds) *Short-time Compensation: A Formula For Work Sharing*, (New York, Pergamon Press, 1984); Fallon, R.H. and Weiler, P.C., '*Firefighters* v. *Stotts*: Conflicting Models of Racial Justice', 1 *Supreme Court Review*, pp. 1–68 (1984).

21. For a discussion of the need for employment law to take a broader perspective and in particular the need to relate to wider economic concerns, see the Editors' Introduction by Davies, P. and Freedland, M. to *Kahn-Freund's Labour and the Law*, (London, Stevens, 1983).

22. At the more general level see the discussion by Hepple, B., 'A Right to Work?', 10 *Industrial Law Journal*, pp. 65–83 (1981).

23. See Hepple, B., 'The Crisis in EEC Labour Law', 16 *Industrial Law Journal*, pp. 69–83 (1986); Szyszczak, E., 'Vulnerable Workers: A European Community Solution?', 9 *Employee Relations*, pp. 41–8 (1987); Deakin, S., 'Towards a Social Europe: Social Policy and Reform Strategies after the Single European Act', 35 *Low Pay Review*, pp. 12–17 (Winter 1988/9); MacNeil, K., 'Social Europe: The Potential and the Pitfalls', 35 *Low Pay Review*, pp. 18–22 (Winter 1988/9); Trades Union Congress, *Maximising the Benefits, Minimising the Costs*, (London, TUC, 1988); Labour Research Department, *Europe 1992: What It Means to Trade Unionists*, (London, LRD, 1989); Hepple, B. and Byre, A., 'EEC Labour Law in the United Kingdom – A New Approach', 18 *Industrial Law Journal*, pp. 129–43 (1989); Buchan, D., 'Storm Cloud Gathers over the Social Charter', *Financial Times*, 12 June 1989.

24. See *inter alia* Pollert, A., 'The "Flexible Firm": A Model in Search of Reality (Or a Policy in Search of a Practice?)', *Warwick Papers in Industrial Relations*, No. 19 (University of Warwick, SIBS, 1987); Atkinson, J. and Gregory, D., 'A Flexible Future: Britain's Dual Labour Force', *Marxism Today*, (April 1986); Atkinson, J. and Meager, N., 'Is "Flexibility" Just a Flash in the Pan?', *Personnel Management* (September 1986).

2

The Contract of Employment:
Historical Perspectives

INTRODUCTION

The device of contract to regulate the employment relationship has been subject to much critical debate, first as to its practical utility[1] and secondly, the ideological consequences.[2] Despite these reservations, modern case-law, statutes and managerial practice confirm the significance of contractual rights in analysing the employment relationship. The importance of law and legal regulation has been questioned also by those who believe that customary rather than legal arrangements dominate this area of social organization. For example, empirical work undertaken by Leighton and Doyle on formation and variation of contracts of employment led them to challenge the role of law in this aspect of the employment relationship:

> The contrasts between the legal model and the industrial realities would suggest that the law is not an adequate cipher for the social norms and rules which govern that relationship and our findings suggest that the law may even be irrelevant to the practices and policies which underline that relationship.[3]

This chapter takes as its premise the proposition that the contractual form plays a significant role in analysing the regulation of, and compensation for, short-time working and lay-off. Contract provides a common thread linking the historical development of the right to lay-off (with or without compensation) at common law through to the present statutory regulation of employment protection rights. Thus, with the exception of the two war periods, where the emergency situation was used to justify the temporary regulation of the labour market, the right to put employees on short-time working and the conditions of short-time working have been governed at a legal level by contractual principles. Three issues have faced lawyers in this area. First, in the absence of an express right to lay-off workers, how far will the law imply a right to lay-off? Secondly, in what circumstances is there a duty to provide work, and thirdly, in what circumstances will lay-off or short-time working be compensated under the contract of employment?

This chapter, together with Chapter 3, will examine how the contractual rules have developed, how much flexibility they have afforded employers to adjust to work shortages and how much protection they have extended to employees. One of the aims of these chapters is to obtain an understanding of the role and importance of contractual rights and to clarify the current legal position, while accepting that law by no means provides the definitive explanation as to how partial unemployment is regulated. In fact, as history reveals, even during recession, few employees resort to their contractual rights. There is also evidence to suggest that agreements are often reached among employers and employees as to how available work will be shared out.[4] Employers, employees, and sometimes the public authorities, seem to observe such agreements as if they would regard themselves as bound by formal legal rules. Yet scant attention has been paid to the *legal* consequences of such arrangements, for example, as to whether the agreements vary, suspend or terminate the original contract.

During the twentieth century two factors have influenced the form of partial unemployment. First, the availability of unemployment benefit has played an important role in determining the regulation of customary and informal short-time working arrangements. Secondly, the growth of statutory employment protection rights has nurtured the idea of a 'property' right in jobs. The availability of compensation for job loss has thus encouraged workers to assert legal rights and increased awareness on the part of employers of the need to firm up legal arrangements so as not to incur legal and financial liability. Equally the recent recession has highlighted the need to retain work that is available or at least receive compensation for job loss, as Dickens, Jones, Weekes and Hart explained:

> In the early 1980s unemployment is high and mass redundancies commonplace. Individuals are not just losing their jobs; jobs as such are disappearing.[5]

An understanding of the role of contractual rights and how these interact with statutory employment protection legislation is fundamental, therefore, in explaining some of the legal and managerial problems encountered by employers in the recent recession.

HISTORICAL BACKGROUND: THE DEVELOPMENT OF THE DUTY TO PROVIDE WORK OR WAGES

Common Law

Initially the contract of employment, based on the wage–work bargain, could deal quite easily with a situation where there was a shortage of work: no work, no pay. The duty to provide work or wages has a curious history. Originally a promise merely to employ someone was considered *nudum pactum* since there could be no consideration for such a promise. In *Sykes* v. *Dixon* (1839)[6] a 'want of mutuality' defence was successfully pleaded against a charge of enticing away and harbouring a servant who had bound himself in writing to work exclusively for a particular master for 12 months. Despite the support from the Master and Servant legislation under which a breach of contract by the employee attracted criminal liability while a similar breach by the employer attracted (often unenforced) civil liability, it was difficult to enforce an obligation to stay in employment when no work (and by implication, no wage) was available. Thus, in order to protect what was seen as the employer's property right in skilled labour and also as a means of disciplining what was perceived as an increasingly militant workforce, the common law developed the idea of a reciprocal duty upon the employer to maintain the employment relationship by providing work or wages. Alongside this duty it was accepted also that a wide prerogative to suspend employment could be properly implied and that the existence of this power of suspension was not in conflict with the concept of reciprocity in a binding contract of employment.

The case of *Pilkington* v. *Scott* (1846)[7] is an illustration of the recognition of a property right in skilled labour. The servant, Joseph Leigh, had agreed to serve the plaintiff for seven years as a Crown glass-maker. During this time he agreed, *inter alia*, not to work for any other person without his master's permission. During any depression in trade it was stipulated in the contract of employment that he should be paid half of his wages. In a successful action against the defendant for unlawfully harbouring the servant the contract was held to be mutual and not in restraint of trade. It was stressed, however, that the contract would be invalid if it withdrew the workman from working in the community generally without any obligation on the employer to employ him.

A later case, *R.* v. *Welch* (1853),[8] is illustrative of the use of the contractual obligation to work being enforced through the use of criminal penalties as a means of disciplining labour. Such criminal penalties were used frequently right up until their abolition in 1875. For example, Fox reports that in 1854 over 3,000 workers were imprisoned for 'leaving or neglecting their work' and in 1872 there were 17,100 prosecutions and 10,400 convictions under the

Master and Servant Act 1867.[9] In *Welch* we see an even wider acceptance of the idea that an employer can reduce work or wages without destroying the employment relationship. Here, it was argued that the contract of employment of a piece-rate tin-plate worker was void for want of mutuality in that there was no express obligation upon the employer to provide a minimum amount of work. This argument was rejected on the ground that the employer was subject to an implied obligation to provide some work but this obligation was defined by Lord Campbell CJ as one of finding reasonable employment according to the state of the trade. Thus the right of the employer to suspend work during times of a trade depression was recognized.

In *Re Bailey* and *Re Collier* (1854)[10] two miners were given two months' hard labour as punishment for absenting themselves from work without permission. Lord Campbell CJ formulated an implied obligation to provide work (for a piece-rate worker) which implied a fairly wide prerogative to suspend work. The employer's duty was not:

> necessarily to find them work day by day; but an obligation to continue the relationship of master and servant, so that if the master causelessly refused to give the servant work whilst the colliery was open he would have broken his contract.[11]

Freedland argues that this decision indicates a right on the part of the employer to suspend working by imposing a temporary closure of the mine perhaps merely by virtue of bad trade conditions.[12]

In another case, where a miner was sentenced to one month's hard labour for absenteeism without good cause, Crompton J suggested that there was an implied obligation to find a piece-rate worker 'a reasonable amount of work if work is to be had' or to provide work 'to a reasonable extent under surrounding circumstances'. The judge was asked by Counsel what would be the situation if work was interrupted by circumstances beyond the employer's control, for example, flooding. Crompton J replied 'the usage of trade would probably determine how the workmen should be employed during that time'.[13]

In *Thomas* v. *Vivian* (1872)[14] there was no objection on the ground of want of mutuality to a contract which entitled an employer to lay-off a furnaceman in the event of an 'unforeseen accident'. Similarly in *Phillips* v. *Stevens* (1899)[15] there was no want of mutuality to a contract and no unreasonable restraint of trade in a contract which bound a daily-rated glass-worker to work only for one employer, while obliging that employer to give him a share of the work equal to that of other employees similarly employed and thus conferring upon the employer an unlimited power to put the employee on short-time working or to lay-off the worker.

Thus, from the point of view of the employer, the contract of employment remained flexible, allowing work shortages to be dealt with by laying-off employees without incurring pecuniary obligations. Given the above examples, few could quarrel with Selznick's observation that by:

> the end of the nineteenth century the employment contract had become a very special sort of contract – in large part a legal device for guaranteeing to management the unilateral power to make rules and exercise discretion.[16]

A major turning point in the common law attitude towards lay-off occurred in *Devonald* v. *Rosser and Sons* (1906)[17] when the Court of Appeal rejected the employer's contention that there was a customary right to suspend employees during a trade depression. The case concerned a tin-plate worker paid on piece-rates, and while it was recognized that there was a custom in the employment to suspend such workers in the event of mechanical failures, this custom could not be extended to a shortage of orders since it would create an unacceptable element of uncertainty into the employment contract. Instead the Court of Appeal found that there was an implied obligation upon the employer to provide a worker paid at piece-rate with enough work to enable him to earn a sufficient amount of remuneration. The rare instances of an obligation to provide actual *work* are discussed later in this chapter. The historical context of this case is significant since the judgment occurred at a time when there was an increased awareness of the need for some kind of compulsory unemployment insurance.

Historical events may also explain the retrograde step for employee's rights taken in *Browning* v. *Crumlin Valley Collieries Ltd.* (1926),[18] a judgment delivered in the year of the General Strike. Here a wide power to lay-off was implied into the contracts of colliery workers when a mine was closed for five weeks in order for repairs to be carried out. It was held that the suspension was 'due to circumstances beyond the employer's control' and therefore the risk of lost wages should fall upon the employees not the employer; the intention of the parties must have been to share the loss of this natural event. As Wedderburn wrily observes: 'Would they have said the same if a crop of diamonds had appeared?'[19]

While *Browning* v. *Crumlin Valley Collieries* has been subject to much criticism it remains a significant precedent in the common law as to when there may be an implied right to lay-off. Its modern application is considered in the next chapter. Before then we will look at the alternative to providing wages in order to maintain the employment relationship: the more difficult duty of actually providing work.

THE OBLIGATION TO PROVIDE WORK

In contrast to the wide implied right to lay-off an employee the common law established a very limited set of circumstances in which there was a legal obligation to provide work. The position is described by Asquith J in *Collier* v. *Sunday Referee Publishing Co.*:

> The contract of employment does not necessarily or perhaps normally, oblige the master to provide the servant with work. Provided I pay my cook her wages regularly she cannot complain if I choose to take any or all of my meals out. In some exceptional cases there is an obligation to provide work.[20]

In delivering the Gresham Lectures in 1947, Sachs identified four special cases where the obligation to provide work existed. These categories have changed very little since that time.[21]

Express Term

The first situation identified by Sachs was where there was an express term in the contract of employment stating that there was a positive duty on the employer to provide work. While this in itself would seem straightforward few contracts would contain such a sweeping and general obligation.

Piece-rate Workers and Commission Earners

The second situation relates to where the remuneration payable under the contract of employment is affected by the lack of provision of work, namely piece-rate earners and people paid by results. Looking at piece-rate workers first, in *Devonald* v. *Rosser*, the plaintiff brought an action for the breach of an implied contractual term when his employers failed to provide him with work during the period of notice given to terminate the contract of employment. The Court of Appeal held that there was an implied obligation on the part of the employer to provide a reasonable amount of work for piece-rate workers but this was not an absolute obligation. Lord Alverstone CJ argued that this obligation to provide work was subject to limitations, for example, where the lack of work was attributable to the breakdown of machinery, shortage of water or materials; in other words factors beyond the employer's control. Then there would not necessarily be an obligation to provide work. Unprofitability was not considered a good excuse for failing to provide work. Interestingly the

Court of Appeal was anxious to confirm the employer's control over the situation. The question of working short time or full time was in the hands of the employer: 'The men have absolutely nothing to say to it,'[22]

Batt, a barrister and Professor of Commercial Law at the University of Liverpool, did not regard *Devonald* v. *Rosser* as laying down a general duty to provide work for piece-rate earners.[23] Each case would turn upon its own facts and the particular construction of the contract of employment. Relying upon the decision in *Turner* v. *Sawdon*,[24] Batt argued:

> Although an obligation to provide an employee with work will be implied in certain cases, it is not to be inferred lightly, and the mere relation of employer and employee does not cast upon the employer the duty of providing work, and the mere fact that the servant receives in addition to a salary, extra payments or commission for work done does not entitle the servant to call upon him to give an opportunity to earn these extra sums.[25]

As regards commission earners, two cases may be contrasted. In *Turner* v. *Goldsmith*[26] the plaintiff agreed to serve the defendant, a shirt manufacturer, as an agent, traveller and canvasser. The terms of the contract were that the agency was determinable by notice given by either party at the end of five years. While the agency existed the plaintiff was to do his utmost to obtain orders and to sell the various goods 'manufactured or sold by the defendant as should from time to time be forwarded or submitted by sample or pattern'. The plaintiff was to be paid on a commission basis. Three years into the agency the defendant's factory burnt down and his business ceased. The plaintiff brought an action for breach of contract for failure to provide sufficient work in order for him to earn his commission. The Court of Appeal upheld the claim, awarding substantial damages. Turning on the construction of the contract it was held that there was an obligation to employ the plaintiff for five years and that this obligation would not be fulfilled unless the plaintiff received a reasonable amount of samples to enable him to earn his commission. The failure to fulfil this obligation was not excused by the fact that the factory had been destroyed by fire since the obligation was to *supply* samples as opposed to manufacturing them. The employer could have bought shirts on the open market in order to meet this obligation. Kay LJ was willing to admit the possibility of *force majeure* in that if the defendant's power to carry on business had been taken away 'by something for which he was not responsible' this would not amount to a breach of contract.[27]

In contrast, in *Turner* v. *Sawdon and Co.*[28] a different conclusion was reached, the case again turning upon the construction of the contract. The Court of Appeal found the claim to provide work 'unique'. Here there was a contract to pay wages by the year, which the employers were willing to do, but because of a depression in the market they were unwilling to allow the salesman to travel promoting and selling their goods. The salesman argued that this was a breach of contract, he should be allowed 'to keep his hand in' otherwise he would not be an efficient salesman. The Court of Appeal was unwilling to stretch the contract this far.[29]

The ratio of *Turner* v. *Goldsmith* was applied in *Bauman* v. *Hulton Press Ltd.*[30] The plaintiff, a journalist and photographer, agreed with the defendant, the publisher of a weekly magazine, that in exchange for a weekly salary of ten pounds plus extra payments for work done he would offer all his 'ideas, stories and so on' to the defendant first, that he would not receive commission from any other magazine and that he would make himself available at all times in order to undertake commissioned work. In February 1951 the defendant informed the plaintiff that he was terminating the contract at the end of the month. In an action for wrongful dismissal, Streatfield J was willing to imply a term into the contract (in order to give it business efficacy) that, for the duration of the contract, the defendant would give the plaintiff sufficient work to enable him to earn what the parties must be taken to have contemplated he should earn.

The case of *Minnevitch* v. *Café de Paris (Londres) Ltd.*[31] provides some discussion as to when circumstances are beyond an employer's control. Here there was a temporary impediment. The news that King George V was seriously ill led to the temporary closure of a restaurant at which the plaintiff was engaged to lead an orchestra under a 'no play, no pay' contract. Macnaghten J accepted that it was not reasonably possible for the restaurant to open for the two nights following the King's death (and this was supported by the fact that other restaurants whose clientele were similar to that of the Café de Paris were closed) but for the following four nights it was possible for the restaurant to reopen. Although it was unlikely that many people would visit the restaurant the defendant was obliged to let the orchestra earn their remuneration. Similar principles have been applied in cases where the employee is remunerated partly by fixed wage or retainer and partly on a commission basis[32] but there are also decisions to the contrary in cases where the remuneration has been fixed in this way.[33]

Publicity and/or Experience

The third situation where there may be a duty to provide work is where it is necessary for the employee to practise her profession to order to gain publicity or experience. Obvious examples in this category are actors,[34] and a band conductor.[35] One case reached the House of Lords and provides a good illustration of the use of the implied term. In *Herbert Clayton and Jack Waller Ltd.*

v. *Oliver*[36] an American actor was engaged to perform in one of the three
leading comedy parts at the London Hippodrome Theatre. Under the contract he was prevented from performing anywhere else during the life of the
contract. The actor objected to the role assigned to him, arguing that it was not
a leading role. The producer refused to re-cast him and the actor refused to
perform his allotted role and sued for breach of contract. The actor won and
was awarded damages for the loss of publicity he suffered. Turning on the
construction of the contract, the House of Lords found that the character of the
employment was an essential part of the contract and the actor was unable to
use his talents elsewhere for the duration of the contract. It was essential then
to provide him with the correct work.

In another case, *Hall* v. *British Essence Co. Ltd.*[37] it was indicated by Henn
Collins J that it would amount to a breach of contract to suspend a director and
a general manager from his duties because of the resulting injury to his
reputation that would arise from the attitudes formed by traders who had dealt
with him.

There is a conflict of authority on the question as to whether the plaintiff is
precluded from claiming damages for loss of existing reputation as opposed to
the loss of the possibility of enhancement of his or her reputation. While the
decision in *Marbe* v. *George Edwardes (Daly's Theatre) Ltd.*[38] suggests that loss of
existing reputation may be included, the decision in *Withers* v. *General Theatre
Corporation*[39] takes the view that this head of damage is excluded. It would
seem that the cases where damages may be recovered for loss of publicity or
experience are very much the exception rather than the rule. Such damages
were refused in *Addis* v. *Gramophone Co. Ltd.*[40] In the more recent case of *Bliss* v.
South East Thames Regional Health Authority[41] the Court of Appeal affirmed that
where damages are assessed for breach of contract it is not permissible to
award general damages for frustration, mental distress, injury to feelings or
annoyance arising from the breach of contract.

The concept of 'keeping a hand in' is not restricted to individual artistic
performances. Two more cases reveal its application to skilled work. *Langston*
v. *Amalgamated Union of Engineering Workers (No. 2) and Chrysler (UK) Ltd.*[42]
concerned the concept of the 'right to work'. Under the Industrial Relations
Act 1971 the appellant sought to exercise the right not to belong to a trade
union. The employer, faced with the threats of strike action from the union,
suspended the employee on full pay pending a discussion with the union. The
employee brought an action against the union arguing that by inducing his
employer to suspend him, the union had induced a breach of contract and were
guilty of an unfair practice under section 96 of the Industrial Relations Act
1971. In the Court of Appeal, Lord Denning, anxious to protect the 'right to
work', adopted a philosophical approach to what he regarded as the changing
nature of why people worked. It was not just to earn pay. It was also to obtain
some satisfaction from work:

It is arguable that in these days a man has, by reason of an implication in the contract, a right to work . . . he has a right to have the opportunity of doing his work when it is there to be done.[43]

When the case was remitted to the National Industrial Relations Court Sir John Donaldson instanced the cases of actors, commission and piece-rate workers as examples where the opportunity to work had to be provided.[44] While Mr Langston, as a spot welder, could be described as a skilled worker, it was felt that he did not have to practise in order to maintain his skills. Sir John Donaldson was prepared to classify him as a piece-rate worker since in addition to his basic pay he earned premiums for working night shifts and overtime and he lost the opportunity to earn these premiums while suspended. Thus a declaration was granted against the union for carrying out an unfair industrial practice which knowingly induced a breach of Mr Langston's right to work under his contract with Chrysler. In doing this the court added workers who regularly work overtime or at night shift premiums to the categories of workers who must be given the opportunity to work.

In *Breach* v. *Epsylon Industries Ltd*.[45] doubts were cast upon *Turner* v. *Sawdon* operating as a general rule. Here the plaintiff was employed as a Chief Engineer. In mid-1974 the work on which the plaintiff was engaged was transferred to Canada and the workforce was run down. By the autumn of 1974 the plaintiff found himself with no work to do but was reluctant to resign his post because he would lose entitlement to redundancy pay. Equally he feared he would quickly lose touch with the expertise required in his industry if he did not work. He resigned, claiming that the failure to provide work amounted to a repudiation of his contract of employment. His subsequent resignation amounted to a constructive dismissal within section 3(1)(c) Redundancy Payments Act 1965.[46] Since the reason for repudiation was a redundancy situation he claimed entitlement to a redundancy payment. In casting doubts upon the relevance of *Turner* v. *Sawdon*, the Employment Appeal Tribunal argued that the decision was out of date and out of touch with modern attitudes. While it could not invalidate the binding effect of a Court of Appeal decision the Employment Appeal Tribunal argued that the correct approach was to look at the facts, in particular the background to the contract, to see how it should be construed and whether, in the circumstances of the particular case, an obligation to provide work ought to be implied. On these grounds the case was remitted to the industrial tribunal since the issue was a question of fact in each case.

In an *obiter dictum*, the Employment Appeal Tribunal pointed to the case of *Collier* v. *Sunday Referee Publishing Co.*,[47] where *Turner* v. *Sawdon* had been successfully distinguished. Phillips J argued that although the *Breach* case did not fall within the ambit of the *Collier* decision he believed that *Breach* could fall within the exceptions to the general principle of *no* obligation to provide work which he characterized as a blend of thought between the cases discussed above, moderated by changes in outlook and opinion and the change in industrial relations since the fifties. Indeed Elias, Napier and Wallington argue that there is a distinct possibility that the decision in *Turner* v. *Sawdon* will be overruled, arguing that the pre-war case reflects 'a very different social relationship between employer and employee and a very different perception of an employee's interest in his job'.[48] This is rather an unusual statement as the case of *Turner* v. *Sawdon* is very much about the obligation to provide actual work; the employers did not dispute the fact that they were obliged to provide remuneration under the contract. While there has been a growing recognition of the need to guarantee earnings it is doubtful if this implies a duty to provide actual work. The trend has been to provide *compensation* for work lost.[49]

An industrial tribunal in *Bosworth* v. *Angus Jowett and Co. Ltd.*[50] took up the suggestion from *Breach* v. *Epsylon* that a right to work may be implied in certain contracts of employment. Four months before Mr Bosworth's fixed-term service agreement was due to expire the employer told him that he need no longer perform his duties as a sales director for the company. Mr Bosworth's claim for dismissal was upheld by the industrial tribunal which found that the employer had repudiated the contract by not allowing the employee to perform the work he was employed to do. Although the employer had continued to pay Mr Bosworth and treat him as still employed the tribunal found that he had a right to work in conformity with the discipline of the company when work was available. In addition to the construction of the contract the tribunal was influenced by the fact that the employee was paid a bonus based upon the profits of the company. Thus by denying him the opportunity to work the employer was preventing the employee from contributing to the profitability of the company and his own salary in addition to risking his reputation in the trade. This case could be regarded as akin to the commission-earner cases or the cases where publicity or experience are a necessary part of the work or it may be that an addition has been made to the categories of employment where there is an obligation to provide work – that of senior management.

Employment in a Specific Post

The fourth situation cited by Sachs is where the employment is for a specific post. This is the example of *Collier* v. *Sunday Referee Publishing Co.*,[51] where the plaintiff was appointed chief sub-editor of a newspaper. When the owner sold the newspaper Collier claimed that there had been a summary dismissal arguing that he had been appointed to a specific post on a specific newspaper and by selling the newspaper the office had been destroyed. Even though the owners paid his wages this was not enough: he was entitled to carry out the work for which he was engaged to do and was not obliged to stay on and work in any other capacity.

The decision in *Collier* is controversial. Freedland points out that there is a difference in the reporting of the case.[52] The authorized report of the case at [1940] 2 KB 647, 657 suggests that the decision is based on the appointment to a specific job or office and that the employee does not need to show a special interest in publicity or experience arising out of the appointment. In contrast, the report of the case at [1940] 4 All ER 234, 236, suggests that the decision is an application of the rule in *Marbe* v. *George Edwardes (Daly's Theatre) Ltd.*,[53] where the employee could claim a special interest in publicity or experience. Today, for example, the kudos attached to editorials in the national press might lead one to argue that if a journalist was appointed to write editorials for an influential newspaper she should be allowed to exercise her talents; mere payment of wages would not be sufficient.

Although *Collier* would seem to form an ambiguous category Freedland[54] argues that it is an important development because it recognizes the significance to the employee of being provided with work for work's sake. Although the principle may be confined only to white collar jobs laying stress upon the proprietory concept of office-holding, Freedland thought that the duty to provide actual work might increase in importance, but this idea has not been followed through in the courts.[55]

ANALYSING THE CONTRACT MODEL

The above discussion suggests that by the twentieth century the common law was beginning to recognize that the contract of employment was based on more than an exchange of work for wages. The employee had an interest in protecting her right to work to earn wages and the employer had an interest in ensuring the availability of skilled labour. This led Freedland[56] to argue that the contract of employment was composed of a two-tier structure:

> At the first level there is an exchange of work and remuneration. At the second level – the promises to employ and be employed – provides the arrangement with its stability and its continuity as a contract.

It could be argued, however, that the model developed by Freedland cannot be applied universally, but in practice has been developed mainly through white collar employment contracts. Neither is the distinction drawn by Freedland evident in the case law of the period. For example, Greer J in *Browning* v. *Crumlin Valley Collieries Ltd.* analysed the bargain struck in the contract of employment as 'the consideration for work is wages, and the consideration for wages is work'.[57] Thus the question of whether wages could be paid if the employee was ready and willing to work but none was available was difficult to fit into the classic contract model.

While Freedland's two-tier structure provides a useful description of the structure of the modern employment contract, we shall see in the next chapter that it is not a classification which the judiciary have openly articulated as a means of explaining the obligation to maintain the reciprocity of the employment relationship. Indeed, as Freedland[58] observes, the wage-work bargain is not a concept which lawyers have analysed in any detail and hence the lack of precision in understanding the legal basis for providing compensation for partial unemployment. Two different perspectives may be added to Freedland's two-tier model. The first is the question as to whether all contracts of employment are homogeneous. Freedland, for example, argues that different principles may apply according to the method of payment. In the above discussion we see the particular duty to provide work or wages seems to be carefully defined only under certain kinds of contract, for example, piece-rate contracts, commission earners or where the person holds a particular post. The second perspective is the issue of whether the two tiers are static. For example, the boundaries may shift according to the particular payment system used. For some contracts the obligation to maintain reciprocity may be a central aspect of the first tier of obligations, for example, with payment by results compensation systems. Another variation may be that the boundaries between the two tiers shift over time. In modern contracts of employment the idea of a guaranteed wage may be a crucial aspect of the first tier obligations.

Two post-war developments have taken the focus away from the central contractual right to lay-off and changed the matter into a more general policy issue. The first development was the growth of collectively agreed guaranteed week agreements and the second development was the increased statutory regulation of lay-offs through National Insurance legislation and employment protection legislation. These developments are discussed in greater detail in Chapters 3, 4 and 5. The move towards more formal contracts of employment as a result of increased rights to employment protection granted by legislation curtailed the scope of implying terms to lay off at will and without pay into contracts of employment. Section 4 of the Contracts of Employment Act 1963 introduced an obligation to supply details of the principal terms and conditions of employment. Subsequent legislation increased employment protection, particularly in the area of termination of contracts of employment, and these developments have increased awareness of the need to define the terms of employment more precisely and to cover contingencies by allowing for flexibility in working arrangements. There is no precise coverage in the legislation of the right to lay-off, and this is still governed by individual or collective negotiation. It is unlikely that the parties to an employment contract will overlook the question of lay-off, but where this does occur or the terms are ambiguous, then the residual rights described above will resume prominence.

Having set the scene in a historical context, the next chapter will examine the right to lay-off or put an employee on short-time working and provide compensation for partial unemployment in a modern context, looking at the right to vary contracts of employment and the consequences of lay-off and short-time working in relation to contractual and statutory employment protection rights.

NOTES

1. See Hepple, B., 'Restructuring Employment Rights', 15 *Industrial Law Journal*, pp. 69–83 (1986).
2. See Fox, A., *Beyond Contract: Work Power and Trust Relations*, (London, Faber and Faber Ltd., 1974); and Selznick, P. *Law, Society and Industrial Justice*, (New York, Russell Sage Foundations, 1969).
3. *The Making and Varying of Contracts of Employment*, (Department of Law Research Paper, The Polytechnic of North London, 1982) at p. 69. See also Leighton, P. 'Observing Employment Contracts', 13 *Industrial Law Journal*, pp. 86–106 (1984).
4. This is discussed in more detail in Chapters 3 and 4.
5. *Dismissed: A Study of Unfair Dismissal and the Industrial Tribunal System*, (Oxford, Basil Black-well, 1985) at p. 1.
6. (1839) 9 Ad and EI 693.
7. (1846) 15 M and W 657.
8. (1853) 2 E and B 357.
9. *Op cit.* at p. 189, note 2. See also Incomes Data Services, 'Lay-offs and Short-time: What the Law Says', *IDS Brief 56*, pp. 15–21 (March 1975); Simon, D., 'Master and Servant', in Saville, J. (ed.), *Democracy and the Labour Movement*, (London, Lawrence & Wishart, 1954).
10. (1854) 3 E and B 607.
11. *Ibid.* at pp. 618–9.
12. *The Contract of Employment*, (Oxford, Clarendon Press, 1976) at p. 88.
13. *Whittle* v. *Frankland* [1862] 31 LJ (NS) MC 81 at p. 84.
14. (1872) 37 JP 228.
15. (1899) 15 TLR 325.
16. *Law, Society and Industrial Justice*, (New York, Russell Sage Foundations, 1969) at p. 135.
17. [1906] 2 KB 728.
18. [1926] 1 KB 522.
19. *The Worker and the Law*, (Harmondsworth, Penguin Books, 3rd edn, 1986) at p. 231.
20. [1940] 2 KB 647 at p. 650.
21. *The Law of Employment: A Summary of the Rights of Employers and Employees*, (London, Pitman, 1947).
22. Note 17 *supra*, per Lord Alverstone at p. 740.
23. Batt, F.R., *The Law of Master and Servant*, (London, Pitman and Sons, 1929) at p. 34.
24. [1901] 2 KB 653.
25. *Op. cit.* note 23 at p. 35.
26. [1891] 1 QB 544.
27. *Ibid.* at p. 551.
28. [1901] 2 KB 653.
29. See also *Lagerwall* v. *Wilkinson, Henderson and Clarke Ltd.* [1899] 80 LT 55 where a commercial traveller unsuccessfully sued for commissions he was unable to earn.

30. [1952] 2 All ER 1121.

31. [1936] 1 All ER 884.

32. See *Re Rubel Bronze and Metal Co. and Others* [1918] 1 KB 315; *Bauman* v. *Hulton Press Ltd.* [1952] 2 All ER 1121.

33. See *Ex parte Maclure* [1870] LR 5 Ch. App. 737; *Re Newman Ltd., Raphael's Claim* [1916] 2 Ch 309.

34. *Fechter* v. *Montgomery* [1863] 33 Beav 22; *Marbe* v. *George Edwardes (Daly's Theatre) Ltd.* [1928] 1 KB 269.

35. *Bunning* v. *Lyric Theatre* [1894] 71 LT 396. This case was distinguished by McCardie J in *Turpin* v. *The Victoria Palace Ltd.* [1918] 2 KB 539. Here a 'variety artist' could not claim damages for loss of publicity through the failure of the defendants to allow her to perform in their music hall because, unlike in *Bunning*, the defendants had not advertised her appearance in newspapers, posters or bills.

36. [1930] AC 209.

37. [1946] 62 TLR 542.

38. [1928] 1 KB 269.

39. [1933] 2 KB 536.

40. [1909] AC 488. Cf. Freedland, *The Contract of Employment* at p. 25 (*op. cit.* note 12), who argues that damages for lack of work need not necessarily be limited in the same way.

41. [1987] ICR 700.

42. [1974] IRLR 15. The earlier decision of the National Industrial Relations Court is reported at [1973] IRLR 82.

43. *Ibid.* at p. 34.

44. [1974] IRLR 182.

45. [1976]IRLR 180.

46. Now section 83(2)(c) Employment Protection (Consolidation) Act 1978.

47. [1940] 2 KB 647.

48. *Labour Law: Cases and Materials*, (London, Butterworths, 1980) at p. 435.

49. See also the views of Hepple, B., 'A Right to Work?', 10 *Industrial Law Journal*, pp. 65–83 (1981).

50. [1977] IRLR 374.

51. *Supra* note 20.

52. *The Contract of Employment op. cit.* note 12 at p. 26.

53. *Supra* note 38.

54. *Op. cit.* note 12 at p. 26.

55. For a more recent discussion and appraisal of the idea of a 'right to work' see Hepple, B. note 49 *supra*.

56. *Op. cit.* note 12 at p. 20.

57. [1926] 1 KB 522.

58. 'The Obligation to Work and to Pay for Work', 30 *Current Legal Problems*, pp. 175–87 (1977).

3

The Contract of Employment:
Modern Developments

THE EXPRESS RIGHT TO LAY-OFF

In a modern contract of employment the express right to lay-off an employee will probably be found in a guaranteed week agreement or a Joint Industrial Council agreement.[1] In order to have contractual effect the terms relating to lay-off must be incorporated into the individual contract of employment. This produces two significant results. First, if the agreement is incorporated into the contract of employment, the parties will be bound by it until the individual contract of employment is varied to provide otherwise. Thus, in *Burroughs Machines Ltd.* v. *Timmoney and Others*[2] the employees were claiming a redundancy payment on the ground that the employer had no right to lay-off employees without pay. In purporting to do so it was alleged that the employers had dismissed the employees. The employers had resigned from the employers' association, the Engineering Employers' Federation (EEF) but a collective agreement between the union and the EEF had been expressly incorporated into the employee's contract of employment. The Employment Appeal Tribunal held that the employers were bound by this agreement as it had been expressly incorporated into the employee's contract of employment. The employers had agreed with the trade union to continue to abide by the collective agreement. While the agreement provided for a guaranteed minimum wage in the event of a lay-off there was also a provision that no guaranteed wage would be payable if the lay-off was due to a trade dispute in a federated firm. Since this was the issue in this case the Employment Appeal Tribunal held that the employers were able to rely upon the exclusion clause in the guaranteed week agreement to avoid making a guarantee payment. The Court of Session overruled the Employment Appeal Tribunal on the point, that by resigning from the EEF, the employers had lost the right to suspend the guaranteed week agreement when the dislocation in production was caused by an industrial dispute in a federated establishment. The Court of Session went on to hold that the employers were not in breach of contract since the right to

guaranteed pay was vested in the contract of employment and the right to
suspend the guarantee continued when the industrial dispute causing the lay-
off occurred within the employers' establishment. It was shown that trades-
men within the firm were on strike thus triggering the suspension clause.

The second result is that non-members of a union may be bound by the
terms of a collective agreement if it has been expressly or impliedly incorporated into their contract of employment.[3] The responsiveness of the common
law to incorporate the pattern of industrial relations and employment practice
at the workplace by allowing the effects of collective bargaining to affect the
individual contract of employment in this way was described by Kahn-Freund
as a form of 'crystallized custom'.[4]

Because many collective agreements are limited in time and amount of
guaranteed pay, the common law rights of employees outlined in Chapter 2
may be altered. The most significant area is the use of suspension clauses, since
evidence suggests that such clauses have assumed a dominant role in the
negotiation of guaranteed week agreements.[5] A High Court decision has
strengthened employees' rights in relation to suspension clauses. In *(1) Bond* v.
CAV Ltd. (2) Neads v. *CAV Ltd.*[6] Peter Pain J was asked to interpret the
suspension clause found in the Engineering Guaranteed Week Agreement of
1964. The dispute involved the question of whether, in order to suspend the
agreement in the event of a dislocation of production in a federated establishment as a result of an industrial dispute, the employer had to show that the
dislocation of production had resulted in a shortage of work for the employees
in question. Davies and Freedland argue that, in holding that there had to be
such an unavailability of work, Peter Pain J was vindicating a broad principle
that there is no *general* right to lay-off at either common law or as a matter of
construction of express agreements.[7] The judge expressly left open the
question as to whether the employer could rely upon the 1964 agreement
where it would derogate from the employee's rights. Davies and Freedland are
not optimistic, however, that the suggestion contained in the judgment, that
the contract of employment might be construed as incorporating the 1964
agreement only in so far as it fulfilled its historical role of improving upon the
common law rights of employees, will be followed generally by the courts. The
tendency has been to regard collective bargaining as *replacing* common law
rights rather than supplementing them.

The judgment in *(1) Bond* v. *CAV Ltd.* is consistent with the modern tendency
to construe the right to lay-off narrowly and with precision.[8] In *A. Dakri and Co.*
v. *Tiffen*,[9] for example, the employee's contract contained a clause providing
that 'if there is a shortage of work or the firm is unable to operate because of
circumstances beyond its control it has the right to lay you off temporarily and
without remuneration'. The Employment Appeal Tribunal held that unless a
time limit is specified in such a clause the lay-off is not to be for more than a
'reasonable' time. What is 'reasonable' is a question of fact for the industrial

tribunal to decide in each case. Here, one month was held to be reasonable for the clothing industry.

Similarly, the precise terms of the lay-off clause must be adhered to. If an employee is laid off and the terms of the agreement are not followed she may be entitled to sue for a breach of contract. It may be that in an emergency situation the employee will agree to an *ad hoc* variation of the contract, but this cannot be an indefinite variation[10] and any employees who did not agree to the variation may either claim unfair dismissal compensation, alleging that there has been a constructive dismissal, or sue for breach of contract. These points are discussed later in this chapter.

The existence of an express right to lay-off still leaves open the question of whether there is a duty to provide wages even though no work has been performed. This brings us back to the problems of analysing the two-tier structure of employment contracts raised by Freedland.[11] Can the consideration for wages be provided only by the employee doing the work or is the consideration met by the employee being ready and willing to work? Napier[12] has argued that doubts should be cast upon the view that *(1) Bond* v. *CAV Ltd.*[13] allows wages to be claimed by an employee who is merely ready and willing to work but does not in fact work unless there is an express agreement to that effect. Napier argues that applying Freedland's two-tier model of the contract of employment, it is the first tier of obligations which applies normally and that the actual performance of work is a condition precedent of the payment of wages.[14] It could be argued, however, that the duty to provide compensation for partial unemployment is not necessarily a component of the second tier of obligations to maintain the reciprocity of the employment relationship but is part of the consideration provided in the first tier of obligations. This is because today it is generally accepted that there is a duty to compensate for lost wages as a result of partial unemployment or other forms of incapacity to work such as sickness or maternity leave. In order to claim either a contractual, collectively agreed or statutory right to a guaranteed wage the employee must show a willingness to be available for work and often must be prepared to accept reasonable alternative work as a condition of eligibility for a guaranteed wage. Thus doubts may be cast upon Napier's analysis that actual performance of work is a residual rule operating as consideration for the wage. For the majority of employees compensation for partial unemployment has become an integral part of the first tier of obligations.

THE IMPLIED RIGHT TO LAY-OFF

In the absence of an express power to lay-off or put employees on short-time working, the employer may be able to show that there is an implied power to

lay-off in the particular circumstances. Despite the modern statutory obligation to inform employees of the principal terms and conditions of employment,[15] the common law may still be invoked to fill the lacunae left by
individual or collective negotiation.

Two cases are cited when comparing the common law position. These are
Devonald v. *Rosser and Sons* and *Browning* v. *Crumlin Valley Collieries Ltd.*[16] In the
Browning case, a mine was closed for five weeks while essential repairs were
carried out. It was held that the employer was not obliged to pay wages as the
closure was due to 'circumstances beyond his control'. Although this exception was expressly recognized in the earlier decision of *Devonald* v. *Rosser*, the
application of the exception in *Browning* has been subject to criticism since it
implies a wide right to lay-off at common law. And although the decision can
be contextualized as part of a hardening of judicial attitudes in the period of
the General Strike, the issue of what are 'circumstances beyond the employer's
control' is not entirely academic since the phrase occurs in many suspension
clauses in modern collectively agreed guaranteed week agreements, and where
these circumstances are not expressly defined the parties may have to resort to
the common law precedents.

The *Browning* case has not been successfully cited since 1945 and its exact
scope is controversial. It may be that it is only limited to natural disasters. Or
does it relate to mechanical failure, shortage of materials, failure of power
supplies? What is certain is that as a result of the decision in *Devonald* v. *Rosser
and Sons*, it will not apply to general conditions where trade is slack[17] or to a
strike within the employer's own firm since this will be within the employer's
control. Equally, unless covered by a guaranteed week agreement, a shortage
of work because of an industrial dispute in another industry will not suspend
the right to remuneration at common law.[18]

A tendency can be discerned to limit the application of the *Browning* decision
to the particular facts and circumstances of the case and, given the modern
Health and Safety at Work legislation, its application now may be even more
limited. The present view would seem to be that the *Browning* decision does not
undermine the general right not to be laid off without express agreement to
that effect. Indeed, in two cases we see the development and adaptation of the
principle laid down in *Devonald* v. *Rosser* within the context of statutory
employment protection rights. In *Johnson* v. *Cross*[19] the Employment Appeal
Tribunal confirmed the primacy of the principle that an employer has no
power to lay-off in the absence of an express or implied agreement but, on the
contrary, the employer was under an obligation to provide reasonable work, or
pay in lieu of work, during the period of notice of termination of employment.
This principle was envisaged to cover lay-offs caused by a shortage of cash,
lack of liquid funds, inclement weather, shortage of work or lack of supplies.

This theme was taken up and reasserted in *(1) Bond* v. *CAV Ltd. (2) Neads* v.
CAV Ltd.,[20] where Peter Pain J adopted the Employment Appeal Tribunal's

view in *Johnson* v. *Cross*, adding that the *Browning* case rested on the terms which were implied in the circumstances of the case and as such did not cast doubt upon the principle established in *Devonald* v. *Rosser*. As Davies and Freedland observe:

> The courts in these two cases seem minded to ensure that no generally implied right of lay-off is available to employers to undermine the substance of the statutory rights to notice that employees now have.[21]

What, then, is the scope of the implied right to lay-off? An industrial tribunal has ruled that such a right can only be implied into the contracts of weekly paid employees.[22] After the introduction of statutory guarantee payments in 1977[23] an industrial tribunal accepted the argument that the statutory measures introduced an implied term into a weekly paid employee's contract that he could be laid off without pay, but this decision was later reversed in the review of the case by the Employment Appeal Tribunal.[24]

The process of implying terms into the contract of employment is not free from controversy, and the prevailing tendency of the courts has been not to invent terms of the contract for the parties. The most recent decision of the Court of Appeal on implied mobility terms reveals the artificial nature of judicial explanations of their conduct and the practical consequences of intervening in contractual relations. In *Courtaulds Northern Spinning Ltd.* v. *Sibson and TGWU*[25] the issue concerned the right of an employer to transfer an employee to another place of employment one mile away following a dispute with his trade union. Sibson's contract was silent on the issue of mobility, but since he brought an action for unfair dismissal alleging that there had been a constructive dismissal, the Court of Appeal had to address the question of whether there had been a breach of contract on the employer's part.[26]

The most pragmatic approach to resolving the issue is not a contractual solution but the test adopted in *Mears* v. *Safecar Security*[27] of looking, with hindsight, at the conduct of the parties during the currency of the contract. This approach was not helpful in the Sibson's case since he had worked at the same site as a lorry driver for 12 years and had not been asked to move during this time. This did not deter Slade LJ from finding that the site was merely a starting and finishing place for Sibson's work. He then went on to argue that post-contractual conduct provided evidence of the reasonable intentions of the parties at the time of the contract formation and that it was likely that the parties would agree that the employer had the power to direct the employee to work at any place within reasonable commuting distance. Furthermore, it was held that that requirement need not be reasonable, nor result from any genuine operational reasons, but could be for any reason. Commenting upon the case Holland and Chandler argue that:

This assumes that the parties, as reasonable men, would have accepted the inclusion of a term which allowed one party absolute discretion over its operation; a discretion that need bear no relation to reasonableness or even managerial necessity.[28]

The traditional technique for implying terms into a contract was the use of the 'officious bystander' test.[29] The demise of the 'officious bystander' test has been noted in the case of *Mears* v. *Safecar Security Ltd.*,[30] when a new technique (coined the 'legal incidents' test) was in evidence. The 'legal incidents' test finds expression in the earlier House of Lords decision of *Liverpool City Council* v. *Irwin*.[31] Here it was established that there are certain contracts which establish a relationship (for example, that of master and servant) and such contracts demand by their nature and subject matter certain obligations which the general law will impose and imply as 'legal incidents' of the contractual relationship. The House of Lords drew a distinction between implying reasonably necessary terms and implying a term merely because it seems reasonable to do so.[32] However, even the concept of necessity may grant a wide discretion to the judiciary to intervene in contractual relationships. As Holland and Chandler point out:

> The drawback to 'necessity' is that it possesses no natural definition. It focuses on the *purpose* for implying terms, not the establishment of criteria defining the content of those terms.[33]

The application of the 'legal incidents' test to give the employer an implied right to lay-off without pay is likely to be very limited since the general view of the 'legal incidents' of employment is that the employment relationship should be maintained and that this necessarily involves the right to be provided with work or wages unless such a right is expressly excluded. However, the case of *Howman and Son* v. *Blyth*[34] is perhaps illustrative of the scope of implying a right to a guaranteed wage. Here a contract contained an obligation to provide sick pay but there was no agreed term as to the duration of the payment. Faced with the ruling in *Marrison* v. *Bell*,[35] that sick pay lasts until the employment is terminated, the Employment Appeal Tribunal decided that before applying the *Marrison* v. *Bell* presumption it was legitimate to imply a term as to duration of sick pay according to the normal practice or custom of the industry. On this basis it was found that the normal practice was to provide sick pay for a limited period only. As we shall discover in the next chapter, guaranteed week agreements are often tailored to the specific needs of different industries, and such an approach would be easy to apply where partial unemployment occurs.

Another way of proving that there is an implied right to lay-off is to show that there is a custom to lay-off without pay in the particular industry. Samuels recognized this right but stated that it must be general, of reasonable antiquity and conformity and sufficiently notorious that people would make their contracts on the supposition that it exists.[36] The use of custom has in fact made little impression upon labour law. Common law cases are rare and few deal with the implied right to lay-off. On the strength of a few examples, however, we find a judicial willingness to assert the employer's control over the employment relationship. For example, it would seem that actual knowledge of the custom is immaterial. In *Carus* v. *Eastwood*[37] the works rules of a mill were posted so that employees passed by them each day on their way to work. One of the rules required 14 days' notice to terminate the employment. The respondent, a piece-rate worker, left without giving the required notice and was prosecuted under the Master and Servant legislation. Although it was not proven that the employee had read the rules or could have read them it was held sufficient to sustain a conviction that the rules had been posted, or alternatively it would be sufficient to show that there was a well-known custom in the district concerning notice.

In *Sagar* v. *Ridehalgh and Son*[38] a weaver challenged deductions from the collectively agreed wage rate for work allegedly not carried out with reasonable care and skill. He argued that such deductions were contrary to the Truck Act 1831. This deduction was held not to be illegal but part of the *calculation* of the wage conforming to the custom observed by most mills in Lancashire in the preceding 30 years. It was argued that the plaintiff was employed on the same terms as other workers; it was immaterial whether or not he knew of the practice, but, as a result of the practice, such a term was incorporated into the *oral* contract of employment without any special mention.[39]

A later case confirms the view that to establish a custom actual knowledge is immaterial. In *Petrie* v. *MacFisheries Ltd.*[40] the plaintiff sought to claim a full weekly wage after being away from work owing to illness. The defendant had posted a notice stating that employees who were absent through illness would be paid half their weekly wage for up to three weeks per year. This was a gratuitous act, not a right. Although it was not proven that the plaintiff had seen the notice it was held that he knew of the custom not to pay the full amount of lost wages and it was on this footing that the contract was made.

Incomes Data Services report that, despite the widespread practice of lay-off during the inter-war years, there were no reported cases where employers had succeeded in proving a custom to lay-off. The absence of litigation can perhaps be attributed to economic factors; for example, the fear of gaining a bad reputation for suing an employer may have led to difficulties in finding local employment, or workers may not have had the financial means or legal knowledge to pursue legal remedies. Or litigation may have been unnecessary since the custom and practice of lay-off was known and accepted.[41]

Incomes Data Services argue that the growth of guaranteed week agreements since 1945 might be seen as a recognition that a custom to lay-off exists and therefore sets the price on it. The difficulty with this approach, as they themselves recognize, is that technically it is the guaranteed week agreement and not custom, which gives the legal right to lay-off.[42]

An application of this approach is seen in *(1) Bond* v. *CAV Ltd. and (2) Neads* v. *CAV Ltd.*,[43] where one of the issues was whether there was a custom in the industry to lay-off without pay in the event of dislocation of production due to an industrial dispute. Peter Pain J held that any custom would have been subsumed into the engineering national agreement of 1964 concerning guaranteed pay and outside of that agreement there was no custom in the industry which satisfied the conditions of reasonableness, certainty and notoriety.

To sum up, in theory at least, custom is still recognized as a legal basis for lay-off. The modern formula is described by Incomes Data Services as follows: the employer would have to show that lay-off without pay is typical of the enterprise or industry and that if the parties had been asked about lay-off without pay before entering into the employment relationship they would have agreed that of course it could happen in the particular circumstances.[44] Despite this affirmation, modern cases alleging custom are rare and the courts have been extremely reluctant to recognize a right to lay-off except in the case of casual work.[45] Custom cannot be based merely upon one precedent,[46] and even if an employee has acquiesced in a previous lay-off it will not prevent her from contesting a new attempt to assert an implied right to lay-off based on custom. For example, *Waine* v. *Oliver (R) (Plant Hire)*[47] concerned a claim for a redundancy payment after a period of lay-off under section 3(1) of the Redundancy Payments Act 1965. The employers contended that they had an implied contractual right to lay-off and that since Mr Waine had accepted a lay-off on a previous occasion he was estopped from denying that there was an implied right to lay-off in his contract. The Employment Appeal Tribunal decided that it could not be deduced from the conduct of the parties in the previous incident that they were acting in accordance with the contract but rather their conduct had been dictated by convenience, commonsense and the good relationship between Mr Waine and his employer. Strict rules had to be complied with for an estoppel to come into existence. The fact that the employee had acquiesced in a previous lay-off did not mean that he was estopped from denying that there was an implied power to lay-off in his contract. For an estoppel to be sustained a representation must have been accepted and acted upon so that the party seeking to establish the estoppel had altered her position on reliance upon that representation.

Applying strict contractual rules the industrial tribunals should be able to imply terms which were the presumed intention of the parties at the formation of the contract. This of course may be difficult to prove and the industrial tribunal is likely to fall back upon the custom or practice of the particular trade. The expectations of the parties may be revealed by their conduct; for example, in *Williamson* v. *William Paton Ltd.*[48] the applicant's employment was 'temporarily suspended' for some time before she was dismissed. When she claimed a redundancy payment her employers argued that her dismissal occurred at the time she was first laid off. The industrial tribunal rejected this argument on the grounds that: 'such a suspension is a common feature of employment of women workers in this industry'. The fact that Mrs William-son had remained on the company books, that she was entitled to participate in the Christmas bonus scheme and the employers could call upon her to return to work was evidence enough to show an implied right to lay-off.

A more recent case indicates that there is a heavy onus of proof upon the employer. In *Freeman* v. *B.S. Eaton Ltd.*[49] the Employment Appeal Tribunal refused to uphold an industrial tribunal's finding that there was a custom to lay-off in the general transport industry when trade was slack:

> If the Tribunal was drawing on its own industrial know-how we think that was going beyond the proper use of that industrial know-how since the nature of such practices are matters which have to be looked at carefully and proved by those in that industry. It may well be that drivers are laid off; but the terms on which they are laid off are matters which would have to be investigated had there been expert evidence.

Quite clearly with the duty to issue details of the employment in the 'section 1' statement of the Employment Protection (Consolidation) Act 1978 and the greater regulation of lay-offs the courts are unwilling to turn what are often uncontested breaches of contract into customary rights.

AD HOC AGREEMENTS AND VARIATION OF CONTRACT

Even where there is an express right to lay-off in the contract of employment situations may emerge where the employer may want to vary the contract to cover new contingencies. In the economic recession of the late 1970s and early 1980s, for example, many employers attempted to shorten normal working hours. In the previous section we have already seen some of the limitations of applying the general rules of contract law to the formation of the employment relationship. These limitations are even more acutely observed when looking at the variation of the terms of a contract of employment. The general law of contract uses difficult and technical distinctions between the various processes and consequences of variation, and the situation is further complicated in the contract of employment by at least three other factors.

The first factor is that the employment relationship is not static; it is a continuing and dynamic relationship. As Fox explains:

> Since no employment contract could anticipate all relevant contingencies arising in work relations, many issues had to be settled during the everyday conduct of business.[50]

The problem for the lawyer is how to fit these practical adaptations into the legal mould. For a valid contractual variation to take place the variation must be agreed and some consideration provided. An important distinction is made between, on the one hand, the variation of an existing contract where fresh consideration must be given for each variation otherwise a claim for breach of contract may arise[51] and, on the other hand, the existing contract may be replaced, by proper notice of termination, with a new contract. Consideration is then said to be provided by the mutual abandonment of the outstanding rights under the former contract.[52] In reality these formal rules are rarely adopted for variations of the employment contract and the limitations of the lawyer's static contractual model are exposed. Recent years have seen a greater tendency on the part of employees to challenge employers' practices, encouraged perhaps by the prospect of compensation for job loss. Equally the deepening of the recession encouraged employees to use legal techniques to protect their employment.

A second factor is that the dynamic employment relationship is complicated even further by the interaction of collective rights and individual rights. While most negotiation over working conditions takes place at the collective level the legal emphasis is still focused upon the notion of individual acceptance of collective bargaining through the idea of incorporation of collective agreements into the individual contract of employment. Thus, while there may be a general acceptance of a variation of working conditions, a variation will not be *legally* valid until incorporated into the contract of employment allowing individual employees the opportunity to object to the variation. Several principles of incorporation have emerged. There may be express incorporation, incorporation by custom or implied incorporation.

Complications may arise if an employee does not object immediately to any change and works under the new conditions for a reasonable length of time. Has the employee accepted the new terms by her conduct? Much will depend upon the facts of the case. For example, we have already seen that an employee's acquiescence in a single lay-off will not give an implied right to lay-off in the contract of employment.[53] In another instance an employee agreed to work shorter hours for a reduced wage during the 'Three Day Week' arising from the fuel crisis in the early 1970s. This arrangement lasted for seven months after the national arrangements ended but the Employment Appeal

Tribunal decided that this arrangement did not constitute a proper contractual agreement to shorten contractual hours.[54]

The situation may be even more complicated where there is multi-union bargaining. For example, in *Rigby* v. *Ferodo Ltd.*[55] both the Transport and General Workers' Union (TGWU) and the Confederation of Shipbuilding and Engineering Union (CSEU) were involved in negotiations over wage cuts. Because of economic difficulties the employer considered that it was necessary to cut production costs without reducing turnover within the firm and so short-time working was not a viable option. The employer proposed to make a 5 per cent wage cut arguing that it would be imposed if the unions did not agree to the cut. The CSEU voted to take industrial action but no vote was taken on whether or not to accept the wage cut. The TGWU consented to the cuts and the reduction in wages became automatically incorporated into the contracts of employment of its members. The plaintiff belonged to the AEU, which is part of the CSEU, which refused to acquiesce in the wage cut and threatened industrial action. This threat was later withdrawn but there was never any acceptance of the wage cuts by the CSEU and the plaintiff succeeded in an action brought in the civil courts to claim the shortfall in his wages that had occurred as a result of the unilateral variation of his contract without his own or his union's consent.

Another illustration is found in *Miller* v. *Hamworthy Engineering Ltd.*,[56] where the employer agreed a variation of the contracts of employment to introduce short-time working with a majority of the unions concerned. The Association of Scientific, Technical, and Managerial Staffs (ASTMS) (to which the applicant belonged) refused to consent to the variation. The Court of Appeal rejected the employer's contention that Mr Miller was bound by the majority decision of the other unions:

> The agreement contains no provision for majority decision; it was signed on behalf of each of the unions concerned, and was obviously entered into with each of the unions concerned. I can see nothing which suggests that merely because a majority of the unions were prepared to accept that proposal it was binding upon the members of a union which flatly refused to do anything of the sort.[57]

The interaction of individual and collective rights was also at issue in *Burdett-Coutts* v. *Hertfordshire County Council*.[58] Faced with public expenditure cuts, the employers initiated negotiations with the appropriate trade unions to vary the terms of employment for school meals supervisors.[59] Such negotiations were usually conducted through the National Joint Councils For Local Authorities' Services. No agreement was reached and the employers wrote to the individual employees giving detailed notice of the variations made to their contracts of employment. When this action was challenged, as being in breach of contract, the employers sought to argue that their action should be construed as a termination of the old employment with an offer to re-employ on the new terms and this new offer had been accepted by the fact that the plaintiff had remained in employment. In the High Court Kenneth-Jones J rejected this interpretation: the letter amounted to an attempt to vary unilaterally the terms of employment resulting in a repudiatory breach of contract. The employees had a choice of accepting or rejecting the termination of the contract arising from the employer's breach. Although the employees had remained in employment they had made it clear that they would not accept the amendments to their contracts.

The third way in which the employment relationship is complicated is by the growth of legislative interventions in the 1960s and 1970s which gave employees greater employment protection rights, particularly in the area of termination of the employment contract. These rights attached greater significance to the conduct of the parties and in particular opened up a claim for compensation for constructive dismissal arising from a unilateral variation of the contract. With the increasing awareness of employment protection rights the 1970s and 1980s have witnessed an increasing volume of litigation and a growing number of publications arising from industrial relations specialists on how to handle variations to contracts.[60]

Legal clarification of the effects of a variation of the contract is particularly important in tracing the relationship between the various components of the statutory provisions. At a general level an agreement to shorten working hours will have repercussions for statutory guarantee payments and other employment protection rights, such as unfair dismissal compensation and redundancy payments, which are contingent upon the amount of contractual pay at the time of lay-off or short-time working or the termination of the employment. At a more specific level, we have witnessed the introduction of employment subsidy schemes such as the Temporary Short-time Working Compensation Scheme, which have affected individual contracts of employment. Despite the warnings issued by Freedland, of the dangers of 'leaflet law', in modifying established employment rights,[61] little attempt has been made to clarify the legal significance of such changes.

One of the main problems encountered by the use of the Temporary Short-time Working Compensation Scheme (see pages 123–134) was the fact that while many manual (i.e. weekly-paid) employees could be laid off through an express or implied contractual right, it was not so easy to lay-off staff employees. Thus in the absence of a power to lay-off the contract of employment had to be varied. Research by Incomes Data Services revealed that some staff employees did agree to a *temporary* suspension of their contract of employment when the Temporary Short-time Working Compensation Scheme was introduced, while other employees entered into arrangements where they received full pay but the staff voluntarily agreed to reimburse the company with a percentage of their salary.[62]

A further problem encountered by the use of the Temporary Short-time Working Compensation Scheme was the question of whether individual employees were bound by the agreement made between the Department of Employment and the employer which implemented the worksharing. The application form for the subsidy (TS1) had to be jointly signed by the employer and the appropriate trade union representatives or recognized employee representatives. As Freedland[63] noted, this wording differed from the usual recognition procedures of trade unions established elsewhere in employment legislation. Incomes Data Services[64] argued that 'recognized employee representative' should be understood to mean that where no union was recognized the employees could nominate a person to sign the application form on their behalf. Department of Employment (DE) regional officers did accept application forms signed only by employers if no unions had been recognized. Such an application was followed by a visit and meeting with the workforce by the DE regional officer to ensure that the workforce agreed to the employer's application for the subsidy. Little evidence is available to show how dissenters were dealt with, although Incomes Data Services suggested that, as a preliminary measure, dissenters should be dismissed once a decision to apply for the subsidy had been made.

The effect of the Temporary Short-time Compensation Scheme on contractual rights did cause some official concern. Where the employer had no power to put employees on short-time working the trade union/employee representative signature would have no contractual effect. If the employees were given reasonable notice of the application and they failed to object within a reasonable time, acceptance of the new terms may have been deemed to have taken place. For this reason Incomes Data Services advised employees to ensure that this was only a temporary and conditional variation. The Department of Employment were also keen to stress that any variation in the contract was temporary. A memorandum sent to local offices of the Department of Employment stated:

> A week's pay will generally be what the employee was receiving before he went on to the scheme because the pay is only temporarily changed, so that the provisions of the (original) contract apply even though the employee does not work throughout the relevant week. If it is suspected that a fresh contract may have been negotiated, then the case should be referred to H.Q.[65]

To ensure the temporary nature of any variation in working arrangements as a result of using the Temporary Short-time Working Compensation Scheme the

Trades Union Congress drafted a model clause for use in negotiations concerning short-time working. It read as follows:

> This agreement is for a temporary period only and is being introduced solely in order to avoid redundancies. This agreement does not affect the existing contracts of employment of any employees: these contracts will remain in force for the duration of short-time working. Should any redundancies still occur during this short-time agreement, the entitlements to redundancy payments shall not be adversely affected by these short-time arrangements and, in particular, the amount of a 'week's pay' used in the statutory calculations for redundancy payments shall be the amount payable under the contract of employment relating to normal working hours.[66]

CONTINUITY OF EMPLOYMENT

Much of the previous discussion has focused upon the paramount role played by contract in establishing rights and obligations in the employment relationship. We have seen that statutory interventions have been minimal in the area of making and varying individual employment contracts. When we look at the *consequences* of a lay-off or short-time working, however, we see that the employment protection legislation assumes a more dominant role and that there is little scope for employer or employee to avoid the statutory consequences of their actions.

In particular, it is important to consider whether or not continuity of employment is maintained during a period of lay-off or short-time working since most employment protection rights are contingent upon the employee satisfying minimum periods of continuous employment.[67] The value of some of these rights, for example a redundancy payment, may also depend upon the length of continuous service. A break in continuity will destroy rights perhaps accumulated over many years.[68] Redundancy payments, unfair dismissal compensation and statutory guarantee payments are the rights most likely to be affected by a period of lay-off or short-time working.

Two issues emerge when we look at the implications of partial unemployment for the continuity of employment. The first is the issue of whether an employee works under a contract of employment providing a sufficient number of hours to be worked in order to qualify for the employment protection guarantees. The second issue is whether the partial unemployment has affected the continuity of employment by either varying or terminating the contract of employment to take the employee either deliberately or inadvertently outside the scope of the employment protection legislation.

Computation of Continuous Employment

According to section 151(1) of the Employment Protection (Consolidation) Act 1978 periods of continuous employment are to be computed in accordance with the provisions of section 151 and Schedule 13 to the Employment Protection (Consolidation) Act 1978. Continuity of employment for statutory employment protection purposes is preserved solely by Schedule 13 to the Employment Protection (Consolidation) Act 1978 and an agreement to preserve continuity in circumstances not covered by Schedule 13 may be contractually enforceable but is ineffective for the purpose of enforcing employment protection rights.[69] Conversely, where continuity is expressly preserved by Schedule 13 the contract of employment cannot exclude the statutory rights.[70] Whether or not employment counts towards a period of continuous employment is determined on a week-by-week basis, as is any question as to whether different periods are to be treated as a single period of continuous employment. A week is defined as a week ending on a Saturday.[71] Thus a lay-off of seven days is not necessarily the same as a *week* that does not count towards continuous employment. A week counts towards continuity if the employee is employed for 16 or more hours[72] or if during the whole or part of the week she works under a contract which normally involves working for 16 or more hours per week.[73]

In certain circumstances, instanced in Schedule 13, paragraphs 5–7 of the Employment Protection (Consolidation) Act 1978, the qualifying hours may fall to eight or more hours' work per week. Difficulties may arise, however, where the number of weekly hours worked under the contract can be varied. In *Secretary of State for Employment* v. *(1) Deary and Others (2) Cambridgeshire County Council*[74] the Employment Appeal Tribunal held that is was necessary to review with hindsight 'the working of the contract throughout its life'. Thus, if hours are drastically reduced in the few weeks prior to a redundancy this variation will not automatically break the period of continuous employment. It is a question of fact for the industrial tribunal to determine as to what were the number of hours *normally* worked.[75]

Another important consequence for lay-off and short-time working is the fact that a week may qualify when the employee has been dismissed with notice and has been paid for the notice period although not actually required to work it. Employment does not terminate until the date on which the notice expires.[76] If an employee is dismissed with less than the statutory minimum period of notice the date of termination is governed by section 55(5) of the Employment Protection (Consolidation) Act 1978, which deems the date on which the minimum notice would have expired to be the date of termination. Schedule 13, paragraph 11 to the Employment Protection (Consolidation) Act 1978 states that the interval between the two dates counts as a period of employment.[77]

Specific provisions to maintain continuity of employment during lay-off and short-time working are contained in Schedule 13 to the Employment Protection (Consolidation) Act 1978. It is necessary to look at the rules relating to lay-off and short-time working separately.

Lay-off

Schedule 13, paragraph 4 of the Employment Protection (Consolidation) Act 1978 provides that:

> Any week during the whole or part of which the employee's relations with the employer are governed by a contract of employment which normally involves employment for 16 hours or more weekly shall count in computing a period of employment.

Thus, if there is a suspensory lay-off, employees who normally work under a contract of employment involving 16 hours or more work per week will maintain continuity. Although the contract of employment is suspended it still governs the employment relationship.

For full-time employees working more than 16 hours per week, continuity of employment will be preserved by paragraph 4 of Schedule 13 to the Employment Protection (Consolidation) Act 1978 even if they are only working part of the week covered by the contract. An employee cannot, however, aggregate a series of contracts even if these are with the same employer in order to prove that she is working full time.[78] Similarly the employee cannot average out the hours worked over several weeks to produce a contract involving 16 or more hours work per week[79] unless the contract is of variable hours so that the industrial tribunal can inquire as to what in practice were the normal hours.[80] Holiday weeks and temporary absences may be included within paragraph 4 provided that the contract of employment continues in existence.[81] The issue of whether the contract of employment normally involves more than 16 hours' work must be determined by looking what the parties did in practice.[82]

Short-time Working

In looking at short-time working we must distinguish between a situation where the contract of employment is not varied and one where it is varied since different consequences emerge from the different situations.

If the contract of employment is *not* varied, when the employee is put on short-time working the normal contract of employment will govern the employment relationship, and provided the contract normally involves 16 hours or more work per week continuity of employment will be guaranteed.[83]

On the other hand, if the contract of employment is varied but still involves at least eight hours' work each week the employee may be able to rely upon Schedule 13, paragraph 5 to the Employment Protection (Consolidation) Act 1978, which states that:

> (1) If the employee's relations with his employer cease to be governed by a contract which normally involves employment for 8 hours or more, but less than 16 hours, weekly and, but for that change, the later weeks would count in computing a period of employment or, as the case may be, shall not break the continuity of a period of employment notwithstanding that change.

Schedule 13, paragraph 5(2) allows weeks to count under sub-paragraph (1) for up to 26 weeks.

If short-time working takes the form of one week at work and one week away from work paragraph 5 will not apply since the employee will not be required to work for at least eight hours on the alternate weeks off. Some help may be found by turning to Schedule 13, paragraph 9(1)(c) which provides that:

> (1) If in any week the employee is, for the whole or part of the week . . .
> (c) absent from work in circumstances such that, by arrangement or custom, he is regarded as continuing in the employment of his employer for all or any purposes . . . that week shall, notwithstanding that it does not fall under paragraph 3, 4 or 5 count as a period of employment.

In *Lloyds Bank* v. *Secretary of State for Employment*[84] an employer was refused a maternity payment rebate in respect of a claim for maternity pay paid to a woman who had been working alternate weeks. The Department of Employment argued that the weeks 'off' did not count as a period of employment and therefore the continuity of employment was not maintained. The Employment Appeal Tribunal held that the employment relationship was not governed by a contract of employment during the week off and continuity of employment depended upon the provisions of paragraph 9(1)(c) of Schedule 13. Under this provision, the week off could be regarded as one during which the employee was absent in circumstances such that, by arrangement or custom she was regarded as continuing in the employment of her employer. Although there is no 26 week limit on such an arrangement, the length of absence will be relevant for determining whether or not the cessation was temporary, and therefore any short-time working arrangements involving long periods of lay-off between short periods of work will not automatically fall within paragraph 9(1)(c) unless it is shown that the parties have entered into an arrangement whereby both parties regard the employment as continuing. Some doubts have been expressed as to whether this interpretation is still valid since the decision has now been impliedly but not expressly overruled by the House of Lords decision in *Ford* v. *Warwickshire County Council*,[85] since their Lordships were unanimous in deciding that an employee cannot rely on paragraph 9 of the Schedule 13 until the contract of employment *ceases*.

Problems with Dismissal and Re-engagement

If the partial unemployment is caused by a lay-off handled by way of dismissal followed by re-engagement a new set of provisions contained in Schedule 13(1), paragraph 9(1)(b) of the Employment Protection (Consolidation) Act 1978 may apply. This allows any week during the whole or part of which the employee is absent from work on account of a 'temporary cessation of work' to count as a period of continuous employment. This has led to litigation over the question of how the words 'temporary cessation' are to be interpreted. In *University of Aston* v. *Malik*[86] the Employment Appeal Tribunal held that there must be a cessation of *paid* work. Also it would seem that the reason for the absence is a matter of fact for determination by the industrial tribunal.[87] In *Hunter* v. *Smiths Dock Co. Ltd.*[88] it was held that, although it was relevant to consider evidence showing that when the cessation of work began, the employer and employee expected and anticipated that it would only be for a relatively short period of time, this was by no means decisive. In *Fitzgerald* v. *Hall Russell and Co. Ltd.*[89] the House of Lords held that evidence in hindsight alone, without evidence of a mutual prior agreement for the resumption of employment, was also acceptable. Essentially it was a question of fact in each case and the tribunal should adopt a 'broad brush' approach taking into account all relevant evidence. It is not necessary for the employer's work to cease completely; only that there is no work available for the employee.

In *Puttick* v. *John Wright and Sons (Blackwall) Ltd.*[90] the employee was employed from 1948 as a boiler scaler but because he had been laid off for short periods during this employment the industrial tribunal held that he did not have the necessary period of continuous employment to qualify for a redundancy payment. The National Industrial Relations Court reversed this finding: in looking at the history of the employment relationship, particularly the basic continuity over 23 years, the fact that the employee had never been given notice of dismissal when laid off, but on the contrary had made himself available for work, meant that it could be said that the contract continued in force throughout so the situation was covered by paragraph 4 and not paragraph 9 of Schedule 13 to the Employment Protection (Consolidation) Act 1978.

Turning to more recent decisions, in *Bentley Engineering Co. Ltd.* v. *Crown and S.M. Miller*[91] the Employment Appeal Tribunal argued that previous case law provided helpful guidelines in posing three questions as an aid to interpreting the statutory wording in order to decide whether or not there was a temporary cessation of work:

> Was there a cessation of the employee's work or job, was the employee absent on account of that cessation, and ... was the cessation a temporary one?

In deciding the last question, the Employment Appeal Tribunal held that the industrial tribunal had set out correctly the relevant criteria to be taken into account:

> The nature of the employment; the length of prior and subsequent service; the duration of the break; what was said when the break occurred; what happened during the break; what was said on re-engagement.[92]

The issue was considered more recently by the House of Lords in *Ford* v. *Warwickshire County Council*,[93] when a part-time teacher who was not employed during successive summer holidays was held to have continuity of employment under Schedule 13, paragraph 9(1)(b) to the Employment Protection (Consolidation) Act 1978. Employing a test of hindsight, similar to that used in *Fitzgerald* v. *Hall Russell and Co. Ltd.*, the House of Lords suggested *obiter* that, provided the length of the period between two successive seasonal contracts is short in comparison with the length of the season of employment and can, therefore, be properly regarded as transient, then continuity of employment will be maintained.

Subsequent court decisions have veered between adopting the 'broad brush' approach of *Fitzgerald* v. *Hall Russell and Co. Ltd.* and the 'mathematical approach' of *Ford* v. *Warwickshire County Council.* The Court of Appeal in *Flack* v. *Kodak Ltd.*[94] expressed a clear preference for the *Fitzgerald* reasoning but the Employment Appeal Tribunal in *Sillars* v. *Charrington Fuels Ltd.*[95] argued that the *obiter* remarks in *Ford* were not intended to lay down a mathematical test in all cases but that in *some* cases such a test would be appropriate. The facts of *Sillars* were similar to those in *Ford*, that is, a regular pattern of work with a temporary break each summer, whereas *Flack* was a case of an irregular pattern of work where it would be inappropriate to apply a mathematical test. The Court of Appeal in *Sillars*[96] held that a seasonal worker employed for 30 weeks and 27½ weeks in the two years prior to his dismissal could not bring the absences from work within paragraph 9(1)(b) of Schedule 13. The industrial tribunal was entitled to apply the mathematical test of *Ford* but the *temporary cessation* of work was to be interpreted as meaning a short time as compared to the period of work. Dismissing the employee's argument that in applying only the mathematical test the industrial tribunal had erred in failing to take into account such matters as the intention of the parties that work would resume in the next season as shown by the retention of payroll numbers, overalls and lockers, the Court of Appeal held that this intention only showed that the break from work was not intended to be permanent. However, the fact that a cessation of work is not permanent does not necessarily show that it is *temporary* for the purposes of paragraph 9(1)(b) of Schedule 13. Woolf LJ did discuss the possibility that a seasonal worker might preserve her continuity of employment by showing that she was absent from work by agreement or custom within paragraph 9(1)(c) of Schedule 13.

In contrast, Balcombe LJ justified the exclusion of temporary workers from the scope of employment protection by arguing that where the worker took two jobs (perhaps to cover the different seasons) she would be in the advantageous position of claiming unfair dismissal compensation or redundancy payments from *both* jobs.

Attempts by employers to share out available work may in the long run be to the disadvantage of individual employees who are subsequently made redundant or dismissed since the variation in employment terms may result in the continuity of employment being broken. In *Byrne* v. *Birmingham City District Council*[97] a local authority employee was employed for one year on a casual basis and then engaged for about six months on a fixed-term contract ending on 31 March 1985. In order to share out the available work the Council had created a pool of workers to whom work could be offered when it was available. Mr Byrne was accepted into this pool as a casual worker on 29 April 1985 and remained in the Council's employment until he was dismissed on 26 July 1985. He was not employed between 31 March 1985 and 29 April 1985. On hearing his complaint for unfair dismissal the industrial tribunal decided that Mr Byrne did not have sufficient continuity of employment to bring a claim since the absence from work between 31 March and 29 April 1985 was not due to a temporary cessation of work within paragraph 9(1)(b) of Schedule 13 to the Employment Protection (Consolidation) Act 1978. The Employment Appeal Tribunal and the Court of Appeal upheld this finding. While it was argued on behalf of Mr Byrne that, following *Fitzgerald* v. *Hall Russell and Co.*, the cessation of work should be viewed from the employee's perspective the Court of Appeal held that in this situation there was no cessation of work since there was work available for the employee but it had been given to someone else.

The disadvantages for the employee of looking at the availability of work from the employer perspective are seen in the application of *Byrne* v. *Birmingham City District Council* by the Employment Appeal Tribunal in *Letheby and Christopher Ltd*. v. *Bond*.[98] Here the applicant was a casual worker for over six years. She ran the bar at race meetings and was employed upon a separate contract lasting one or two days each time there was a race meeting. Normally she took her holidays over the Christmas vacation period when there were fewer meetings. In the year prior to her dismissal she worked for a minimum of 16 hours per week except for two weeks when she did not work at all. For one of these weeks in September 1985 work was available but was not offered to her; in the other week in December 1985 she took a holiday. In addition there were nine weeks in the year when she attended only one race meeting working more than eight hours per week but less than 16 hours. The industrial tribunal looked to see if her continuity of employment was preserved by virtue of the provisions of paragraphs 6 and 9(1)(b) and (c) of Schedule 13 to the Employment Protection (Consolidation) Act 1978. The industrial tribunal found that her absences in September and December when compared with the total employment were short and furthermore it could be argued that the September absence could be regarded as a temporary cessation of work within the meaning of paragraph 9(1)(b) of Schedule 13 and in the case of the December holiday, an absence by arrangement or custom. The industrial tribunal also held that it was implicit in her contract that when she attended for only one race meeting a week her normal period of employment was for more than eight hours as required by paragraph 6(1) of Schedule 13. Thus her continuity of employment was preserved. The Employment Appeal Tribunal upheld the employer's appeal. Applying *Byrne* it was held that where work was available to an employee but was not offered there could not be a cessation of work within paragraph 9(1)(b) of Schedule 13. This decision also weakens the employment protection status of casual workers since in addressing the question of whether there was an absence from work due to a custom or arrangement in December it was held that paragraph 9(1)(c) of Schedule 13 did not apply. It was not possible to show that the employment was continuing after the cessation of the previous contract since the applicant was employed under separate contracts. Furthermore it was not possible to show a normal pattern of working by reference to what happened weekly, thus the nine weeks in which she worked less than 16 but more than eight hours per week were not governed by the provisions of paragraph 6(1).

If the employee engages in other employment during the temporary cessation of work this will not automatically result in continuity being broken. For example, in *Thompson* v. *Bristol Channel Ship Repairers and Engineers Ltd*.,[99] the employee was laid off and told he would be re-employed 'in a few weeks' time'. While laid off he took up employment with another employer but went back to his old employment when asked to do so. Later he was made redundant and the employer sought to argue that the continuity of employment had been broken when the employee had sought work elsewhere. The industrial tribunal rejected the employer's claim on the grounds that the alternative employment was merely 'bridging a gap' and the new work did not prevent the employee from resuming old duties when called upon to do so. A similar approach is seen in *Jolly* v. *Spurlings*,[100] but in *Yates* v. *Ruston Diesels Ltd.*[101] continuity was found to be broken when the employee was shown to regard the new employment as permanent. Here the employee had 19 years' service with the firm and had been absent for only 36 days.

Finally, if the employee receives a redundancy payment and is later re-engaged, continuity of employment will be broken[102] and the qualifying period for employment protection rights will commence from the date of the new contract.

Where a contract has been varied against the employee's will further redress may be sought by a return to common law principles and an action for breach of contract. The value of this is seen in *Secretary of State for Employment* v. *(1) Deary and Others (2) Cambridgeshire County Council*,[103] where the school meals supervisors worked under a 'variable hours' contract. The number of hours worked was reduced so that often the women worked less than eight hours per week. In 1982 the women were finally made redundant but they were refused a redundancy payment claim on the ground that they had insufficient continuity of service. The Employment Appeal Tribunal adopted a flexible approach, by not regarding the first dip below the eight-hour qualifying threshold as breaking the continuity of employment. It was held that the employer's reduction of the hours of work was a unilateral breach of contract in this particular case and that the number of hours the women were normally requested to work was always over eight. The next section will explore in greater detail the remedies available for a wrongful lay-off and breach of contract.

EMPLOYEES' REMEDIES FOR A LAY-OFF IN BREACH OF CONTRACT

If there is no contractual right to lay-off without pay but the employer purports to do so, or where there is a right but the agreed conditions are not met, the employer will be acting in breach of contract. An employee may decide to continue with the contract of employment and sue for a breach of contract, or alternatively she may elect to treat the act as a termination of the contract and bring a claim for unfair dismissal alleging that a constructive dismissal has occurred, or claim a redundancy payment.

Suing for a Breach of Contract

It is generally conceded that the 'floor of rights' approach to employment protection has led to many shortcomings in the extent of statutory job protection. The problems concerning continuity of employment, the low level of compensation awards, the under-use of the remedies of re-engagement and re-instatement in unfair dismissal claims and the perceived 'management bias' in the interpretation of the employment protection legislation are some of the reasons put forward to explain why some employees have attempted to assert common law rights and equitable remedies in the ordinary courts.[104]

As Ewing and Grubb point out, this resort to such judicial protection results in a double paradox:

> It was the failure of the common law which was partly responsible for the introduction of the statutory jurisdiction in the first place. Now it is the failure of the statutory jurisdiction to meet expectations which is leading people to fall back on the possibility of greater common law protection. . . . Some of the weaknesses of the present unfair dismissal law exist because of the hostile intervention of the senior judges dealing with appeals from the specialist tribunals. Yet it is to the same judges that employees are now turning for more substantive rights and more effective remedies than the legislation currently provides.[105]

Many of the cases invoking the equitable remedies of an injunction or an order for specific performance involve dismissals taken as disciplinary measures in which it is alleged that the employer has committed a breach of procedure. Such cases may have consequences for claims arising from partial unemployment, perhaps where there has been a failure to consult or follow contractual implementation of redundancy procedures. Even the courts remain hesitant as to whether the pursuance of such remedies is the correct course of action and, particularly in relation to the use of equitable law remedies, academic commentators have also expressed their doubts.[106]

In relation to legal issues arising from partial unemployment, greater success is likely to be found by suing for damages in either the County Court or the High Court if the employee believes that there has been a breach of contract.[107] However, the use of declarations and injunctions may also be available where there is a dispute over contractual rights or the employee believes that the employer's conduct may amount to a termination of the contract of employment.

The fullest discussion of the right to receive pay under the contract of employment when work has not been carried out arises in a series of cases presented to the courts by workers suing for the return of wages deducted or withheld during limited industrial action falling short of a strike. The right to make deductions from wages has now been added to the employer's armoury of tactics in handling industrial action. Other remedies available to the employer include a right to sue for damages for breach of contract,[108] the right to prevent the workforce from working at all[109] and, provided that the employer does not act in a discriminatory way, the right to 'accept' the repudiation of the contract and terminate the contract by a dismissal.[110] To these remedies (and in the face of much criticism)[111] the right to make deductions from an employee's pay has now been added.[112]

The courts have not been consistent, however, in their reasoning for granting this additional remedy. The Court of Appeal in *Henthorn and Taylor* v. *Central Electricity Generating Board*[113] refused the claims by employees denied wages on days they were taking limited action. The basis of the decision was that in order to claim money due under a contract the plaintiffs had to prove that they were ready and willing to perform their contracts of employment. Employees taking industrial action would not be in a position to discharge this burden of proof.

A different position was taken by the High Court in *Royle* v. *Trafford Borough Council*.[114] Here the plaintiff had complied with a union resolution and for six months had refused to take an additional five pupils into his class of 31 pupils. As a result five children were sent home and the education authority was prevented from fulfilling its statutory obligations of providing full-time education for children in its catchment area. The Council warned teachers that they would not be paid for periods when they refused to obey instructions and even though Mr Royle continued to perform all his other duties his salary was withheld for six months. After examining the authorities, Park J held that there was no directly applicable authority on the question of 'partial pay partial work'. Instead he referred to *Chitty on Contracts* for the appropriate general contractual principles as to an innocent party's options in the face of a repudiatory breach of contract:

> Affirmation may be express or implied. It will be implied if, with the knowledge of the breach, he does some unequivocal act to go on with the contract regardless of the breach, or from which it may be inferred that he will not exercise his right to treat the contract as repudiated. Affirmation must be total. The innocent party cannot approbate and reprobate by affirming part of the contract and dis-affirming the rest, for that would be to make a new contract. Mere inactivity after breach does not of itself amount to affirmation; nor it seems does the commencement of an action claiming damages for breach. But if the innocent party continues to press for performance, or accepts performance by the other party, after becoming aware of the breach, he will be held to have affirmed the contract.[115]

Since the employers had accepted the imperfect performance of the contract by allowing Mr Royle to continue teaching they could not refuse to pay him. However, since the plaintiff had not performed his full range of contractual duties the court allowed a 5/36th deduction from his salary.[116] No legal basis for this deduction is made. *Henthorn* is distinguished on the grounds that that decision simply meant that a worker claiming unpaid wages had to prove that she was entitled to be paid for work carried out under the contract of employment. As Morris points out:

> Clearly, however, this begs the question of when, and on what basis, entitlement to sue arises in the first place.

It would have been more consistent with other reasoning in the case to require the employer to initiate a separate claim for damages for breach of contract.

A fuller discussion of the legal basis for deductions from pay during indus-trial action emerged in the judgment of Scott J in *Sim* v. *Rotherham Metropolitan Borough Council.*[117] This again concerned a teaching dispute. The union, the National Union of Teachers, instructed its members not to perform a range of duties, including, *inter alia* the provision of cover for absent colleagues. The Council deducted a sum of money from the plaintiff's salary intended to represent the failure to provide cover for a 35-minute period. The plaintiff argued that she was not under any contractual obligation to provide cover and even if there was such an obligation the Council's remedy lay only in damages.

Scott J held that since teachers were professional workers they owed a general contractual obligation to co-operate in the running of schools in accordance with reasonable directions given by the head teacher. It was held that the provision of cover fell within the scope of such reasonable directions and in failing to comply with the request to supply cover the plaintiff was in breach of contract. This finding has important implications for workers claiming wages where there is a lay-off or short-time working since many guaranteed week agreements and the statutory scheme of guarantee payments allow the employer to offer reasonable alternative work. Equally it provides flexibility for management to argue for a broad range of contractual obli-gations in the contracts of so-called 'professional' workers where the contrac-tual duties are not clearly laid out.[118]

On the second point Scott J held that the plaintiff was entitled to her salary since she had been allowed to continue working. However, the employers had presented a cross-claim for damages flowing from the breach of contract, and the doctrine of equitable set-off was utilized to justify deductions from the salary, the argument being that it would be unjust to allow the plaintiff to proceed without taking into account the loss incurred by the employer. It was agreed that the amount deducted did not exceed the amount the Council could have claimed in damages. This was the first time the doctrine of equitable set-off has been applied to employment contracts.[119] From the employee's perspective the difficulties of allowing this remedy are revealed in the submission made by counsel in *Sim*. Even where there was a dispute over whether the contract had been broken employers were free to impose deductions from pay and the onus would be upon the employee to pursue her remedies before the courts in order to prove the illegality of the action.

The House of Lords was finally invited to discuss the issue of salary deductions in *Miles* v. *Wakefield Metropolitan District Council*.[120] The plaintiff, as a superintendent of births, deaths and marriages, was an office holder paid by the Council. He was engaged to work 37 hours per week, three of these hours were to be worked on Saturday mornings. As a result of a dispute between the National and Local Government Officers' Association union (NALGO) and the local authority over salary rates NALGO instructed its members not to conduct marriage ceremonies on Saturday mornings. Mr Miles obeyed this instruction by attending work on Saturday mornings but refused to officiate at marriage ceremonies. He was informed by the Council that he would not be paid and would not be required to turn up to work at all unless he performed his full range of duties. In taking disciplinary action the Council withheld 3/37th of Mr Miles' pay. He then sued the Council for the wages withheld. Nicholls J held that although there was no express power to deduct sums from the salary due to an office-holder, since Mr Miles was not carrying out all of his statutory duties the Council correspondingly was not under an obligation to pay all of his salary.

In holding that Mr Miles was an office-holder and not an employee the Court of Appeal held that the Registration Service Act 1953 (as amended) under which Mr Miles held his office did not permit deductions from salary. The remuneration was attached to the office and was not a reward for service. Two members of the Court of Appeal did consider what the position would have been if Mr Miles had been an employee.[121] Eveleigh LJ found that it was impossible to lay down a general rule:

> ... other than that there is no rule of law to prevent him [the employer] from ... withholding part of the salary for part performance, but that each case depends upon the particular terms of engagement.[122]

Parker LJ gave the matter more consideration:

> I find it unnecessary to decide whether, if the appellant had been an employee of the respondents, they would have been entitled to withhold part of his salary, but I do not accept that they would. Had that been the case, the respondents would no doubt have had a claim for any damages they could prove but, in the absence of a breach amounting to a repudiation accepted by dismissal or a specific right to suspend, there

appear to be strong grounds for saying there is no right to withhold payment and take the benefit of all work in fact done during the period in which the refusal to perform a particular function was operative. *Gorse* v. *Durham CC*[123] appears to me to be authority for the proposition that there is no such right. The right is asserted on the basis that an employee, in order to recover unpaid salary, must show that in the relevant period he was ready and willing to perform his contract and that, if he was not, he can recover nothing even if his unwillingness did not go to the root of the contract or, albeit that it did, it was not accepted as a repudiation. The validity of this proposition may have to be decided in the future. As it was not fully argued before us and does not require decision now. I say only that I regard the proposition of doubtful validity.

The House of Lords, in holding that Mr Miles' position was analogous to that of an employee, was obliged to address the issue squarely.

In *Miles* it was admitted that the plaintiff was in breach of contract. *Henthorn and Taylor* v. *Central Electricity Generating Board*[124] was relied upon by the House of Lords to uphold the view that there is no right to wages unless they have been earned or the worker indicates that he is ready and willing to perform the services required. Napier[125] points out, however, that there is a distinction between a claim for damages for *breach of contract* brought by an employee and a claim for *arrears of wages in debt*. In the former claim the claimant must show that she is ready and willing to perform the duties imposed by the contract of employment whereas in the latter claim the employee merely has to show that payment was *due* under the contract. Thus Napier argues that in *Henthorn* the court failed to distinguish between the claim for damages and the claim for debt.

A further difficulty in *Miles* was that he had rendered *partial* performance of the contract but the Council had indicated that partial performance was not acceptable. Their Lordships differed in their *obiter* opinions as to the situation where an employer accepted partial performance of the contract (although in *Miles* it is difficult to see how it could be said that the Council did not accept the partial performance). Lord Templeman and Lord Brightman were of the opinion that wages would not be payable because the employee was not ready and willing to perform the services required of him. However, they thought that if he had provided some service he might be able to sue the employer separately on a *quantum meruit* basis.[126] The other Law Lords were not so clear that wages should be denied to an employee who had rendered partial performance where the employer had *not* made it clear that this was not acceptable. Lord Oliver and Lord Brandon left the point open while Lord Bridge claimed that he failed to comprehend the basis on which employees should be entitled to payment on a *quantum meruit* basis rather than remuneration at the contractual rate.

From the House of Lords speeches Smith argues that rather than addressing the specific 'no work no pay' situation of *Miles* the House of Lords addressed the 'whole gamut of "no work no pay" scenarios'.[127] These are described as:

(i) Where there is partial performance but the employer clearly indicates that part performance will not be accepted. The part performance may either be a refusal to do certain tasks or a refusal to work for a defined number of hours.

(ii) Where the part performance is expressly or impliedly accepted by the employer as if it were a performance which satisfied the terms of the contract.

(iii) Where the part performance is accepted by the employer but really only 'of necessity'[128] or (in the words of Lord Templeman) 'in order to avoid greater damage [the employer] is obliged to accept the reduced work'.[129] We might call this 'forced acceptance'.

(iv) Where there is just a 'go slow' or the employees deliberately work 'inefficiently'.

In analysing the four situations depicted by Smith the application of *Miles* would result in the employee being unsuccessful in the first situation but successful in the second since Lords Brightman, Oliver and Brandon agreed that if the employer accepted part performance without treating it as a breach of contract then the employer could not deduct sums by way of damages.[130] Here the doctrine of substantial performance could be used effectively. Although there is the requirement of completion of entire contracts in full before payment can be made arising from *Cutter* v. *Powell*[131] this has been mitigated by the doctrine of substantial performance[132] where as a matter of fact there has been substantial performance of the contract, full payment of wages are due.[133]

In relation to the third situation, only Lord Brightman expressly found that where acceptance of part performance was effectively forced upon an employer would that employer be entitled to refuse to pay wages.[134]

The fourth situation poses real problems and it is difficult to discern any uniformity or majority opinion on the question. Lord Templeman argued that a 'go slow' would justify deductions from wages (or indeed the payment of no wages). Lord Brightman agreed with this, while Lord Bridge preferred not to express an opinion[135] and Lord Oliver did not express any overt opinion on the matter.[136] Lord Brandon agreed with Lord Oliver and Lord Templeman. In view of the reliance placed upon the readiness and willingness to work in order to receive wages in *Miles* the employee will probably have a heavy burden of proof to discharge in the fourth situation.[137] Of course, if the employee fails to render any service due to industrial action there can be no claim against non-payment of wages or any deductions from wages. The employee will have failed to provide actual work[138] and cannot prove she was ready and willing to work.[139]

Morris criticizes the use of the doctrine of equitable set-off since it leaves workers exposed to arbitrary treatment by employers.[140] First of all, as was pointed out earlier, there may be a dispute as to whether there is a breach of contract. This will be a particularly difficult question in cases concerning a dislocation in production where the employer claims that there is a duty under the contract of employment to undertake reasonable alternative work. Secondly, how are the employer's damages to be assessed? For example, the measure of damages may be difficult to assess for non-production workers. For production workers the loss flowing from a breach of contract may be enormous. No clear guidelines seem to have been established. Scott J in *Sim* held that the deduction from pay must relate to the employer's loss rather than the time for which the employee was in breach of contract but in *Sim* the deduction related to the 35 minutes for which the plaintiff had refused to cover and in *Royle* the deduction related to the number of pupils the plaintiff had refused to teach.

The far-reaching effects of *Miles* are seen in the Court of Appeal ruling in *Wiluszynski* v. *London Borough of Tower Hamlets*,[141] another dispute between a local council and the union, NALGO. NALGO took limited industrial action which involved Estates Officers boycotting enquiries from Council members. This work was part of Wiluszynski's contractual duties but occupied only a small amount of his working time. When the industrial dispute was over it took only approximately two-and-a-half to three hours to reply to the enquiry backlog. The Council warned the employees that if they did not comply with the contractual requirement to carry out their full range of contractual duties they would be sent away from the Council premises and would only be paid if they continued to work normally. Later, in a letter sent to the employees, the Council expressed the view that if the employees continued to offer only partial performance of their contract this work would be regarded as unauthorized and undertaken in a voluntary capacity and for which they would not be paid. The industrial action lasted for five-and-a-half weeks and during the period the employees were not paid any of their salary. The High Court upheld Wiluszynski's claim for his *full* salary during the industrial action because it was found that he was substantially performing his contract, higher management were aware of his action and acquiesced in it and the Council took the benefit of the work. While it was hinted that the Council might have legally deducted a small amount of money from Wiluszynski's salary for breach of contract there was no ruling upon the point since it had not been argued by the Council.

The Court of Appeal allowed the Council's appeal and refused leave to appeal to the House of Lords. Despite the small amount of time taken to catch up with the work which had been boycotted, Fox LJ found that the employee's breach of contract was not insubstantial: it was of considerable importance. Firstly, because of the constitutional responsibilities of councillors to their constituents it was important that they should be supplied with information. Secondly, the fact that this particular form of industrial action was an effective form of industrial action deployed by the union revealed its significance in terms of a breach of contract. Nicholls LJ found that Wiluszynski had committed a repudiatory breach of contract entitling the Council to dismiss him. Support can be found in the speeches of Lord Bridge and Lord Brightman in *Miles* to endorse the view put forward by Nicholls LJ that it was possible for the Council to decline to accept the partial performance offered by Wiluszynski *and* to continue to hold out to him that the Council was willing and ready to continue the contract of employment if Wiluszynski chose to do so as well. Nicholls LJ did not accept the argument put forward by the employee that the Council had altered its position from the warning letter, and on the facts there was no question of a waiver of rights or an estoppel.

On the question of whether the Council had accepted the benefit of the partial performance of the contract, Fox LJ and Nicholls LJ agreed that the Council had not, and it was not necessary to take drastic action such as a lockout since some of the employees were working normally and it was unrealistic to expect the Council to introduce a policing system or attempt to use legal action such as applying for an injunction since this would worsen industrial relations. Regarding the issue of whether there had been acquiescence in the breach of contract since Wiluszynski's superior had given him work in breach of Council instructions, Fox LJ and Nicholls LJ were prepared to agree with the High Court finding that one could not safely conclude that a member of the Council's senior management gave any direction to Wiluszynski's superior to give him work. The mere fact that the Council took the benefit of the work was not enough to disentitle the Council from arguing that they refused to accept partial performance of the contract and the fact that the Council had taken the benefit of Wiluszynski's work was not enough to show that they had acquiesced in the breach of contract.

Nicholls LJ discusses the issue of what amounts to an 'acceptance' of partial performance:

> But a person is not treated by the law as having chosen to accept that which is forced down his throat despite his objections. The rationale underlying the principle of waiver is that a person cannot have it both ways: he cannot blow hot and cold; he cannot eat his cake and have it; he cannot approbate and reprobate. But this does not mean that an employer of a large workforce is required physically to eject a defaulting

employee from his office, or prevent him from going round the estate of houses for which he is responsible, on penalty that if he, the employer does not do so he must pay the employee for the work which the employee insists on carrying out contrary to the employer's known wishes.[142]

Thus it is a question of fact in each case: the court will look to see if the employer has given an expression of a genuine attitude and that there is no question of the employee being misled or confused by the employer's actions. No guidance is given, however, as to how and on what basis an employer could make *partial* deductions from pay if she decides to accept partial performance.

The explanation for reaching this conclusion put forward by Nicholls LJ in *Wiluszynski* is given in an explicitly industrial relations context. While an employee would normally work for money and be paid, in this situation the employee deliberately chose to follow a path where he knew he was not entitled to be paid. Thus it seems that the courts are not prepared to sanction the use of effective industrial action by upholding the right to pay on either a *pro rata* or *quantum meruit* basis.

Although these cases are concerned mainly with industrial action resulting in the employee not working (either fully or partially) they may have significance for the issues raised by work shortages resulting from partial unemployment. Particularly where a lay-off or short-time working results from industrial action or where the employees are asked to carry out alternative work because of a work shortage, a dispute may arise as to whether the employer has a contractual right to order the employees to carry out different work under the contract. Many collective guaranteed week agreements and the statutory guarantee payments scheme allow the employer some discretion in ordering employees to carry out 'reasonable alternative work' during a temporary dislocation in production.

Turning to the cases where the contractual remedies have been pursued by employees not engaged in industrial action but where they have received a reduction in wages because of economic factors, we see again that the use of contractual remedies has been pursued by trade unions as an additional collective bargaining/industrial relations tactic. In *Miller* v. *Hamworthy Engineering Ltd*.[143] the employee succeeded in a claim to recover the shortfall in his wages when the employer unilaterally imposed short-time working. In *Rigby* v. *Ferodo Ltd*.[144] the employer attempted to argue that damages were only available to cover the amount of wages underpaid equivalent to the proper notice period. The House of Lords rejected this argument in holding that the contractual rate of pay is payable until the contract has been terminated or varied in the correct way. If the employment is terminated at the time of the breach of contract (because the employee has accepted the repudiation) the employee may only claim damages equivalent to the correct amount of notice time. In *Rigby* v. *Ferodo*, however, the employer deliberately intended to keep the workforce at work in order to cut production costs and did not intend to terminate the contracts of employment.

Obviously, the cases which have resulted in litigation are those where drastic economic measures have been used by employers in order to respond to industrial and economic situations. From case studies conducted on the Short-time Working Project at the University of Kent 1983–5 and through an analysis of redundancy agreements made available to us and through surveys conducted by Industrial Relations Services and Incomes Data Services, measures other than variations in hours or wages are used to respond to partial unemployment. One of the most common occurrences where it was convenient was to vary employees' holidays either by lengthening them or altering the time at which they should be taken. While such measures could be found in redundancy handling agreements it was often uncertain whether it was a valid exercise of management discretion. Faced with the prospect of a holiday or no work few employees bothered to question the legality of such arrangements. Another tactic, of which there is only anecdotal evidence, is that with the introduction of statutory sick pay employers could ask employees not to attend work when there was a work shortage but claim that they were sick. The employer was reimbursed any sick pay made to employees. Again the legality of such a move has not resulted in any litigation.

Equitable Remedies for Breach of Contract

Finally, we can briefly consider the relevance of the equitable remedies for breach of contract. Normally the equitable remedy of an order for specific performance is not available for a breach of a contract of employment. As Carty observes, the reasons given for this rule are diverse: enforced serfdom, lack of mutuality, difficulty of supervision and the notion of not forcing a relationship.[145] This rule is no longer an absolute rule[146] and injunctions have been granted restraining dismissals,[147] and recently an order has been issued in relation to an employer's refusal to appoint an employee to a post she had been offered.[148]

There is no reason in principle, therefore, why an order of specific performance should not be available requiring an employer to keep to the agreed terms of a contract until such time as the contract has been properly varied or terminated.[149] In this respect, an injunction may also be sought to restrain a threatened breach of contract where the employer is attempting to break an employment contract, for example, by reducing hours of work.

In *Hughes* v. *London Borough of Southwark*[150] a local authority was restrained from forcing hospital social workers to transfer to a community district. An injunction was granted since there had not been a breakdown of mutual trust and confidence between the parties. However, this remedy will not be readily available; difficulties may arise as to the exact scope of the contractual obligations, as is seen in the refusal to grant a mandatory injunction in *MacPherson* v. *London Borough of Lambeth*,[151] where employees sought protection in the High Court to require the employer to observe the terms of the contract of employment and to continue paying wages. This dispute arose from a new-technology agreement reached between the union, NALGO, and the Council, when it was felt that because of increased workloads it was necessary to computerize the administration of the housing stock in Lambeth. Clause 4(1) of the agreement provided that the parties should reach agreement prior to the purchase and installation of new-technology equipment. Other clauses provided for the regrading of jobs and for the maintenance of the status quo (unless specific arrangements had been made and jointly agreed) until new arrangements could be implemented in the future. This agreement worked well until 1986, when the Council proposed a new method of computerization to deal with the administration of housing benefit and rent collection. Since the Council had been rate-capped it argued that it had to act quickly and could not follow the agreed procedures. An initial agreement was reached with the union NALGO, but key matters such as terms and conditions of employment and pay were omitted from this agreement. By March 1988 a deadlock was reached in the relations between NALGO and the Council, and the Council issued a statement to the employees stating that they must operate the new computer system otherwise the Council would have no alternative but to stop all pay. Lawyers acting for the employees replied saying that the employees would report for work and were willing to work according to their contracts but they were not prepared to use the new computer. Before the High Court the issue was whether the new-technology agreement had been incorporated into the employees' contract of employment. The Council argued that the court could not grant a mandatory injunction to compel the Council to pay money. The plaintiff's correct remedy was to issue proceedings for each instalment of pay as it fell due.

Echoing the decision in *Cresswell* v. *Board of Inland Revenue*,[152] it was found that the plaintiff could not perform his duties without using the new computer and that the Council was not obliged to pay the plaintiff unless he was willing and able to discharge his obligations under the contract. If, as the plaintiff alleged, the Council had introduced the new computer system in breach of their contractual obligations,[153] the plaintiff was entitled to terminate the contract of employment and sue the Council for breach of contract. It was not possible, however, for the plaintiff to claim he was still able and willing to perform his contractual obligations by working in the way in which he worked before the new computer was introduced knowing full well that it was impossible for him to do so. It was impossible to operate the new housing benefits scheme manually once it had been computerized.

The decision of the High Court in *Wiluszynski* was distinguished in that there was no evidence in *MacPherson* that the Council had accepted the plaintiff's services as substantially complying with the contract of employment. On the contrary, they had done everything to make it clear, including defending the legal action, to show that they would not accept the plaintiff's work and would not pay for it.

Thus, similar criticisms to those voiced by Morris on the *Miles* decision, of the lack of protection afforded to employees alleging that there has been a breach of contract, may be levied in relation to the application of injunctive relief. There are other limitations in using the equitable remedies, for example, the remedies of an injunction and specific performance are only available at the discretion of the court. However, on a more positive note it should not be forgotten that there are a range of remedies available to be pursued since an employee may also seek a declaration of the parties' legal rights. In particular, an employee may apply for a declaration of her continuing entitlement to wages.[154] Again, in order to succeed in such an action the employee must be ready and willing to work.[155]

Of course, the use of equitable remedies may work both ways. An employee may find that the shortage of work lowers her earnings or prevents her from exercising skills in the labour market. She may want to transfer her employment, while the employer may regard the work shortage as temporary and want to retain trained staff for when the work picks up. Or the employer may want to prevent employees taking skills and perhaps trade secrets to rival competitors. The courts have not abandoned the rule against specific performance entirely, as is seen in *Warren* v. *Mendy and Another*,[156] where it was confirmed that an injunction to restrain a breach of contract for personal services will not be granted where its effect will be to require specific performance of a contract. In this case the plaintiff sought to restrain the defendant from inducing a breach of a boxing management contract. While the courts have been willing to enforce negative covenants in the contract of employment (for example, restraining the performance of services for a competitor), problems arise where the services are tied up with the exercise of a special skill or talent. Nourse LJ argued that such negative covenants will not be enforced if they effectively compel the employee to perform a positive obligation. The issue of whether there is compulsion depends upon the facts of the case, although Nourse LJ sets out the principles on which this may be judged. He argues that a realistic regard must be taken of the probable reaction to the injunction on the psychological, material and sometimes physical needs of the employee to maintain a skill or talent. The longer the time for which the injunction is sought, the more readily will compulsion be found.

The Advantages and Disadvantages of Using Common Law and Equitable Remedies

To summarize, there are disadvantages in bringing a claim for breach of contract. For example, the proceedings may be subject to delay and formalities leading to the necessity of engaging a lawyer for legal representation (although legal aid may be available), and there is the risk of having to pay the employer's costs if the case is lost. There are some advantages, however. If the action is successful the employee may recover all wages lost and, technically (although it is highly improbable), the employer may be fined and even face imprisonment if she fails to obey the court order. If the employer is unable to pay the wages, a claim for redundancy pay may be made and if the employer is insolvent an application for payment of contractual and statutory debts may be made to the Secretary of State for payment from the Redundancy Fund under section 122 of the Employment Protection (Consolidation) Act 1978.

The main advantage of common law and equitable remedies is that the employee does not have to terminate the contract of employment and prove that there has been a repudiatory breach of contract by the employer. The remedy is particularly useful for employees who are outside the scope of the employment protection legislation and therefore cannot qualify for a redundancy payment or unfair dismissal compensation and for employees who want to keep their jobs. While this claim may appear an attractive way of ensuring employment *and* wages it has been relatively under-used. Various explanations can be put forward to explain why this is so. It may be that resort to individual legal remedies is less effective than collective action in the form of strikes or working to contract in the world of industrial relations. Economic realities must also play a major part. In times of prosperity an employee may decide to cut her losses and move on to another job; in times of recession it is unlikely that an employee who has a reputation for suing for lost wages will be easily re-employed.

With the weakening of the status of individual employment and trade union rights it may be that this is another tactic to be deployed by trade unions. Other groups of workers may choose to pursue claims through the civil courts and it may not be just a lack of employment protection that the contractual remedy assumes prominence. The employer's action in *Burdett-Coutts* was in response to public expenditure cuts. The advantages of using a contractual remedy over the statutory remedy of unfair dismissal in this case are clear. If the women had chosen to treat the case as one of a repudiatory breach of contract it is doubtful if they would have won a claim for unfair dismissal since the courts and tribunals have tended to accept as reasonable a termination which the employer argues is necessitated by economic stringencies.[157] Furthermore, even if they had been successful the remedy would most likely have resulted in the women receiving a small lump-sum payment as compensation with the prospect of long-term unemployment.

Unfair Dismissal and Redundancy Pay

As an alternative to a claim for breach of contract an employee may claim that the variation in the contract amounts to a dismissal in law. If she decides to leave the employment she may argue that she has been constructively dismissed. The continuous service qualification for an unfair dismissal claim is now two years for all employment contracts commencing after 1 June 1985.[158]

For some time an idea gained currency that the test for constructive dismissal was not limited merely to cases of repudiation or fundamental breach of contract but also extended to any case where the employer's conduct could be said to be unreasonable, judged by reference to the test of unfairness now contained in section 57(3) of the Employment Protection (Consolidation) Act 1978. This approach was laid to rest by the Court of Appeal in *Western Excavating (EEC)* v. *Sharp*,[159] which reaffirmed the traditional ground of repudiation of contract.[160]

The position in relation to wrongful lay-off is stated in *Jewell* v. *Neptune Concrete Ltd.*:[161]

> In law, the right to suspend can only be exercised by an employer in cases where the contract of employment expressly or impliedly gives the employer that right. An employer is not entitled unilaterally to suspend an employee and, if he does so, the employee is entitled to say 'I treat this as a repudiation by you of my contract of employment'.

An example, of a successful claim of constructive dismissal is seen in the case of *Grimes* v. *E. Marshall Smith Ltd.*[162] Mr Grimes was laid off without pay for up to six weeks because of a shortage of work. The employers had no express or implied right to lay him off without pay. When Mr Grimes objected to the lay-off his employers dismissed him. In a claim for unfair dismissal and a redundancy payment it was held that he was unfairly dismissed because his refusal to go along with the unlawful lay-off could not be regarded as a substantial reason justifying dismissal. The real reason for the lay-off and the dismissal was a shortage of orders, entitling the employee to claim a redundancy payment.

An example of a breach of lay-off conditions can be found in the case of *A. Dakri and Co.* v. *Tiffen*,[163] where there was a contractual right to lay-off but the employees were not informed as to when there would be a return to work. The company then closed its factory and moved without informing the employees. Nine of the employees terminated their contracts and claimed a redundancy payment. Although no time limit for the lay-off was fixed in the agreement the Employment Appeal Tribunal was prepared to hold that the law implied that such a lay-off would not extend beyond a reasonable time. What was a reasonable amount of time would depend upon the circumstances of the case and was a matter of fact to be determined by the industrial tribunal.

It may be that the courts are moving towards adopting a *subjective* test of the employer's intention and thus diluting the employer's liability for a significant breach of contract. This view is aired in the judgment of Sir John Donaldson MR in *Bridgen* v. *Lancashire County Council*.[164] Although the ratio of this particular decision did not adopt such a test, it has been argued that the adoption of a subjective approach could have far-reaching consequences, particularly in the defence of unfair dismissal claims.[165] An employer may try unilaterally to impose new terms into the contract of employment believing she was entitled to introduce new terms in the interests of 'managerial flexibility' as a reason for the dismissal under section 55(2)(c) of the Employment Protection (Consolidation) Act 1978.

There is a mixture of authority as to whether a lay-off in breach of contract amounts to a dismissal by the employer. Some judges adopt the normal 'elective theory'; that is, a repudiatory breach of contract is of no effect until it has been 'accepted' by the innocent party.[166] The competing theory is the 'automatic termination theory'; that is, that a repudiation by one party to the contract automatically terminates the contract.[167] Despite the Court of Appeal ruling in *Gunton* v. *Richmond-upon-Thames London Borough Council*,[168] the more recent discussion of the issue in *Rigby* v. *Ferodo*[169] suggests there is still no firm confirmation of the majority decision in *Gunton*. It is disappointing that the House of Lords in *Rigby* refused to accede to the Court of Appeal's request for guidance on the matter. The House of Lords felt that it was inappropriate to comment upon the competing termination theories since in *Rigby* there was no outright termination by the employer. Reading the judgments in *Rigby* it would seem that in the case of an 'outright dismissal' (on the part of the employer), or 'walk-out' (on the part of the employee), a repudiation *may* automatically terminate a contract of employment. If there is a repudiatory breach falling short of these situations the innocent party can choose whether or not to accept it. Conceptually this distinction is important because it allows the employee to waive the breach of contract and seek remedies under the existing contract, for example, sue for lost wages (as in *Rigby* v. *Ferodo* and *Burdett-Coutts* v. *Hertfordshire CC*) or claim guarantee payments under a collective guaranteed week agreement or the statutory guarantee pay provisions.

If the employer's breach of contract does not terminate the contract automatically but leaves the employee with the option of terminating or affirming the continuing existence of the contract the employee may do nothing about her rights for several weeks. It would seem that cogent evidence is required to show that an employee is aware of her rights and has decided not to exercise them. In *Friend* v. *PMA Holdings*,[170] for example, the employee agreed to work less hours for less money during the fuel crisis in 1973. When the national crisis was over, the employers were unable to resume full-time working and the employee remained on the reduced hours for seven more months. The Employment Appeal Tribunal held that it could not be inferred from the employee's delay alone that she had agreed to accept the new employment terms.[171] A similar conclusion was reached in *Powell Duffryn Wagon Co. Ltd.* v. *House*.[172] Mr House was laid off without pay because an industrial dispute involving British Rail dried up the supply of work. The employment was governed by a guaranteed week agreement but the employers refused to make a guarantee payment. After a four-month delay Mr Powell made a claim for a redundancy payment. The National Industrial Relations Court found that the employees had agreed to waive their rights to terminate the contract provided the stoppage was temporary. After four months without pay, their right to a guaranteed wage or to terminate the contract revived and therefore Mr House could claim to be dismissed by reason of redundancy. The court acknowledged that the fallback wage was intended to protect employees in precisely the situation that Mr House found himself in. The employer had to decide quickly whether or not to uphold the obligations under the guaranteed week agreement or opt for a redundancy situation. Cogent evidence would be demanded to support the proposition that employees had agreed to forgo their rights.

In *Bocarisa and Garcia* v. *B. Simmonds Ltd.*[173] the employer altered the employee's method of payment from a weekly basis to a piece-work basis with a guarantee that employees would earn not less than two-thirds of their previous weekly pay. The employees were laid off owing to a shortage of work and the guarantee was not paid. The industrial tribunal found that the employer's failure to pay the guaranteed wage did not amount to a repudiation of contract and thereby it was found that there was no intention to dismiss the employee. In finding that the action did in fact amount to a constructive dismissal, entitling the employees to claim a redundancy payment, the Employment Appeal Tribunal stated that the position taken by the industrial tribunal was:

> a misapprehension of the law of repudiation. If one party to a contract commits a fundamental breach of it, the other party is entitled to treat the breach as a repudiation of the contract and to accept such a repudiation: thereupon the contract is at an end. It is not necessary that the person committing the breach should himself have intended to put an end to the contract.

Not every breach of contract will give rise to a claim of constructive dismissal since the employee's resignation must be in response to a particular breach of contract. In *Freeman* v. *B.S. Eaton Ltd.*[174] the employers had acted in breach of contract on three occasions. On the first occasion the employers failed to pay the employee an additional £100 which had been promised to the employee for working when other employees had been given a holiday. On the second occasion he was suspended without pay as a disciplinary measure when the employer had no power to do so. On the third occasion he was laid off without pay when there was no express or implied term in the contract of employment to do so. The industrial tribunal held that these 'incidents' did not amount to a breach of contract. Although the Employment Appeal Tribunal held that the employers were in breach of contract on each occasion and that the lay-off amounted to a fundamental breach of contract allowing a claim for constructive dismissal, the Employment Appeal Tribunal upheld the industrial tribunal's finding of fact that Mr Freeman's resignation was not in response to the breaches of contract but was for another reason.

Finally, the interaction of the claim for unfair dismissal and a claim for sex or race discrimination should be noted. These issues are discussed more fully in Chapter 6 when considering the alternatives to seniority systems of lay-offs. It is interesting to note that the first case taken by the Women's Legal Defence Fund was based upon a variation of a contract to introduce short-time working. The claim was brought by Maxine Ballard, whose working week was cut back by one day (with an almost equivalent pay cut) in response to financial difficulties encountered by her employers. Three other female colleagues were subject to a similar cutback but all the male employees remained on normal working arrangements. A complaint was made to the Equal Opportunities Commission in the hope that a formal investigation would take place, and industrial tribunal proceedings were initiated under sections 1 and 6 of the Sex Discrimination Act 1975 together with a claim that the pay reduction amounted to a constructive dismissal.[175]

A disadvantage of the claim alleging that there has been a constructive dismissal is that the employee can only bring a claim for a redundancy payment or unfair dismissal compensation. The maximum amount in 1989–90 that can be awarded for a compensatory award for unfair dismissal is £8,925.[176] This may be contrasted to the situation where reinstatement is requested but not granted in matters relating to trade union dismissals. Here the minimum special award is £12,550 and the maximum amount of the award is £25,040. In cases where reinstatement is awarded but not complied with the minimum amount of the unfair dismissal award is £18,795.[177] In even starker contrast is the fact that the median award of unfair dismissal compensation for successful applicants to industrial tribunals in 1987/8 was a mere £1,865.[178]

Statutory redundancy payments are calculated on the number of years of service. These are calculated, working backwards, as one-and-a-half weeks' pay for each year of service between the ages of 41 and 60 (for women) and 65 (for men),[179] one week's pay for each year of service between the ages of 22 and 41; and half-a-week's pay for each year of service between the ages of 18 and

21. The statutory redundancy award is subject to a maximum calculation of 20 years at a maximum rate of £172 per week.[180] In addition, there may be entitlement to a contractual redundancy payment which improves upon the statutory provisions.

The industrial tribunal cannot award compensation for back pay. This anomaly could be eased by the implementation of the proposal, originally put forward in the Department of Employment Consultative Document on the Employment Protection Bill of 1974,[181] (and now contained but not implemented in section 131 of the Employment Protection (Consolidation) Act 1978) that industrial tribunals should have jurisdiction to deal with certain claims for damages for a breach of the contract of employment. As the Consultative Document acknowledged, this would simplify litigation since industrial tribunals often hear evidence relevant to the claim for a breach of contract while dealing with unfair dismissal and redundancy claims. The Department of Employment has circulated a Consultative Document inviting comments on whether or not the powers contained in section 131 of the Employment Protection (Consolidation) Act 1978 should be exercised. Initially these powers were not implemented when a draft order prepared by the Labour government in 1978 was opposed by the Trades Union Congress which feared that the industrial tribunals would become too legalistic when confronted by breach of contract claims. In particular the TUC was concerned that the tribunals should not develop the bad points of the court system such as delays in achieving hearings and long and expensive proceedings.

Following recommendations by the Justice Report (1987), in 1989 the Department of Employment sought views on firstly, whether the powers under section 131 should be exercised at all. Secondly, if so, whether the industrial tribunals should be given power to hear claims: (a) where the claim arises or is outstanding on the termination of employment; and (b) where the claim arises in circumstances which have also given rise to separate proceedings brought before a tribunal (for example, where there is a redundancy or unfair dismissal claim), or whether the requirement under (b) should be a necessary prerequisite for a claim being heard under (a). Thirdly, whether certain actions involving particular complexity should be exempted from the scope of tribunal jurisdiction. The Trades Union Congress has now altered its position on the implementation of section 131, accepting that it will simplify the procedures for dealing with breach of contract claims and help clarify the situation regarding contractual claims under the Wages Act 1986.

At the same time the government has introduced measures in the Employment Act 1989 which will make the presentation of claims to industrial tribunals more difficult. For example, the Act removes the requirement that small businesses with fewer than 20 employees provide details of disciplinary procedures in section 1 of the Employment Protection (Consolidation) Act 1978 statement of particulars of terms and conditions of employment, and the length of continuous service has been raised to two years in order for employees to be eligible for a written statement of reasons for dismissal under section 53 of the Employment Protection (Consolidation) Act 1978. Both these provisions may have consequences for employees who are seeking to bring unfair dismissal claims as a result of dismissals, constructive or otherwise, arising from partial unemployment. The introduction of the power to order deposits of up to £150 for industrial tribunal proceedings may also deter applicants.

CONCLUSIONS

Contractual principles, it was argued, provide the historical link in the regulation of partial unemployment. We have seen that in the past the simple solution to adjusting to market changes by hiring and firing at will was not always so easy to apply, particularly where the employer wished to retain an interest in skilled labour. The reaction of the law was to adapt the contract of employment in a somewhat paradoxical fashion: first, by implying a duty to maintain the employment relationship and secondly, by introducing a certain amount of flexibility into the contract to allow an implied right to lay-off in certain circumstances. As such the contract of employment provided a framework for the adjustment of labour to fluctuations in demand. The lack of any coherent unemployment insurance programme and an unsympathetic judiciary left the employee largely unprotected in both a financial and a legal sense. The idea of the employer providing compensation for periods of unemployment took some people a long time to accept. For example, Sachs writing in 1947 commented:

> The general rule is that so long as the employer pays whatever is due under his contract, he is, in the absence of some express stipulation, under no obligation to provide actual work. This may result in the highly unsatisfactory position of the employee receiving his salary or wages but not being able to exercise his occupation. At least it is a position which I think most people, even in these days, would think unsatisfactory – though there are some who are not averse to receiving money for doing nothing.[182]

Today the employment relationship is far more complex. Davies and Freedland provide a useful description in stating that the relationship is a *combination* of common law, collective bargaining and statutory regulation.[183] These three strands are clearly visible in the current regulation of partial unemployment.

While the right to lay-off or put employees on short-time working and the conditions of lay-off and short-time working are governed by the contract of employment, this in itself is likely to be influenced by collective bargaining. The *consequences* of partial unemployment are regulated by statutory interventions, but despite the importance of statutory rights these are defined and mediated through contractual rights.

As we have seen, the use of contract to regulate the employment relationship reveals limitations in this device to adapt to changes in the labour market and provide protection for employees. As Carty argues:

> In essence, therefore, the employer had the best of both worlds: the law might only imply a minimal commitment from him but it required a wide notion of 'fidelity' from his employees.[184]

From a regulation perspective an inherent limitation is the individualistic approach taken by the law towards the employment relationship and the inflexibility of the contract model to allow simple variations of contract. The result has been that *ad hoc* variations have taken place without much thought as to the legal significance of the changes; economic pressures seemingly more immediate than legal niceties. These responses have been affected in the post-1945 period by developments in collective bargaining and the growing influence of the state. The former has never been comprehensive and has never been satisfactorily reconciled with the individualistic notion of the employment contract. While the right to insist upon contractual rights is a useful remedy for those employees not covered by collective bargaining it has also been used by trade unions as an industrial relations tactic in cases such as *Rigby* v. *Ferodo, Miller* v. *Hamworthy Engineering Ltd., Wiluszynski* v. *London Borough of Tower Hamlets*, and *MacPherson* v. *London Borough of Lambeth*.

The involvement of the state in this area is also significant for contractual rights. It was suggested earlier that the increase in statutory employment protection rights has focused attention upon the employment relationship.[185] This aspect of state intervention is also linked to the fact that the state has become directly involved in providing compensation for unemployment. While this has become a central concern of social policy the direct and indirect costs have become a politically sensitive aspect of public expenditure. Although few people today would register the same distaste as Sachs in recognizing the need to provide compensation for partial unemployment, *how* this should be achieved is still a matter of debate. In order to discharge some of the financial and administrative burdens of partial unemployment the state has sought to transfer some of the costs to individual employers in the form of redundancy payments, guarantee payments and unfair dismissal compensation. The result of this policy has been an increasing counter-pressure from employers to reduce the fixed costs of labour, to reduce the liability to make

National Insurance contributions, and to make the labour force adjustment more flexible and adaptable to fluctuations in demand. Although the Conservative government has helped this process by embarking upon a policy of 'deregulation' of the labour market since 1979, we now see a parallel tendency for employers to take greater care in drafting employment contracts to allow for flexibility as well as reducing liability for employment protection rights by the use of part-time work,[186] home-based work, task contracts or encouraging self-employment.

NOTES

1. Wages Councils also played an important role in guaranteeing the wages of the low paid and non-unionized sectors of the labour market. Their role has diminished since proposals to reduce their powers were put forward in 1985. Section 12(2) of the Wages Act 1986 removed people under the age of 21 from the scope of Wages Council regulation and section 14 limited Wages Council Orders to fixing a basic minimum hourly rate, overtime entitlement and a limit on deductions from pay that an employer can make for living accommodation. At the time of writing a Consultative Paper has been issued proposing the total abolition of the Wages Councils. See Keevash, S., 'Wages Councils: An Examination of Trade Union and Conservative Government Misconceptions about the Effect of Statutory Wage Fixing', 14 *Industrial Law Journal*, pp. 217–32 (1985).

2. [1977] IRLR 404.

3. *Land and Wilson* v. *West Yorkshire Metropolitan County Council* [1981] IRLR 87.

4. Davies, P. and Freedland, M. (eds) *Kahn-Freund's Labour and the Law*, (London, Stevens, 3rd edn., 1983) at p. 168.

5. Incomes Data Services, 'Short-time to Save Jobs', *Incomes Data Services Study 241*, (May 1981).

6. [1983]IRLR 360.

7. *Labour Law: Text and Materials*, (London, Weidenfeld and Nicolson, 2nd edn., 1984) at p. 359.

8. See *Jewell* v. *Neptune Concrete Ltd.* [1975] IRLR 147.

9. [1981] IRLR 57.

10. *Friend* v. *PMA Holdings* [1976] ICR 330.

11. *The Contract of Employment*, (Oxford, Clarendon Press, 1976) at p. 20.

12. 'Aspects of the Wage–Work Bargain', 43 *Cambridge Law Journal*, pp. 337–48 (1984).

13. *Supra* note 6.

14. Cf. Elias, P., 'The Structure of the Employment Contract', 35 *Current Legal Problems*, pp. 95–116 (1982).

15. Section 1 of the Employment Protection (Consolidation) Act 1978.

16. [1906] 2 KB 728; [1926] 1 KB 522. Discussed in Chapter 2.

17. [1906] 2 KB 728.

18. See Incomes Data Services, *Lay-offs and Short-time*, (London, Incomes Data Services Handbook Series No. 19, 1981) at p. 6.

19. [1977] ICR 872.

20. *Supra* note 6.

21. *Op. cit.* note 7 at p. 358.

22. *Jones* v. *Harry Sherman Ltd.* [1969] 4 ITR 63.

23. Discussed in Chapter 5.

24. *Namyslo* v. *Secretary of State for Employment* [1979] IRLR 333.

25. [1988] ICR 451.

26. See *Western Excavating (ECC) Ltd.* v. *Sharp* [1978] ICR 221.

27. [1982] ICR 626.

28. 'Implied Mobility Clauses', 17 *Industrial Law Journal*, pp. 253–56 (1988).

29. See, for example, Lord Wright in *Luxor Eastbourne Ltd.* v. *Cooper* [1941] AC 108.

30. [1982] ICR 626. See the note by Leighton, P. and Doyle, B. 'Section 11, Sick Pay and the Demise of the Officious Bystander', 11 *Industrial Law Journal*, pp. 185–88 (1982). They argue that *Mears* applies a flexible approach to the construction of contracts to a 'static' term of the contract. Previously this approach had been applied to evolving aspects of the employment relationship such as the 'job definition' aspects. Cf. Davies, P. and Freedland, M., *Labour Law: Text and Materials*, (London, Weidenfeld and Nicolson, 1984) at p. 305 who challenge the division of the contract of employment into 'static' and 'evolving' terms.

31. [1977] AC 239.

32. Cf. the use of 'reasonableness' rather than 'necessity' by Slade LJ in *Courtaulds Northern Spinning Ltd.* v. *Sibson, supra* note 25.

33. *Op. cit.* note 28 at p. 255.

34. [1983] ICR 416.

35. [1939] 2 KB 187.

36. *The Law Relating to Industry*, (London, Pitman, 1931) at p. 10.

37. (1875) 32 LT 855.

38. [1931] 1 Ch. 310.

39. See also *Hart* v. *Riversdale Mill Co.* [1928] 1 KB 176.

40. [1940] 1 KB 258.

41. 'Lay-offs and Short-time: (1) What the law says', *IDS Brief 56*, (March 1975) at p. 15.

42. *Sneddon* v. *Ivorycrete (Builders) Ltd.* [1966] 1 ITR 538.

43. *Supra* note 6.

44. *Supra* note 18.

45. *Puttick* v. *John Wright and Sons (Blackwall Ltd.)* [1972] ICR 457.

46. *Jones* v. *Harry Sherman Ltd.* [1969] 4 ITR 63.

47. [1978] IRLR 434.

48. [1966] 1 ITR 149.

49. Unreported, EAT 416/82.

50. *Beyond Contract: Work, Power and Trust Relations*, (London, Faber and Faber, 1974) at p. 183.

51. *Stilk* v. *Myrick* (1809) 6 Esp 129.

52. *Strange (SW) Ltd.* v. *Mann* [1965] 1 WLR 629.

53. *Waine* v. *Oliver R. (Plant Hire)* [1978] IRLR 434.

54. *Friend* v. *PMA Holdings* [1976] ICR 330.

55. [1988] ICR 29.

56. [1986] IRLR 461.

57. *Ibid.* Lord Justice Fox at p. 464.

58. [1984] IRLR 91.

59. See also *Kerr and Williams* v. *Council of Hereford and Worcester* (Unreported) [1985] *IRLIB* 287. Employee and trade union response to the variation of employment contracts as a result of expenditure cuts on local authorities has been varied. A claim for unfair dismissal was brought in *Kent County Council* v. *Gilham* [1985] IRLR 18, while in *R.* v. *Birmingham CC ex parte NUPE* (Unreported) and *R.* v. *Hertfordshire CC ex parte NUPE* [1985] IRLR 177 an application for judicial review was made.

60. See for example, Industrial Relations Services, 'Changing Terms of Employment Contracts: 1', *Industrial Relations Legal Information Bulletin 340*, pp. 2–10 (3 November 1987), and Part 2 at *IRLIB 341* pp. 2–10 (17 November 1987).

61. 'Leaflet Law: The Temporary Short-time Working Compensation Scheme', 9 *Industrial Law Journal*, pp. 254–8 (1980).

62. 'Short-time to Save Jobs', *Incomes Data Services Study 241* (May 1981).

63. *Supra* note 61.

64. *Supra* note 62.

65. Source, Incomes Data Services, *supra* note 62 at p. 15.

66. Source, Incomes Data Services, *supra* note 62 at p. 3.

67. See Szyszczak, E., 'Employment Protection and Social Security', in Lewis, R. (ed) *Labour Law in Britain*, (Oxford, Basil Blackwell, 1986).

68. *Todd* v. *Sun Ventilating Co. Ltd.* [1974] IRLR 4.

69. *Secretary of State for Employment* v. *Globe Elastic Thread Co.* [1979] IRLR 327.

70. Section 140(1) Employment Protection (Consolidation) Act 1978. See *Hanson* v. *Fashion Industries (Hartlepool)* [1981] ICR 35; *Smith* v. *Carlisle City Council* Unreported EAT 453/83.

71. Schedule 13, para 24(1) Employment Protection (Consolidation) Act 1978.

72. Schedule 13, para 3 Employment Protection (Consolidation) Act 1978.

73. Schedule 13, para 4 to the Employment Protection (Consolidation) Act 1978.

74. [1984] IRLR 180.

75. This only applies for paragraph 4 purposes and does not apply to paragraph 3.

76. *Adams* v. *GKN Sankey Ltd.* [1980] IRLR 416.

77. *Hobden* v. *Longview Conservative Club*, Unreported COIT 1045/80.

78. *Lewis* v. *Surrey CC* [1987] IRLR 509.

79. *Opie* v. *John Gubbins (Insurance Brokers) Ltd.* [1978] IRLR 540 (EAT); *Mailway (Southern) Ltd.* v. *Willsher* [1978] IRLR 322 (EAT).

80. *Secretary of State for Employment* v. *Deary* [1984] IRLR 180 (EAT); *Dean* v. *Eastbourne Fishermen's and Boatmen's Protection Society and Club Ltd.* [1977] IRLR 143 (EAT); *Larkin* v. *Cambos Enterprises (Stretford) Ltd.* [1978] ICR 1247 (EAT).

81. Cf. the application of paragraph 9 of Schedule 13 to the Employment Protection (Consolidation) Act 1978, which can only apply when the contract of employment has ended.

82. *Wilson* v. *Maynard Shipping Consultants AB* [1977] IRLR 491 (CA); *ITT Components (Europe) Ltd.* v. *Kolah* [1977] IRLR 53 (EAT). Normally voluntary overtime will be ignored, but see *Girls Public Day School Trust* v. *Khanna* [1987] ICR 339. (EAT).

83. Schedule 13, para 4 to the Employment Protection (Consolidation) Act 1978.

84. [1979] IRLR 41.

85. [1983] ICR 273. Discussed below.

86. Unreported 580/83 (EAT).

87. *H. McAree* v. *GKN Sankey Ltd.* [1976] IRLR 58.

88. [1968] 1 WLR 1865.

89. [1969] 3 All ER 1140.

90. [1972] ICR 457.

91. [1976] IRLR 146.

92. *Ibid.* at p. 148.

93. [1983] ICR 273.

94. [1985] IRLR 443.

95. [1988] ICR 505.

96. [1989] IRLR 152.

97. [1987] ICR 519.

98. [1988] ICR 480.

99. [1970] 1 Lloyds Rep. 105.

100. [1967] ITR 117.

101. Unreported COIT 1487/213.

102. Schedule 13, paragraph 12 to the Employment Protection (Consolidation) Act 1978.

103. [1984] IRLR 180.

104. See Carty, H., 'Dismissed Employees: The Search for a More Effective Range of Remedies', 52 *Modern Law Review*, pp. 449–68 (1989).

105. 'The Emergence of a New Labour Injunction?', 16 *Industrial Law Journal*, pp. 145–63 (1987) at p. 145.

106. See Fredman, S. and Lee, S., 'Natural Justice for Employees: The Unacceptable Face of Proceduralism', 15 *Industrial Law Journal*, pp. 15–31 (1986); Wedderburn, Lord, *The Worker and the Law*, (Harmondsworth, Penguin Books, 3rd edn., 1986) at pp. 153–71.

107. See Lloyd-Jones, C. and Chapman, V., *Small Employment Claims in the County Court – A Guide for Employees and Their Advisors*, (London, Tower Hamlets Law Centre and the Low Pay Unit, 1988).

108. *National Coal Board* v. *Galley* [1958] 1 WLR 16.

109. *Cresswell and Others* v. *Board of Inland Revenue* [1984] IRLR 190, where civil service employees who refused to operate new computerized methods of work were sent home without pay and could not recover the wages lost. See the comment in *Chitty on Contracts*, 25th edn., Vol. 2, para

3457, where it is suggested that this indirectly gives the employer a power of lock-out which is not directly conceded by the common law of implied terms of the contract of employment.

110. *Simmons* v. *Hoover Ltd.* [1977] ICR 61. Under section 62 of the Employment Protection (Consolidation) Act 1978 an unfair dismissal claim may succeed if the employee can show that not all those employees taking part in the industrial action have been dismissed.

111. See McMullen, J., 'The Legality of Deductions from Strikers' Wages', 51 *Modern Law Review*, pp. 234–40 (1988); Morris, G., 'Deductions from Pay for Industrial Action', 16 *Industrial Law Journal*, pp. 185–88 (1987).

112. The Wages Act 1986 purports to prevent arbitrary deductions from pay but section 1(5)(f) of the Act expressly excludes deductions where the employee has taken part in a strike or other industrial action and the deduction is made on account of the employee having taken part in the strike or industrial action. For a comment on the Wages Act 1986 see Dolding, L., 'The Wages Act 1986: An Exercise in Employment Abuse', 51 *Modern Law Review*, pp. 84–97 (1987).

113. [1980] IRLR 361.

114. [1984] IRLR 184.

115. *Chitty on Contracts* 25th edn., Vol. 1, para 1593 at 879.

116. This represented the five additional students he was expected to teach.

117. [1986] IRLR 391.

118. See the discussion of implied terms earlier in this chapter.

119. Scott J sought to explain the judgment in *Royle* v. *Trafford Borough Council* on this basis, however, and also referred to *obiter dicta* of Lord Hanworth in *Sagar* v. *Ridehalgh and Son Ltd.* [1931] Ch. 310 (discussed earlier) to support his decision.

120. [1987] IRLR 193.

121. Fox LJ did not comment on the question; in his view the statute was absolute. *Ibid.* at p. 114.

122. *Ibid.* at p. 115.

123. [1971] 2 All ER 666.

124. *Supra* note 113.

125. 'Aspects of the Wage–Work Bargain', 43 *Cambridge Law Journal*, pp. 337–48 (1984).

126. This is the approach adopted in Australia; see *Pavey and Matthews Pty Ltd.* v. *Paul* (1987) 69 ALR 577 discussed in Smith, G.F., '"Part Work No Pay?": The Obligations to Pay Wages for Part Performance of Contracts of Employment', Working Paper No. 39, *Labour Studies Programme*, (Faculty of Economics and Commerce, University of Melbourne, June 1988). See the discussion in Sales, P., 'Contract and Restitution in the Employment Relationship: No Work, No Pay', 8 *Oxford Journal of Legal Studies*, pp. 301–11 (1988). Contrast Birks, P., *An Introduction to the Law of Restitution*, (Oxford, Oxford University Press, PB ed 1989) at p. 464.

127. *Ibid.* at p. 11.

128. [1987] 2 WLR 795, per Lord Brightman in *Miles*, at p. 799.

129. *Ibid.* at p. 807.

130. Another answer might be that the employer has impliedly agreed to a variation of contractual duties, see *Bond* v. *CAV Ltd. supra* note 6.

131. (1795) 6 TR 320.

132. *Hoenig* v. *Isaacs* [1952] 2 All ER 176. See also *McClenaghan* v. *Bank of New Zealand* (1978) 2 NZLR 529; *Welbourn and Others* v. *Australian Postal Commission* (1984) VR 257.

133. *Bolton* v. *Mahadeva* [1972] 1 WLR 1009.

134. At p. 799. Smith points out that Lord Templeman may have implicitly agreed with Lord Brightman when, in relation to the fourth situation, Lord Templeman held that wages were not payable when work was forced upon an employer during industrial action. Smith argues that 'If this is the result when an employer is "obliged to accept" inefficient work it follows that there will be a similar result if an employer is "obliged to accept" part performance ...' *op. cit.* note 126 at p. 12.

135. At p. 798.

136. However, later on in his speech Lord Oliver impliedly rejects the view that an employer can take the benefit of a 'go slow' and refuse to pay wages.

137. See *Cresswell* v. *Board of Inland Revenue*, note 109 *supra*.

138. *Gunton* v. *Richmond-upon-Thames London Borough Council* [1980] ICR 755.

139. *O'Grady* v. *M. Saper Ltd.* [1940] 2 KB 469; *International Correspondence School* v. *Ayres* (1912) 106 LT 845.

140. *Op. cit.* note 111.

141. [1989] IRLR 259.

142. At p. 265.

143. [1986] IRLR 461.

144. [1988] ICR 29.

145. 52 *Modern Law Review* 449–68 (1989) at p. 450.

146. *Hill* v. *C.A. Parsons and Co. Ltd.* [1971] 3 All ER 1345. Cf. *Sanders* v. *Ernest A. Neale Ltd.* [1974] 3 All ER 327.

147. *Hill* v. *C.A. Parsons and Co. Ltd.* [1971] 3 All ER 1345.

148. *Powell* v. *London Borough of Brent* [1988] ICR 176.

149. See *Dietman* v. *Brent LBC* [1987] ICR 737, where the need to obtain injunctive relief was emphasized in order to show that an employee has not accepted an employer's unilateral repudiation.

150. [1988] IRLR 55.

151. [1988] IRLR 470.

152. [1984] IRLR 190.

153. It was argued that it was not clear if the new technology agreement had been incorporated into the contract of employment.

154. *Cresswell* v. *Board of Inland Revenue* [1984] IRLR 190; *Cadoux* v. *Central Regional Council* [1986] IRLR 131.

155. *Warburton* v. *Taff Vale Railway Co.* [1902] 18 TLR 420; *Hanley* v. *Pease and Partners* [1915] 1 KB 698.

156. [1989] IRLR 210.

157. *Supra* note 58. *Hollister* v. *National Farmers' Union* [1979] ICR 542; *Genower* v. *Ealing Hammersmith and Hounslow Area Health Authority* [1980] IRLR 297. Cf. *Kent County Council* v. *Gilham* [1985] IRLR 18, when the Employment Appeal Tribunal and the Court of Appeal disagreed upon the question of whether the dismissals fell within section 57(1)(b) of the Employment Protection (Consolidation) Act 1978. Cf. the industrial tribunal's finding that the dismissals were not reasonable under section 57(3) of the Employment Protection (Consolidation) Act 1978 since local consultations on the variation of the contract had not been exhausted and there had also been a serious breach of a national agreement.

158. Unfair Dismissal (Variation of Qualifying Period) Order SI 1985 No. 782.

159. [1978] ICR 221.

160. See the discussion by Elias, P., 'Unravelling the Concept of Dismissal', 7 *Industrial Law Journal*, pp. 16–29 and 100–12 (1978).

161. [1975] IRLR 147 at p. 149.

162. Unreported COIT 328/76 (1975).

163. [1981] IRLR 57.

164. [1987] IRLR 58.

165. Neal, A.C., 'Recent Developments in Unfair Dismissal – Part II', 137 *New Law Journal*, pp. 669–71 (1987).

166. *Gunton* v. *Richmond-on-Thames LBC* [1980] ICR 755. See also Templeman LJ in *London Transport Executive* v. *Clarke* [1981] IRLR 166; Warner J in *Irani* v. *Southampton HA* [1985] ICR 590, 597; *Burdett-Coutts* v. *Hertfordshire CC* [1984] IRLR 91.

167. See Sir John Donaldson in *Sanders* v. *Ernest A. Neale* [1974] 3 All ER 327; *R.* v. *East Berkshire Health Authority, ex p. Walsh* [1984] 3 WLR 818.

168. *Supra* note 138.

169. *Supra* note 144.

170. [1976] ICR 330.

171. Cf. *Burdett-Coutts* v. *Hertfordshire County Council supra* note 58, where the employees had remained in the employment but had made it quite clear they did not accept the variations to their contracts by instructing solicitors to write to the employers informing them of this fact.

172. [1974] ICR 123.

173. Unreported 466/80 (EAT, 1981).

174. Unreported 416/82 (EAT).

175. Women's Legal Defence Fund, *Between Equals* Issue 1, Summer 1989.

176. Terms and Conditions of Employment The Unfair Dismissal (Increase of Compensation Limit) Order 1989, SI 1989/527. Note, however, that if the claim is based upon sex discrimination an industrial tribunal in *Marshall* v. *Southampton and South West Hampshire Area Health Authority (No. 2)* [1988] IRLR 325 has ruled that the present statutory limits do not provide an adequate remedy for victims of sex discrimination as required by Article 6 of Council Directive 76/207/EEC (OJ L 39/40 14 February 1979) and the ruling in Case 14/83, *Von Colson and Kamann* v. *Land of North Rhine-Westphalia* [1986] 2 CMLR 430. In *Marshall* compensation of £19,400 was awarded. The decision is under appeal at the time of writing.

177. Terms and Conditions of Employment The Unfair Dismissal (Increase of Limits of Basic and Special Awards) Order 1989 SI 1989/528.

178. Department of Employment, 'Industrial Tribunal Statistics', 97 *Employment Gazette*, pp. 257–61 (May 1989).

179. Schedule 4, para 2 Employment Protection (Consolidation) Act 1978. Note that as a result of the Employment Appeal Tribunal decision in *Hammersmith and Queen Charlotte's Special Health Authority* v. *Cato* [1987] IRLR 483 the qualifying age for women is to be extended up to the age of 65 (Hansard Written Answer col. 292, 28 October 1987). Section 16 of the Employment Act 1989 implements this amendment.

180. Terms and Conditions of Employment The Employment Protection (Variation of Limits) Order 1989 SI 1989/526.

181. September 1974, paragraph 81.

182. *The Law of Employment: A Summary of the Rights of Employers and Employees*, (London, Pitman, 1947) at p. 22.

183. *Op. cit.* note 7 p. 110.

184. *Op. cit.* note 104 at p. 449.

185. See also the discussion in Carty *op. cit.*

186. Cf. Hakim, C., 'Employment Rights: A Comparison of Part-time and Full-time Employees', 18 *Industrial Law Journal*, pp. 69–83 (1989) with Disney, R. and Szyszczak, E., 'Part-time Work: Reply to Catherine Hakim', 18 *Industrial Law Journal* pp. 223–8 (1989).

4

State Intervention: Pre-1975

INTRODUCTION

This chapter and Chapter 5 turn our attention away from the individual employment relationship and towards the wider social policy issues and economic factors which determine the amount of state involvement and direction in regulating partial unemployment. This chapter examines the use of the social security system to compensate partial unemployment: it also shows how the state attempted to transfer some of the financial burdens of partial unemployment on to individual employers, both by encouraging collective bargaining in the form of guaranteed week agreements and by imposing a liability to make a redundancy payment available for prolonged lay-off or short-time working. However, this transfer of responsibility has not been an entirely successful exercise, and with the deepening of the recession in the mid-1970s and early 1980s we see that the state has been compelled to regulate partial unemployment more closely by introducing statutory guarantee payment provisions as well as utilizing temporary employment subsidies.

There has been, therefore, a continued tension between attempts by the state to maintain an abstentionist role in employment law, and the response to situations which requires that it must adopt a more interventionist and directive role in the labour market. The year 1975 is by no means a watershed in these different approaches: it merely provides a convenient place at which the state openly adopted this directive role while continuing to subsidize compensation for partial unemployment through the National Insurance Fund and the use of employment subsidies.

THE USE OF THE SOCIAL SECURITY SYSTEM TO COMPENSATE PARTIAL UNEMPLOYMENT

A Brief History of the State Unemployment Benefit Scheme[1]

Prior to the introduction of the state scheme of unemployment benefit, trade unions and Friendly Societies had established their own forms of unemployment compensation funded from employees' contributions. There is evidence also of worksharing established in occupations with firm-specific skills, and some of these occupations, particularly cotton spinning, resisted the idea of a compulsory system of social security compensation.[2]

A compulsory scheme of insurance against unemployment was first established by Part II of the National Insurance Act 1911, and contributions first became payable on 15 July 1912 and benefit on 15 January 1913.[3] The scheme covered about two-and-a-quarter million workers aged 16 or over in the building, construction, shipbuilding, mechanical engineering, ironfounding, vehicles and sawmilling trades. From 4 September 1916 the scheme was extended to other groups of employees thought likely to suffer from unemployment after the war. An extra one-and-a-half million people were placed within the ambit of the scheme and the extension covered munitions workers and the metal, chemical, leather, rubber and ammunition trades. These were essentially capital goods industries prone to extreme cyclical fluctuations in employment and employing predominantly male workers. This period also saw the compulsory notification of vacancies linked to the compensation for unemployment scheme. Unemployment benefit was limited to 15 weeks' benefit per year and was contingent upon the employee having an adequate National Insurance record. One week's benefit was payable for five weeks' National Insurance contributions. Thus in general the treatment of short spells of partial unemployment was more generous than the provision made for the long-term unemployed.

The reasons for state intervention are complex. The traditional economist's explanation of market failure does not apply easily here since the state scheme tended to replicate existing private arrangements to compensate for unemployment, and even after the introduction of the state scheme private insurance schemes continued to exist, usually providing more generous benefits. An alternative explanation for the growth of the comprehensive social security scheme has suggested that the state used the extensions to the basic scheme to raise revenue, to bring the privately funded employee (and in some cases employer) contributions into the public exchequer.[4]

At an early stage in the war, the government had announced that ex-servicemen who were unemployed in the period immediately following their discharge from the Forces would receive an 'out of work donation' not dependent upon payment of contributions. Shortly before the Armistice it was decided that as the Unemployment Insurance scheme covered only a small proportion of civilian workers the 'out of work donation' should also be available to civilian workers in the changeover from the state of war to peace. Thus it was necessary to bring as many contributors into the state scheme as possible in order to fund these additional payments. The scheme came into operation from 25 November 1918 and for the ex-servicemen and women payments continued up until 31 March 1921. For civilian workers covered by the 1911 and 1916 Acts, payments finished on 24 November 1919.

The Unemployment Insurance Act 1920 repealed the earlier statutes and extended the contributory scheme of Unemployment Insurance to all manual workers not earning more than £250 per year. Certain groups of workers were excluded, such as agricultural workers, private domestic servants and certain classes of permanent employees, for example, permanent civil servants, pensionable teachers and permanent employees of local authorities and railway companies. These groups were not considered to be vulnerable to periodic unemployment. Between 1921 and 1931 more than 20 Acts were passed refining and adjusting the social security scheme. None of these measures was able to deal adequately with the severity of the Great Depression and eventually the National Insurance Fund ran into debt.[5]

In May 1936 the Unemployment Insurance (Agriculture) Act extended Unemployment Insurance to agricultural and horticultural workers, and in April 1938 some 242,000 domestic workers were brought within the ambit of the Unemployment Insurance Acts for the first time. Non-manual workers earning between £250 and £420 per year became insurable in 1940. Finally, an all-inclusive National Insurance scheme was introduced in July 1948.

Development of Occupational Unemployment Benefit Schemes in the Inter-war Period

While the state attempted a comprehensive coverage of unemployment risks some firms endeavoured to retain skilled labour by entering into explicit contracts establishing additional occupational benefit schemes. In 1930 Gilson and Riches reviewed the 15 additional schemes established outside the operation of the Unemployment Insurance Acts.[6] These schemes were by no means homogeneous in either their coverage or the financing of the unemployment benefits. Only one, the Match Industry Scheme, covered a whole industry. Other schemes were funded entirely by employers' contributions: for example, in the confectionery industry, the Rowntree Company, Cadbury Brothers Ltd., J.S. Fry and Sons Ltd.; in the stationery industry, E.S. and A. Robinson; and in soap manufacturing, Lever Brothers Ltd. Other funds were established using part or wholly funded contributions from workers: for example, Needlers Ltd; and in steel manufacturing, Redpath Brown and Co. Other schemes involved an employment guarantee: for example, ICI Ltd., John Mackintosh and Sons Ltd. Here the cost of the scheme did not involve a special fund but was regarded as a payroll tax. Equally there was no contractual obligation on the part of the employer to continue with the scheme. The purpose of these schemes was not only to compensate for partial unemployment but was also seen as a way of raising the status of some 'loyal' manual workers who were of value to the firm by reason of their skills, training and familiarity with the work. These schemes were, in fact, quite sophisticated for their time, both in their administration and the level of protection provided for partial unemployment. It is perhaps likely that the experience of such private 'unemployment benefit' schemes paved the way for more extensive collective bargaining over guaranteed week conditions in the post-1945 period.

The Use of the State Unemployment Benefit Scheme to Compensate Partial Unemployment

The development of a comprehensive state system of compensation for partial unemployment resulted in widespread use, and what was later seen as abuse, of the scheme to organize worksharing patterns to deal with work shortages. Some examples of the use of the unemployment system in the inter-war period are given by Bakke,[7] when one colliery company circulated a leaflet stating:

> The pits will be so worked as to enable the employees to qualify for three days' unemployment benefit in alternate weeks. The unemployment benefit will therefore more than cover the reduction in wages.

At another colliery:

> Five hundred men who had signed the unemployed register on Thursday and Saturday of one week, sent a deputation to the management asking that on the Wednesday following, the afternoon shift should not work because it would be impossible if they had worked on that day to draw unemployment pay for the two days in the previous week when they had been unemployed. Six days would have passed and the two days in which they had been unemployed would be non-effective. The manager telephoned to the Employment Exchange, found out that the workers were right and consequently dismissed the men for the afternoon shift on Wednesday.[8]

Benjamin and Kochin[9] refer to the widespread practice of short-time working in the inter-war period which came to be known as the 'OXO' system. This was the frequently observed arrangement where workers would form 'pools' in which members of the pool would alternate between days of work (O) and days of unemployment (X). Such a system allowed continuous eligibility for wages and unemployment benefit. The use of the social security system brought with it a fierce debate which has continued to recent times as to how far the availability of unemployment benefit actually increased unemployment in the inter-war years.[10] The perceived 'abuse' of the social system in this way was finally outlawed by a series of decisions by the Umpires and Referees.

Although the unemployment benefit system was used extensively in the inter-war years to compensate short-time working, several doubts began to emerge over the utility of such a policy in the post-1945 period. To deal with the administrative problems of paying unemployment benefit to a worker who still had a contract of employment, an 'astonishing labyrinth' of administrative rules developed which became 'extraordinarily intricate and unwieldy'.[11] Prior to an inter-departmental working party investigation into the composition of the unemployment statistics in 1972, the 'temporarily stopped' were included in the unemployment total thus swelling this figure considerably.[12] Critics felt that these employees would not register as 'unemployed' at all except to claim benefits under the complex set of rules and suggested that the number of the 'temporarily stopped' was a by-product of the benefit rules and not an accurate index of a particular form of unemployment. It was not until the eighties that changes were made (in order to reduce administrative costs) so that employees working short time did not have to register as unemployed.

Conceptual problems notwithstanding, other factors militated against the use of the National Insurance Fund to compensate for short-time working. From an economic point of view it was seen as undesirable that all contributors to the Fund should subsidize firms which regularly laid off workers:

> It does not seem sense economically, nor is it right socially, that the contributions of the general mass of workers – many of whom earn less full time than others are getting when they are employed part time or on short time – should be used in this way to subsidize earnings in certain industries . . . it would be quite wrong to pay benefit for part of the week to people who still have a job and have earnings during the rest of the week.[13]

Such criticism of cross-subsidization was far from new, having been addressed almost half a century earlier in the Royal Commission on Unemployment Insurance when short-time working was particularly widespread and extensive.[14]

Calculations carried out on the Short-time Working Project at the University of Kent[15] show that there is no doubt that industries which use the unemployment benefit system to compensate for short-time working do so regularly. However, these calculations suggested that the cross-subsidization criticisms should not be over-emphasized. For example, in the metal goods industry the estimated total value of National Insurance contributions paid into the Fund in 1975 amounted to £153.8 million. In the course of the year the total number of claims for unemployment benefit due to male workers claiming unemployment benefit for short-time working amounted to 366,193; for females, 58,157 claims were made. On the assumption that each claim represented one complete week of unemployment benefit, the total value of the claims amounted to £3.8 million, which represents only 2.45 per cent of the total value of National Insurance contributions. Thus it would seem that contributions paid into the National Insurance Fund by this sector of industry comfortably covered the benefits drawn to compensate short-time working.

A second criticism against using the National Insurance Fund to compensate short-time working was an efficiency argument. The administrative costs of paying unemployment benefit for short spells of unemployment were thought to be disproportionately high,[16] thus diverting funds and personnel from those who may have more urgent claims, to workers on short time who already have an employer and whose attendance at the unemployment benefit office:

> ... has little or nothing to do with looking for another job. In some cases, indeed, we have found that the guaranteed week agreement, which ought to be the workers' protection against short-time working, is reduced or suspended by arrangement between the parties so that more benefit can be drawn.[17]

An emergency arrangement was implemented when particularly extensive short-time working was imposed on the British economy between 31 December 1973 and 8 March 1974 ('The Three-Day Week'). Employers were asked to make the payment of unemployment benefit due to their workers when paying wages. The peak number of employees recorded as claiming benefit during this period was almost 1.6 million in the week beginning 14 January 1974 and it was estimated that over 80 per cent of these received unemployment benefit entitlement from their employer.[18] Surprisingly this scheme has not been implemented on a more permanent basis to provide compensation for lost wages due to lay-off or short-time working. Since 1982, however, once it has been established that the claimant is entitled to unemployment benefit it is not necessary for the claimant to register weekly with the unemployment benefit office provided the Secretary of State is satisfied that the award and payment of unemployment benefit can be controlled adequately.[19]

The use of the National Insurance Fund to finance short-time working compensation received criticism not only from the government but also from the Trades Union Congress (TUC) evidence to the Department of Employment on the following grounds.[20] First, there was no financial support for short-time working for the first three 'waiting' days of unemployment benefit. Secondly, the complexity of the administrative rules surrounding a claim for unemployment benefit resulted in anomalies. For example, a worker on a five-day week was better placed than a worker on a six-day week. The worker working a five-day week lost a greater proportion of her weekly earnings than did a six-day worker in order to receive the same amount of proportionate compensation from the unemployment benefit system. Only in the case of losing a whole week, in which case the 'full extent normal' rule[21] was satisfied, did the five-day week employee enjoy the same proportion of earnings loss and unemployment benefit gain. For the six-day worker there was always a one-to-one proportionate compensation.

A third criticism voiced by the TUC echoed that of the employers, that the pattern of short-time working was commonly fixed to reflect the administrative rules of the unemployment benefit scheme rather than suit the needs of industry.

Finally the TUC reflected upon the government's fears that the system of compensation for short-time working might have undesirable consequences for the work ethic. Although many people on short-time working received much less than normal earnings, others, especially those with dependants, received more in wages plus unemployment benefit (because the latter was, until November 1982, tax free) than in net earnings for a normal week. It is unlikely that the TUC fears would have gone as far as reiterating the anecdotal evidence provided by Barney Hayhoe to the Standing Committee on the Employment Protection Bill:

> We have not too far away from us the memory of the Jaguar case where there appeared to be a curious collusion between the employers and employees so to design short-time working so that the maximum amount of money would end up in the pockets of employees, which would be ordinary pay plus overtime for some days in the week, plus non-taxable unemployment pay for the rest. This curious combination resulted in people being better off if the arrangement was made in this way.[22]

In the light of these criticisms the state began to reconsider the use of the National Insurance scheme to finance partial unemployment compensation.

THE GROWTH OF GUARANTEED WEEK AGREEMENTS

Despite the importance of the role of contract discussed in Chapters 2 and 3, the notion of freedom of contract did not always enjoy prominence in the twentieth century. In those two chapters we suspended from our discussion two important periods when the state actively intervened in order to regulate employment during war time emergencies. We can now return to examine these periods since they introduced the idea of state intervention as a means of guaranteeing an adequate supply of labour as well as guaranteeing wages. In so doing, these forms of regulation provided the genesis for the guaranteed week agreements that emerged in the post-1945 period.

In the first war-time experiment, during the First World War, labour was regulated under the Munitions of War Acts 1915–19.[23] If an employee was working in a controlled establishment she was obliged to obtain a 'leaving certificate' from the employer before moving on to alternative work. The purpose of this was to stabilize the supply of labour and prevent the poaching of labour. A failure to obtain a leaving certificate resulted in a penalty of six weeks' unemployment.[24] This regulation caused problems when workers were laid off because of a shortage of work. Employers could attempt to lay-off workers and refuse a leaving certificate. To remedy such an abuse section 5(2) of the Munitions of War (Amendment) Act 1916 provided compensation to be paid where an employee did not have the opportunity of earning wages for more than two days. The employee could apply to the local munitions tribunal and claim that the refusal of a certificate was unreasonable. The tribunal had the capacity to issue a leaving certificate and order the employer to pay a sum of money not exceeding £5 to the worker.[25] Despite this guarantee, it was felt that the leaving certificate scheme severely hampered the free movement of labour and the government was obliged to concede to its abolition in 1917.[26]

Although this form of regulation was only justified and existed to cover the war-time emergency, Rubin[27] has argued that this period of history may have some relevance in looking at how the judiciary approached the nature of statutory regulation and its interaction with customary work practices, as well as the way some of the difficult common law concepts such as the right to work or entitlement to wages were handled under the regulations. In fact the right to work or wages was discussed in a number of decisions arising from the regulation of leaving work. In *Hinchley* v. *A.V. Roe and Co. Ltd.*,[28] for example, the issue of pay for days when there had been a suspension of work (at issue in the later decision of *Minnevitch* v. *Café de Paris (Londres) Ltd.*[29]) was raised by Atkin J (as he then was). Atkin J considered that there was a distinct possibility that where the workers had not agreed to the suspension but had waived their right to the breach of contract the workers could bring a claim for wages in the absence of a contractual provision excluding the right to work or wages.

Of more significance for our discussion of the development of collective guaranteed week agreements were the regulations of the Second World War period. Essential Work Orders were introduced from March 1941 under Defence Regulation 58A in order to stabilize labour. This was achieved by curtailing an employer's freedom to discharge an employee from a 'scheduled' employment and at the same time restricted an employee's freedom to leave such an employment. In return for the assurance of a permanent and mobile workforce the employer was obliged to guarantee a weekly or a daily wage for piece-rate workers provided the employee was capable and available to work and was willing to perform reasonable alternative work if the usual work was not available.[30]

The Second World War period also saw the end of casual labour in the docks, a cause for which Ernest Bevin had fought for more than 30 years, often facing opposition from trade unions as well as the employers.[31] The National Dock Labour Corporation administered the scheme of registering dockers and ensuring their mobility. Dock workers were paid a guaranteed wage [32] plus payment by results above the minimum wage in return for working when and where they were required in order to unload ships and get the ports cleared.

The principle of de-casualization remained the basis for the post-war reconstruction of the industry. The Dock Labour Scheme was established in 1946 and remained in operation until it was abolished by section 1 of the Dock Work Act 1989. By 1989 Normal Fowler, the Minister for Employment, considered the idea of guaranteed wages as a total anachronism.[33] In particular it was argued that the scheme was costly to maintain – in 1988 employers had paid the National Dock Labour Board more than £4.7 million to cover its activities and administrative costs and it cost the 'tax payer' £770 million to maintain the voluntary severance terms 'to prop up the 46 British scheme ports'. In addition the White Paper argued that labour surpluses and inefficient work practices added over 20 per cent to the wages bill of the scheme ports.[34] Arguing that 50,000 jobs would be created without the restrictions of registered dock work the Conservative government rushed the Bill through Parliament. Despite a successful House of Lords ruling[35] allowing a national dock strike to go ahead the subsequent opposition to the Dock Work Act 1989 by the TGWU crumbled in August 1989 and the scheme was abolished.

Returning to the immediate post-war period, the end of the war saw the re-emergence of the notion of freedom to contract as the means of regulating the employment relationship. Given the apparent ease with which employers had been able to lay-off employees without pay and the difficulties of enforcing contractual obligations in the inter-war years, the Minister of Labour, Ernest Bevin, set about encouraging an, albeit reluctant, trade union movement to include guarantees of work or wages into collective agreements for other areas of industry. Although the Essential Work Orders had been subject to much criticism by the Trades Union Congress, Bevin singled them out during a speech to the TUC Conference on 7 September 1944 as an example where the TUC could take the initiative and provide practical self-help in order to improve social conditions:

> Does anybody ... want to go back to the hourly payment? I cannot believe it. This standing on and off, this going to the factory door in the morning and 'Nothing doing, Tom, go home' – surely nobody wants to

go back to that again. But could I make this suggestion, if you will allow me. Do not rely on the Government to maintain it. Why not weave it into your collective agreements at the earliest opportunity? We are not anxious to have the duty of enforcing it by law. Do not turn the rising generation too much to law and not enough to you.[36]

Bevin, of course, was eager to keep the concept of a weekly engagement and guaranteed wages in order to prevent industry from slipping back into the pre-war habit of part-time working 'when the Unemployment Act was merely a subsidy to meet what was growing into a conspiracy between the trade unions and the employers'.[37]

Thus the terms and conditions of lay-off became partly regulated and the necessity of relying entirely upon common law rights diminished, particularly for manual workers. The regulation of lay-offs through collective bargaining was actively encouraged by the state, which saw the advantages in financial and administrative terms of employers, rather than the National Insurance Fund, bearing the cost of short spells of temporary unemployment.

Although such collective agreements did materialize, particularly in the building, construction and engineering industries, the continuing existence of the National Insurance Fund provided a convenient fallback and most of the guaranteed week agreements were riddled with exclusion, limitation and suspension clauses. An important legacy from the Essential Work Orders was the use of 'flexibility' clauses whereby workers were bound to undertake reasonable alternative work if the ordinary work was not available. As we shall see in the next chapter, this idea has been followed through in the statutory scheme of guarantee payments. Few so-called guaranteed week agreements guaranteed a full week's pay although some contained clauses improving the conditions of the guarantee for workers with long service. Temporary and part-time workers were usually excluded from the schemes as were what were perceived as 'unreliable' employees with bad time-keeping or absenteeism records. Most guaranteed week agreements contained exclusion clauses covering lack of work due to circumstances outside the employer's control and in later years wider clauses covering industrial action have been drawn up. In addition to the exclusion clauses and the exceptions there were often provisions allowing the employer to suspend the guaranteed week agreement and the agreements were always limited in time. The modern surveys conducted by Incomes Data Services and Industrial Relations Services reveal these limitations as well as the wide divergencies across industries on the nature and extent of the guarantees.[38]

Although trade unions were aware of the increased emphasis on guaranteed week agreements in the rest of Western Europe,[39] little progress was made with employers in extending the coverage and terms of guaranteed week agreements in Britain, and their widespread use did not materialize at a pace and at a level that was acceptable to the state. In order to reduce the burdens on the National Insurance Fund the state took more drastic measures to shift the burden of partial unemployment compensation away from the National Insurance system by discounting the first six days of lay-off in the computation for the earnings-related supplement to unemployment benefit when it was introduced in 1966.[40] It was also proposed that unemployment benefit would not be available for the first six days of unemployment:[41] these are known as 'waiting days'.[42] A three-year transitional period was envisaged to facilitate the negotiation of guaranteed week agreements but these agreements did not materialize on a widespread scale and the 'six waiting days' rule was postponed.[43] Although the Conservative government announced that it would resurrect the rule, to come into operation on 1 January 1972, this course of action was postponed after strong representations from both sides of industry.[44] Instead the Labour government put forward proposals for a mandatory guaranteed wage which formed the basis of the statutory guarantee payment provisions. These are discussed in the next chapter.

REDUNDANCY PAYMENTS FOR SHORT-TIME WORKING AND LAY-OFF

In the post-1945 period the state began to take an active interest in providing compensation for 'no-fault' job loss. One of the earliest measures was the Redundancy Payments Act 1965, which introduced the statutory right to a redundancy payment for employees satisfying the general conditions of eligibility and who had been dismissed by reason of a cessation or diminution of the work they were normally required to perform under the contract of employment.[45] The idea of the provisions was to facilitate the restructuring of British industry and to provide compensation for job loss due to economic factors. Although many firms have negotiated redundancy procedures and compensation payments over and above the statutory framework[46] the method and form of state regulation of redundancy has not passed without criticism.[47]

It would be easy for an employer to avoid making redundancy payments by putting employees on prolonged periods of short-time working or lay-off. This possibility was recognized when the statutory scheme of redundancy payments was introduced and provisions were included for employees finding themselves on short-time working or lay-off for unacceptable periods to terminate the contract of employment on their own initiative without losing their entitlement to a redundancy payment.[48]

The provisions of sections 87–89 of the Employment Protection (Consolidation) Act 1978 seek to maintain, what at times must seem an unwieldy balance, between, on the one hand, the needs of an employer who wishes to retain skilled labour, and on the other hand, the needs of the employee, whose earnings need to be maintained and who wishes to seek alternative work. The procedures have given rise to little reported litigation and it is difficult to discover how often they are utilized since such redundancy payments are not identified in redundancy payment statistics. The small amount of reported litigation may be because employees do not pursue claims under these provisions, perhaps because they are unaware of their rights or their claims for a redundancy payment are easily defeated because of the complex system of rules surrounding the redundancy claim. Other measures to compensate partial unemployment, such as employment subsidies and statutory guarantee payments, may have eclipsed the use of the redundancy procedures and may also have prevented the substantive rules defining when a redundancy-lay-off occurs from operating. A more realistic assumption is that in times of recession and shortage of alternative work employees are more ready to fall back on compensation for partial unemployment and keep the prospect of work open rather than accept a lump-sum redundancy payment with the prospect of long-term unemployment attached.

While it may be that the provisions are not frequently used and the conventional employment law texts give little space to the interpretation of the rules, it is worth while discussing the rules in some detail to assess their significance and to see whether they should be retained or amended to encourage greater use.

Definition of Lay-off and Short-time Working for the Purposes of a Redundancy Payment

'Lay-off' and 'short-time' working are given a strict statutory definition for the purposes of a redundancy payment claim. The interaction of these rights with contractual and collective rights should first be mentioned. If employees are laid off or put on short-time working in breach of contract this may result in a claim for unfair dismissal alleging that there has been a constructive dismissal enabling an employee to make a claim for a redundancy payment in the normal way. This is a useful fallback if the employee fails to obey the complex procedures for redundancy-lay-off. The second point to note is that some collective agreements and individual contracts of employment fail to specify the length of time an employee may be legitimately laid off. The redundancy payment provisions give a concrete definition to the idea of a 'reasonable' length of time outlined by the Employment Appeal Tribunal in *A. Dakri and Co.* v. *Tiffen*.[49] By specifying that after four consecutive, or six weeks in 13 weeks, of lay-off or short-time working the employee may take steps to mitigate the consequences of the work shortage the onus is upon the employee to initiate the redundancy-lay-off procedures in order to claim a redundancy payment. She cannot rely solely upon the fact that the period of lay-off has become unreasonable and claim a redundancy payment without following the 'labyrinthine legislative provisions'.[50]

Lay-off and short-time working are defined differently in the redundancy provisions.

Lay-off

The redundancy payment provisions only apply to a suspensory lay-off agreed under a contract of employment. If there is a lay-off dismissal with the prospect of re-engagement the normal redundancy rules will apply. This is a logical consequence of the procedural rules contained in sections 88 and 89 of the Employment Protection (Consolidation) Act 1978 since they specifically demand that the employee, not the employer, terminates the contract of employment. Section 87(1) of the Employment Protection (Consolidation) Act 1978 defines a lay-off as:

> Where an employee is employed under a contract on such terms and conditions that his remuneration thereunder depends on his being provided by the employer with work of the kind which he is employed to do, he shall, for the purposes of this Part, be taken to be laid-off for any week in respect of which, by reason that the employer does not provide such work for him, he is not entitled to any remuneration under the contract.

It was originally thought that section 87(1) could only apply to piece-rate workers[51] but subsequent decisions have applied the section to time-rate workers.[52] If an employee receives any contractual remuneration, for example, from an employment subsidy or a guaranteed week agreement, she will not be 'laid-off' within the meaning of section 87(1) unless she waives her right to such a payment.[53] Non-contractual payments, such as statutory guarantee payments, social security benefits or tax rebates, will not disqualify an employee from falling within the ambit of section 87(1).

Short-time working

Short-time working is defined in section 87(2) of the Employment Protection (Consolidation) Act 1978:

> Where by reason of a diminution in the kind of work provided for an

employee (being work of a kind which under his contract the employee is employed to do) the employee's remuneration for any week is less than half a week's pay, he shall for the purposes of this Part be taken to be kept on short-time for that week.

Again the focus of attention is upon loss of remuneration. If an employee is receiving payment under an employment subsidy or guaranteed week agreement which amounts to more than half a normal week's pay she will fall outside the provisions of section 87(2). There is a noticeable change of wording between this sub-section and section 87(1). Here the words 'the employee's remuneration' are used, whereas under section 87(1) the words 'remuneration under contract' are used. This could be interpreted to mean that statutory guarantee payments should be taken into consideration when determining if the employee is on short-time working although Grunfeld disagrees with this view.[54] Social security payments and tax rebates will not be regarded as remuneration under this sub-section.

Section 87(1) and (2) should be read in the light of section 89(3) of the Employment Protection (Consolidation) Act 1978 which states that:

No account shall be taken of any week for which an employee is laid off or kept on short-time where the lay-off or short time is wholly or mainly attributable to a strike or lock out ... whether the strike or lock out is in the trade or industry in which the employee is employed or not and whether it is in Great Britain or elsewhere.

To summarize, a lay-off involves the loss of an entire week's contractual remuneration, whereas short-time working involves a diminution of work with the consequence that an employee earns less than a normal week's remuneration. In both cases it is the loss of remuneration that is the crucial factor.

Length of Lay-off or Short-time Working

Section 88(1)(a) and (b) provides two alternative lengths of lay-off and short-time working to trigger the redundancy payment provisions. This may be a period of four or more consecutive weeks or a series of six weeks of which not more than three were consecutive within a period of 13 weeks. Section 89(2) allows a combination of whole weeks of lay-off and whole weeks of short-time working to be used, subject to the provisions of section 89(3) which states that weeks in which the lay-off or short-time were caused by a strike or lock-out shall not count towards the calculation of the requisite period. A 'week' is calculated according to section 153 of the Employment Protection (Consolidation) Act 1978 as a week ending on payday for weekly paid employees or, for other employees, a week ending upon a Saturday.

Procedural Requirements

Once the substantive requirements for a redundancy claim have been satisfied the procedural requirements must be followed. Under section 88(1) of the Employment Protection (Consolidation) Act 1978 the employee must serve a notice in writing to the employer indicating her intention to claim a redundancy payment. The timing of the notice is crucial. If the employee is relying upon section 88(1)(a) the notice must be served within four weeks of the end of the four consecutive weeks of lay-off or short-time working. In *Allinson* v. *Drew Simmons Engineering Ltd.*[55] the Employment Appeal Tribunal held that the employee's premature notice, given one day before the four weeks had elapsed under section 88(1)(a), did not comply with the statutory procedure.

If the employee is relying upon section 88(1)(b), the notice of intention to claim must be given within four weeks of the last day of the period of lay-off or short-time working, *not* the last day of the 13-week period. The 13-week period is calculated backwards from the last day of lay-off, not forwards, from the first day of lay-off.

Despite the complexities of the preceding procedural rules it seems that no particular terms of art are required in writing the notice provided the letter is not unambiguous or unequivocal about the employee's intentions. In *Walmsey* v. *C. and R. Ferguson*[56] an employee who had been laid off for four consecutive weeks claimed a redundancy payment. After consulting an official from the Advisory Conciliation and Arbitration Service (ACAS) he wrote the following letter to his employers:

> As I have now been laid off for 4 consecutive weeks with no work, I have been advised by ACAS that after such time you must either re-employ me full-time for a minimum period of 13 weeks or make me redundant. If you do not wish to do any of the above, then I am left with no option but to resign and instigate industrial tribunal proceedings against you. I look forward to hearing from you within 7 days.

The Court of Session reversed the Employment Appeal Tribunal's finding that there was nothing in the letter to indicate that the employee was giving notice.

On receiving the notice of intention to claim a redundancy payment the employer may contest the claim by serving a counter-notice, or she may do nothing, or she may dismiss the employee. Each of these possibilities will be discussed in turn.

THE EMPLOYER'S COUNTER-NOTICE

An employee is not entitled to a redundancy payment if at the date on which she serves the notice of intention to claim it was reasonably to be expected that she would enter into a period of employment of not less than 13 weeks' duration during which time she would not be laid off or put on short-time working.[57] These provisions are presumably a reference to section 87(1) and (2) of the Employment Protection (Consolidation) Act 1978 and thus normal working is not guaranteed; rather, the employee must expect to earn at least half a week's pay. Unlike the normal redundancy provisions[58] an offer of alternative work cannot be made; the work must be work the employee is normally employed to do under the contract of employment.[59] From this condition it might be implied that full normal remuneration should also be received, but this is by no means certain. The purpose of this provision is to improve industrial relations since it will deter employees from serving a notice of intention to claim when they know work is likely to become available and encourages employers to keep the workforce informed of the situation.[60]

In order to assert that there is a reasonable expectation that work will be available section 88(4) of the Employment Protection (Consolidation) Act 1978 states that the employer must serve a written counter-notice upon the employee within seven days of receiving the notice of intention to claim a redundancy payment. Although it is not provided for in the statute, an industrial tribunal in *Hulse* v. *Harry Perry*[61] and the Employment Appeal Tribunal in *Fabar Construction* v. *Race and Sutherland*[62] held that the work which is expected to materialize must be described in some detail; a mere promise of some work is not sufficient. If the employer does serve a counter-notice the redundancy claim must then be referred to an industrial tribunal in order to determine whether the employee is entitled to a redundancy payment.[63] If work does not become available within the four-week period, section 89(1) of the Employment Protection (Consolidation) Act 1978 offers a conclusive presumption that work is not available. If the industrial tribunal finds in favour of the employee, she must then proceed to terminate the contract of employment within three weeks of the industrial tribunal decision.[64] The employer may revoke the counter-notice by a subsequent notice in writing. The employee may then go on to terminate the contract of employment within three weeks of the service of the notice of withdrawal.[65]

THE EMPLOYER DOES NOTHING

If the employer takes no action after receiving the notice of intention to claim, the employee must then take steps to terminate the contract of employment. This must be done within strict time limits as set out in section 89(5)(a) of the Employment Protection (Consolidation) Act 1978, which allows four weeks after the service of the notice of intention to claim. The employee must give at least one week's notice[66] to terminate the contract of employment. Although the notice may be given orally it must show a clear intention to terminate the contract of employment.[67]

THE EMPLOYER DISMISSES THE EMPLOYEE

If the employer dismisses the employee then the employee is no longer entitled to a redundancy payment under the lay-off/short-time working provisions,[68] but the employee may be able to claim a redundancy payment under the normal redundancy-dismissal provisions. This will involve the employer issuing a notice of dismissal and, where appropriate, entering into consultations with trade unions[69] and notifying the Department of Employment.[70] The point has been raised as to whether an employer may dismiss an employee after the notice to terminate the contract of employment has been given under section 88(2)(a) of the Employment Protection (Consolidation) Act 1978. If a summary dismissal in breach of contract occurs during the employee's notice period and the employee does not receive a redundancy payment the employee may sue for breach of contract, counting as a head of damage the redundancy payment that would otherwise have been received in pursuance of the notice of intention to claim a redundancy payment.[71]

The Calculation of the Redundancy Payment

To be eligible for a statutory redundancy payment the employee must have at least two years' continuous service calculated at the 'relevant date'.[72] Normally the 'relevant date' is the date on which the dismissal takes effect; however, section 90(2)(a) and (b) of the Employment Protection (Consolidation) Act 1978 defines the 'relevant date' for a redundancy-lay-off payment as the date when the last of four or more consecutive weeks or the last of the 'six in 13 weeks' period of work shortage came to an end.

The calculation of the redundancy payment is made in the same way as for a redundancy-dismissal payment, based on age, length of service and a maximum amount of weeks' pay.[73] Perhaps the most important element is the question of whether the continuity of employment has been maintained through prolonged periods of work shortages[74] and what is the correct calculation of the week's pay. A week's pay is calculated at the rate of pay in force at the 'calculation date',[75] which is the date the minimum statutory notice[76] would have been given had the contract been terminated by the employer.

Using this method, it is most likely that the 'calculation date' will fall during a period of short-time working or lay-off. Where the employee's hours do not normally vary from week to week, the week's pay is calculated at the amount payable under the contract of employment. Thus the employee's redundancy payment will not be affected by the work shortage. Where the employee's hours do vary from week to week, the week's pay is calculated as the average weekly pay over the period of 12 weeks preceding and ending on the 'calculation date'. If the employee has been laid off during this period (thus not receiving any remuneration) then it is possible to include remuneration from earlier weeks in the calculation.[77] This rule does not apply, of course, to employees on short-time working (who by definition receive less than half their normal pay) and therefore the amount of the redundancy payment will be reduced as a result of the short-time working. Workers with normal working hours whose pay does vary according to the amount of work done are covered by paragraph 3(3) of Schedule 13 to the Employment Protection (Consolidation) Act 1978. A week's pay is calculated as the amount of remuneration for the number of normal working hours calculated by the average hourly rate of remuneration payable by the employer in respect of a period of 12 weeks ending either on the last week of the calculation date or the last complete week before the calculation date.

Retention of Redundancy Payments for Lay-offs and Short-time Working

In his proposals in 1969 for reforming the Redundancy Payments Act 1965, Rideout argued that the redundancy-lay-off provision 'causes relatively few problems'.[78] In subsequent years this view has not been borne out by commentators or the industrial tribunals and appellate courts and tribunals which adhere rigidly to the procedural rules but frequently comment with some apprehension at the complexity and hardship they cause. Lord McDonald, for example, in the Scottish Employment Appeal Tribunal in *Kenneth McRae and Co. Ltd.* v. *Dawson*,[79] lamented the fact that:

> The provisions of s.88 and their predecessors have been the despair of all who have been concerned with the interpretation of industrial legislation since the scheme of statutory entitlement to a redundancy payment was introduced in 1965.

The few reported cases reveal that in the situation of work shortages the parties often act in an informal way. On to this behaviour the law must mould its formal legal procedures in order to apply (or not to apply) the redundancy provisions. At a practical level the procedures could be simplified perhaps by the adoption of formal printed notices which the parties must use and which state the procedures and time limits to be observed. While criticism and reform of redundancy law generally must take on board the special problems posed by redundancy-lay-off it could be argued that more could be made of the existing provisions in the industrial relations setting. In theory, at least, the provisions provide a residual remedy for the employee who has been laid off with little or no pay for a prolonged period. The provisions give the employee the chance to claim a lump sum payment and seek alternative employment while providing a bargaining weapon, to force the employer's hand and compel her to provide work or compensation for job loss. The financing of the redundancy payments provisions may have some effect upon the willingness of employers to accept that there is a redundancy situation in the future. The redundancy rebate paid to employers who make a redundancy payment has gradually been reduced[80] and section 17 of the Employment Act 1989 abolishes the rebate altogether. In order to avoid fully experience-rated redundancy payments there is thus an incentive for employers to choose employees with less continuous service qualifications to bear the brunt of partial unemployment, but this may open up liability for a claim based on sex or race discrimination. These issues are discussed in Chapter 6.

CONCLUSION

In this chapter we have seen that by 1975 the state had initiated a series of legislative interventions in order to regulate partial unemployment. The result was a complex system of different schemes, some subsidized by the state, some funded by employer and employee contributions and some funded solely by employers. None of the schemes provided comprehensive coverage for partial unemployment and the interaction of the schemes resulted in fragmentation of the funds available to compensate for partial unemployment rather that maximizing the coverage. Instead of rationalizing this complex situation we shall see in Chapter 5 that the state responded to the rise in partial unemployment in the late 1970s by adding even more schemes instead of streamlining and maximizing the available resources.

NOTES

1. For a more detailed account, see Fraser, D., *The Evolution of the British Welfare State: A History of Social Policy since the Industrial Revolution*, (Basingstoke, Macmillan, 1973); Gilbert, B.B., *The*

Evolution of National Insurance in Great Britain, (London, Batsford, 1966); Fulbrook, J., *Administrative Justice and the Unemployed*, (London, Mansell, 1978).

2. See Whiteside, N., 'Welfare Legislation and the Unions during the First World War', 23 *Historical Journal*, pp. 857–74 (1980).

3. See Richards, J., 'The Use of the Unemployment Benefit System for Short-time Working in Great Britain', Working Paper No. 8, Short-time Working Project 1983–85, (Canterbury, University of Kent, August 1984); Richards, J. and Carruth, A., 'Short-time Working and the Unemployment Benefit System in Great Britain', 48 *Oxford Bulletin of Economics and Statistics*, pp. 41–60 (1986).

4. Disney, R., 'Theorising the Welfare State: The Case of Unemployment Insurance in Britain', 11 *Journal of Social Policy*, pp. 33–57 (1982).

5. Deacon, A., 'Systems of Interwar Unemployment Relief', in Glynn, S. and Booth, A. (eds) *The Road to Full Employment*, (London, Allen and Unwin, 1987).

6. 'Employers' Additional Unemployment Benefit Schemes in Great Britain', 21 *International Labour Review*, pp. 348–94 (1930).

7. *Insurance or Dole? The Adjustment of Unemployment Insurance to Economic and Social Facts in Great Britain*, (New Haven, Yale University Press, 1935) at pp. 63–4.

8. *Ibid.* at p. 64.

9. 'Searching for an Explanation of Unemployment in Inter-War Britain', 87 *Journal of Political Economy*, pp. 441–78 (1979).

10. See *inter alia*, Benjamin, D.K. and Kochin, L.A. *ibid.* Cf. Metcalf, D., Nickell, S. and Floros, N., 'Still Searching for an Explanation of Unemployment in Inter-War Britain', 90 *Journal of Political Economy*, pp. 386–99 (1982).

11. Ogus, A.I., 'Unemployment Benefit for Workers on Short-time', 4 *Industrial Law Journal*, pp. 12–23 (1975).

12. Report of an Inter-Departmental Working Party, *Unemployment Statistics*, Cmnd 5157, (London, HMSO 1972).

13. Miss Herbison, 724 HC Deb., col. 43, (7 February 1966).

14. Royal Commission on Unemployment Insurance, First Report, Cmnd 3872 (1931).

15. Richards, J. and Szyszczak, E., 'Guarantee Pay and Unemployment Benefit: Criticisms and Evidence', Working Paper No. 18 Short-time Working Project 1983–85, (Canterbury, University of Kent, May 1985).

16. See National Insurance Act 1946. Benefit for Very Short Spells of Unemployment or Sickness. Cmnd 9609 (London, HMSO, 1955).

17. Miss Herbison, 724 HC Deb, col 143, (7 February 1966).

18. DHSS Annual Report 1974, Cmnd 6130, pp. 10–11, (London, HMSO 1975).

19. The Social Security (Claims and Payments) Amendment No. 2 Regulations 1982 (SI 1982 No. 1344) and the Social Security (Unemployment, Sickness and Invalidity Benefit) Amendment No. 2 Regulations 1982 (SI 1982 No. 1345), Report of the Social Security Advisory Committee, Cmnd 8667, paras 7–9, (London, HMSO, September 1982).

20. Department of Employment, *Compensation for Short-time Working: A Consultative Document*, (London, April 1978).

21. These rules are discussed in greater detail in Chapter 5.

22. Standing Committee F, Employment Protection Bill, 11th Sitting, 17 June 1975, col. 533.

23. For a full discussion of this aspect of regulation see Rubin, G.R., *War, Law and Labour: The Munitions Acts, State Regulation and the Unions 1915–21*, (Oxford, Clarendon Press, 1987); Fyfe, T.A., *Employers and Workmen under the Munitions of War Acts 1915–17* (London and Edinburgh, William Hodge and Co., 3rd edn, 1918); Tillyard, F., *The Worker and the State: Wages, Hours, Safety and Health*, (London, Routledge, 1923).

24. Section 5(2) of the Munitions of War (Amendment) Act 1916.

25. See *Dodds* v. *Thomson* (1917) 2 Mun. App. Rep. 63; *Waugh* v. *Duncansons Ltd.* (1916) Sc. Mun. App. Rep. 46.

26. See Rubin, G.R., *War, Law, and Labour*, *op. cit.* note 23, Chapter 8.

27. 'The Munitions Appeal Reports 1916–20: A Neglected Episode in Modern Legal History', 3 *The Juridical Review*, pp. 221–37 (1977).

28. (1918–19) 3 Mun. App. Rep. 50.

29. [1936] 1 All ER 884. Discussed in Chapter 2.

30. Article 4 of the Essential Work (General Provisions) (No. 2) Order 1942 (SR and O 1942 No. 1594). For a fuller discussion of the operation of Essential Work Orders see Ministry of Labour and National Service Report for the Years 1939–46, Cmnd 7225 (London, HMSO, September 1947).

31. Dock Labour (Compulsory Registration) Order SR and O 1940 No. 1013 18 June 1940.

32. This was £4 2s 6d for a 44-hour week.

33. White Paper, Employment in the Ports: The Dock Labour Scheme, Cm 664 (1989).

34. Two particular practices were singled out for special criticism: 'bobbing' - where a staffing level was too high some dockers 'bob(bed?) off', and 'ghosting' - where non-registered dockers were hired to handle specialized cargo registered dock workers were paid at the normal rates whether they were working or not. The Transport and General Workers' Union argued that such practices were not widespread: TGWU, *Dockwork Bill: Abolition of the Dock Labour Scheme* (1989).

35. *Associated British Ports and Others* v. *TGWU* [1989] IRLR 399; [1989] IRLR 291 (High Ct); [1989] IRLR 305 (CA).

36. See Bullock, A., *The Life and Times of Ernest Bevin: Vol. II, Minister of Labour 1940–5*, (London, Heinemann, 1967) at p. 274.

37. *Ibid.* at p. 198.

38. For surveys see Incomes Data Services, 'Guaranteed Pay in a Changing Situation: A Study of Conditions', *IDS Report 24*, (June 1967) pp. 16–20, 'The Guaranteed Week - Part 1', *IDS Study No. 20*, (January 1972), 'The Guaranteed Week - Part 2', *IDS Study No. 22*, (February 1972), 'The Guaranteed Week - Part 3', *IDS Study No. 81*, (August 1974), 'Lay-offs (2) Guaranteed Week Agreements', *IDS Brief 57*, (March 1975) pp. 12–17, 'The Guaranteed Week', *IDS Study 128*, (August 1976), 'Guaranteed Week and Lay-off', *IDS Study 192*, (April 1979), 'Guaranteed Week and Lay-off', *IDS Study 297*, (September 1983). Industrial Relations Services, 'Guaranteed Pay Agreements', *Industrial Relations Review and Report No 23*, pp. 3–8 (January 1972), 'Guaranteed Week Agreements 1: Pay and Eligibility', *Industrial Relations Review and Report 324*, (24 July 1984) pp. 2–7, 'Guaranteed Week Agreements 2: Suspension of Guarantees, *Industrial Relations Review and Report 325*, (7 August 1984), pp. 2–9; 'Guaranteed Week Agreements', *Industrial Relations Review and Report 416* (17 May 1988) pp. 2–10.

39. See *The Guaranteed Week: A Study Commissioned by the General Federation of Trade Unions*, (Ruskin College, Oxford, Trade Union Research Unit, 1973).

40. Section 2 of the National Insurance Act 1966. The earnings-related supplement was payable between 1966–81. It was phased out and finally abolished by section 4 of the Social Security (No. 2) Act 1980.

41. 724 HC Deb, cols 43–4, 7 February 1966.

42. During periods of high unemployment in the inter-war years the waiting day period was one week, but since 1937 (SR and O 1937 No. 194, Reg. 2(b)) it has been three days.

43. 775 HC Deb, col. 1579, 19 December 1968.

44. 814 HC Deb, cols 401–2, 31 March 1971; 828 HC Deb, cols 143–4, 15 December 1971. (Written answer).

45. The relevant provision relating to the definition of redundancy is now section 81(1) Employment Protection (Consolidation) Act 1978. For a fuller discussion of the law relating to redundancy see Grunfeld, C., *The Law of Redundancy*, (London, Sweet and Maxwell, 3rd edn, 1989); Bourn, C.J., *Redundancy Law and Practice*, (London, Butterworths, 1983).

46. For surveys see Incomes Data Services, 'Redundancy Schemes', *IDS Study 250* (September 1981), 'Redundancy Terms', *IDS Study 280* (December 1982), 'Redundancy Terms', *IDS Study 327*, (December 1984), 'Redundancy Terms', *IDS Study 369*, (September 1986); Booth, A., 'Extra-statutory Redundancy Payments in Britain', 25 *British Journal of Industrial Relations*, pp. 400–18 (1987).

47. Fryer, R.H., 'Redundancy and Public Policy', in Martin, R. and Fryer, R.H. (eds) *Redundancy and Paternalist Capitalism*, (London, Allen and Unwin, 1973); Lewis, P., 'Twenty Years of Statutory Redundancy Payments in Great Britain', Occasional Papers in Industrial Relations, Universities of Leeds and Nottingham (1985); Daniel, W.W., 'Great Britain', in Cross, M. (ed) *Workforce Reduction: An International Survey*, (London, Croom Helm, 1985). Cf. Grunfeld, C., *The Law of Redundancy*, (London, Sweet and Maxwell, 3rd edn, 1989) Chapter 1.

48. Sections 5, 6, 7 Redundancy Payments Act 1965, now sections 87–89 Employment Protection (Consolidation) Act 1978.

49. [1981] IRLR 57. Discussed in Chapter 3.

50. *Kenneth McRae and Co. Ltd.* v. *Dawson* [1984] IRLR 5.

51. *Hanson and Others* v. *Wood (Abington Process Engravers)* [1968] ITR 46.

52. *Hulse* v. *Harry Perry t/a Arthur Perry and Son* [1975] IRLR 181; *Powell Duffryn Wagon Ltd.* v. *House* [1974] ICR 123; *Puttick* v. *John Wright and Sons (Blackwall) Ltd.* [1972] ICR 457; *Neepsend Steel and Tool Corp. Ltd.* v. *Vaughan* [1972] ITR 371.

53. See *Powell* v. *Duffryn Wagon Ltd. ibid.*

54. *Op. cit.* at p. 160.

55. [1985] ICR 488.

56. [1989] IRLR 112.

57. Section 88(3) Employment Protection (Consolidation) Act 1978.

58. Section 82(3) and (5) of the Employment Protection (Consolidation) Act 1978.

59. See *Reid* v. *Arthur Young and Son* Unreported EAT 714/82 (10 March 1983); *Neepsend Steel and Tool Corp. Ltd.* v. *Vaughan* [1972] ITR 371.

60. 'Lay-off; Part 3 Redundancy Payments', *Industrial Relations Legal Information Bulletin 236* (July 1983) at p. 6.

61. *Hulse* v. *Harry Perry, supra* note 52.

62. [1979] IRLR 232.

63. Section 89(4) Employment Protection (Consolidation) Act 1978.

64. Section 89(5)(c) Employment Protection (Consolidation) Act 1978.

65. Section 89(5)(b) Employment Protection (Consolidation) Act 1978.

66. Section 88(2) Employment Protection (Consolidation) Act 1978. Note that there may be a contractual obligation to give more than the minimum period of notice. If this is the case this must be the length of notice given the proviso to section 88(2).

67. *Fabar Construction Ltd.* v. *Race and Sutherland* [1979] IRLR 232.

68. Section 88(2)(b) Employment Protection (Consolidation) Act 1978.

69. Section 99 Employment Protection Act 1975.

70. Section 100 Employment Protection Act 1975.

71. *Supra* note 60 at p. 8.

72. Section 81(4) Employment Protection (Consolidation) Act 1978. Continuous service is calculated in accordance with Schedule 13 to the Employment Protection (Consolidation) Act 1978. Note that service before the age of 18 does not count towards continuous service for a redundancy payment.

73. At present subject to a statutory maximum of £172 per week; The Employment Protection (Variation of Limits) Order 1989, SI 1989/526.

74. These issues were discussed in Chapter 3.

75. Schedule 14 para 7(1)(1) and (2).

76. As defined in section 49 Employment Protection (Consolidation) Act 1978 and Schedule 14 para 6(3) Employment Protection (Consolidation) Act 1978.

77. Schedule 14 para 6(3) Employment Protection (Consolidation) Act 1978.

78. *Reforming the Redundancy Payments Act*, (London, Institute of Personnel Management, 1969) at p. 34.

79. [1984] IRLR 5 at p. 6.

80. Originally the rebate varied from two-thirds to seven-ninths of the redundancy payment according to the redundant employee's age. The highest rebates were recoverable in respect of older employees. From March 1969 the rebate was set at a uniform 50 per cent and then reduced to 41 per cent, then to 35 per cent (Redundancy Payments (Variations of Rebates) Order SI 1985/250). Where the statutory redundancy payment was legally reduced (for example, because of the employee's age), the rebate was also reduced proportionately (Schedule 6, paragraphs 2, 3, and 4 to the Employment Protection (Consolidation) Act 1978). Section 27 of the Wages Act 1986 introduced section 104A(1) of the EP(C)A 1978 so that the rebate was no longer available for employers employing more than ten people.

5

State Intervention: Post-1975

We have seen, in the previous chapter, that various debates took place in the post-1945 period over the appropriate way of compensating partial unemployment. In particular, serious criticisms were levelled against the policy of using unemployment benefit to compensate for short periods of unemployment. The administrative costs were high and there were objections to using the National Insurance Fund to subsidize industries which regularly laid off workers. Evidence also suggests that employers tried to organize short-time working to attract the maximum amount of unemployment benefit even though this might have disadvantages from the employer's point of view in that it might involve the reorganization of work patterns which were then unsuitable for the particular industry. The inability of industry to agree on a comprehensive form of guaranteed wage compelled the Labour government to include guarantee payments in its security of earnings measures contained in the employment protection legislation of the 1970s.

STATUTORY GUARANTEE PAYMENTS

The statutory right to a guarantee payment was introduced in sections 22–28 Employment Protection Act 1975. As a social measure guarantee payments formed part of the 'floor of rights' which was extending away from concentrating on the termination of the contract of employment to focusing upon the *content* of the employment contract.[1] These provisions were subsequently re-enacted as sections 12–18 Employment Protection (Consolidation) Act 1978, which has been amended by the Employment Acts of 1980 and 1982. Although the idea of guarantee pay was hardly novel, since most European Economic Community countries had introduced the principle long before 1975 and Britain had witnessed the growth of collectively bargained guaranteed week agreements, the introduction of a statutory scheme was surrounded by fears over the extra expenses employers would incur.[2] These fears led the Labour government to delay the introduction of the statutory provisions until 1 February 1977.

Considerable interest was shown in the guarantee payment provisions of the Employment Protection Bill. The following quotations offer a flavour of some of the issues raised. John Evans (Labour) stated:

> The Bill refers to a guarantee payment to the employee, and I confess that I feel this does not go far enough. The principle is sound, and many firms have already agreed to some such arrangement. But I ask the Minister to give some consideration to the £6 a day clause. I ask him to withdraw the word 'maximum' and to substitute 'minimum' ... I also ask him to bear in mind that many employers have long ago conceded much higher payments than £6 a day. I suggest, therefore, that the word 'minimum' is preferable in this context.[3]

In contrast James Prior (Conservative) argued:

> It would be much better to place a general requirement on the employer to negotiate guarantee pay arrangements with recognized trade unions and then allow them to work out their own arrangements in the conduct of collective bargaining.[4]
>
> These proposals transfer all the responsibility, or a great deal of the responsibility, for providing social security benefit from the state to the employer ... this will lead to considerable financial problems particularly for the small company and the small employer, and certainly in those industries which are prone to fluctuations in demand and trade disputes.[5]

Albert Booth (Minister for Employment) drew attention to the costs of the provisions:

> I would not argue that the cost of the guarantee provision is small or minimal because it is unquestionably the most expensive provision in the Bill. It costs about four times as much as the other provisions put together.[6]

Contrary to the initial fears, few employers expressed anxiety over the statutory scheme of guarantee payments when Daniel and Stilgoe[7] surveyed the impact of the employment protection legislation. This survey found that the guarantee payment provisions had no effect in 83 per cent of firms surveyed in the manufacturing sector employing between 50 and 5,000 workers. Furthermore, in 36 plants suffering a loss of demand in the previous three years, 82 per cent reported that the statutory guarantee payments had no effect and yet these are the firms where the impact would have been felt. Various reasons can be put forward to explain this result. A significant factor is the timing of the study. It was carried out only six months after the introduction of the provisions. Surprisingly the Department of Employment has not commissioned any research on guarantee payments and does not keep statistics on the level and number of payments made. Thus no overall appraisal of the impact or working of the statutory scheme has been made.

Another limitation is that the study focused upon large firms which had probably experienced collective agreements on guarantee pay. A study of smaller firms a year after the Daniel and Stilgoe survey suggested that very few firms in that study had to make guarantee payments, but 8 per cent of the respondents reported that statutory guarantee pay would be the most troublesome of the new employment protection provisions and 18 per cent thought the statutory guarantee payments provisions were among the three most troublesome of the new employment protection provisions; unfair dismissal and maternity provisions were consistently ranked above statutory guarantee payments in terms of their impact upon small firms.[8]

A further explanation for the reported lack of impact of the statutory provisions is that the duration and level of compensation for short-time working is not very high. Initially statutory guarantee payments were to be subject to a maximum weekly limit of £30 with the ultimate aim to provide the equivalent of a full week's pay. This aim was never realized. The Secretary of State has the power to vary the limits set on guarantee payments taking into account the national economic situation as a whole and other matters thought to be relevant by him or her.[9] The various up-datings of the limits are to be found in Appendix A.

In research carried out on the Short-time Working Project at the University of Kent the up-rating of guarantee payments was compared in relation to other key economic variables such as inflation, unemployment benefit and average earnings. It was found that the maximum limits set for guarantee payments have declined in relation to all three key variables since their introduction in 1977.[10] Furthermore, not only was the maximum ceiling on guarantee pay fixed so low as to lie below many of the pre-existing collective arrangements on guarantee pay, but even in the low-paid and least unionized sectors of employment the ceiling was inadequate. In order to explore the issue in more detail, the rates of weekly pay were examined in the sectors of employment covered by Wages Councils which operate in sectors where, because of insufficient trade union organization, collective bargaining does not exist. These were sectors of low-paid employment comparable to the sectors of employment the statutory guarantee payments were designed to have most effects in. Further analysis revealed that although the guarantee pay ceiling was set in 1977 at a figure commensurate with minimum rates laid down by Wages Councils, by 1981 only one sector covered by Wages Council Orders –

Hairdressing – had a minimum weekly wage set *below* the statutory guaranteed wage figure. This suggests that, by 1985, the maximum guarantee had fallen below many of the minimum rates of pay established in sectors where collective bargaining is typically weak.

In addition to the lack of impact felt by employers the provisions have given rise to little litigation. This is probably due to the limited financial nature of guarantee payments, the absence of legal aid to pursue claims before an industrial tribunal, the existence of more favourable collectively bargained agreements, and also to the fact that while the incidence of short-time working has increased in recent years the employer's obligation to make guarantee payments has been cushioned by the introduction of employment subsidies.

ELIGIBILITY FOR A GUARANTEE PAYMENT

In order to qualify for a statutory guarantee payment an employee must be continuously employed under a contract of employment for a period of one month ending the day before the day for which a guarantee payment is claimed.[11] Certain groups of employees are excluded from guarantee payments. These comprise part-time employees working under a contract of employment involving less than 16 hours per week,[12] casual workers,[13] the armed forces,[14] employees who ordinarily work outside Great Britain,[15] share fishermen,[16] and the police.[17] Registered dock workers were excluded from the statutory scheme[18] but will now be covered as normal employees by the extension of employment protection rights under the Dock Work Act 1989. Employees who are employed under a contract of employment for a fixed term of three months or less, or employees employed for the performance of a specific task which is expected to be completed within three months, are also excluded from the statutory scheme of guarantee payments.[19] In order to prevent employers avoiding liability for guarantee payments by putting their workforce on a series of short contracts, or if the employment lasts longer than expected, section 13(2) of the Employment Protection (Consolidation) Act 1978 allows an employee to claim a guarantee payment if she is in fact continuously employed for more than three months. It is unclear, however, whether the removal of the exclusion applies *ab initio* or only from the elapse of the first three months.

The statutory scheme of guarantee payments applies only where there is a subsisting contract of employment. This excludes a guarantee payment where a lay-off results in the termination of the contract of employment with the prospect of re-engagement or a constructive dismissal where the employer's breach of contract is accepted by the employee. Guarantee payments may be claimed by employees laid off under a suspensory contractual provision or where a lay-off is in breach of contract but the breach is waived by the employee.

The statutory guarantee pay provisions do not imply that the employer has a right to lay-off employees where there is no right to do so in the contract of employment, and the statutory scheme of guarantee payments does not affect any contractual right to a guaranteed minimum wage,[20] although provision is made for mutual set-off of statutory and contractual pay.[21]

Section 12 of the Employment Protection (Consolidation) Act 1978 defines the right to a guarantee payment. Broadly speaking a guarantee payment is only available for normal working days on which there is no work available. Section 12 has been subject to interpretation by the industrial tribunals and certain phrases merit special attention.

Definition of a Workless Day

A workless day is defined in section 12(1) of the Employment Protection (Consolidation) Act 1978 as:

> Where an employee throughout a day during any part of which he would normally be required to work in accordance with his contract of employment is not provided with work by his employer by reason of: (a) a diminution in the requirements of the employer's business for work of the kind which the employee is employed to do; or (b) any other occurrence affecting the normal working of the employer's business in relation to work of the kind which the employee is employed to do, he shall subject to the provisions of this Act be entitled to be paid by his employer a payment referred to in this Act as a guarantee payment in respect of that day.

The use of the words 'throughout a day' suggests that the guarantee payment provisions apply only to *whole* days without work. Thus an employer may try to avoid liability for a guarantee payment by providing some work each day. By reducing the number of hours worked each day, however, an employer may be in breach of contract and a right to claim a redundancy payment could also arise under section 88 Employment Protection (Consolidation) Act 1978.

A day is defined by section 12 as a period of 24 hours from midnight to midnight. If an employee works shifts extending over midnight the employment is treated as occurring only on the day the duration of employment is longer; that is, before or after midnight. The effect of this rule on shift working is seen in *Trevethan* v. *Sterling Metals Ltd.*[22] The applicant was a regular night shift worker who worked four shifts between 8.00 p.m. and 6.30 a.m., starting at 8.00 p.m. Monday and finishing at 6.30 a.m. on Friday. In contrast, the day shift workers worked a five-day week consisting of eight-hour shifts each day from Monday through to Friday. The applicant was laid off on 15 and 23 February and 1 and 8 March and received the maximum guarantee payment for these days. He was again laid off on 10 March and received no guarantee payment, as his employer argued that he had used up his entitlement for that quarter. The industrial tribunal upheld this view, because, according to what is now section 12(2) Employment Protection (Consolidation) Act 1978, the employee only worked four days per week and therefore was only entitled to a guarantee payment for four days under section 15(3)(a) of the Act. The employer's representative argued that the day shift would have been similarly disentitled if employees had chosen to cram their 40-hour week into four days. The disadvantage of this interpretation is that a guarantee payment is calculated on an hourly rate multiplied by the number of hours in a working day but subject to a daily maximum. Thus even when a day will count as a 'workless' day a shift worker will not be fully compensated for all the hours of work lost.

Days Normally Required to Work

The workless day must be a day on which the employee is normally required to work under the contract of employment. This definition precludes days on which an employee is away from work owing to sickness or holiday. In *York and Reynolds* v. *College Hosiery Co. Ltd.*[23] the factory was left open on a limited basis during the annual holiday shutdown and employees were able to go in to work if work was available. An industrial tribunal denied a claim for a guarantee payment during this period because these were not days on which employees were normally required to work.

Workers who work on an intermittent basis may find it difficult to prove their eligibility for a statutory guarantee payment. The first hurdle to overcome will be showing that there is a 'mutuality of obligation' in order to achieve employee status.[24] The decision of the Court of Appeal in *Nethermere (St Neots) Ltd.* v. *Taverna and Gardiner*[25] (a case concerning the employment status of homeworkers) may have mitigated some of the harsher effects of the earlier ruling in *O'Kelly* v. *Trusthouse Forte Plc* by regarding 'an irreductable minimum of obligation' as the determining factor of employee status. Here it was found that while there were weeks when the applicants did not work and they could indicate to the delivery driver how much work they wanted, there was a required minimum of work in that they had to make it worthwhile for the driver to call. However, the interpretation of section 12 means that casual workers who can prove that they are working under a contract of employment may still have difficulty in showing there are specific days on which they are required to work.[26] Problems also arise if the employer has enforced a reduction in the working week, thus varying the hours normally required to work. In *Daley* v. *Strathclyde Regional Council*[27] the industrial tribunal took the view that where the working week has been reduced and the employees have worked the shorter hours they may lose their right to a guarantee payment when they are no longer required to work during the whole of the week. Here the 17 applicants were employed as night shift workers at a College of Technology. Until April 1977 they were employed on a 40-hour week consisting of five eight-hour shifts. Following public expenditure cuts, two of the three unions representing the employees agreed to an alteration of the working week. The new arrangements provided for one week of five eight-hour shifts and one week of four eight-hour shifts, Monday to Thursday, giving alternate normal weekly working hours of 40 hours one week and 32 hours the next week. The applicants were all members of the National Union of Public Employees which had organized a strike against the cuts in hours, but after the strike the applicants had worked the shorter hours and a revized statement of particulars showing the reduced working hours was issued under section 1 of the Employment Protection (Consolidation) Act 1978. The applicants then tried to claim a guarantee payment for the alternate Friday when they were no longer supplied with work. The industrial tribunal rejected the claim on the basis that the alleged workless day was no longer a day on which the employees would normally be required to work and so section 15(4) did not apply:

> It is true that the change had been met with a protest and a strike. Since the end of the strike the applicants had been working the varied hours. They did not claim that the respondents had repudiated their contracts and resign to seek whatever remedies might (or might not) have been open to them. The effect is that the applicants had contracts of employment which do not normally involve their working on alternate Fridays. The change is not a short-term or a temporary one. It is an alteration in their normal working arrangements which they must be held to have accepted.

A similar approach was adopted in *Clemens* v. *Peter Richards Ltd.*[28] Here the applicant began work in 1974 on a five-day week but this was reduced to a four-day week one year later. Business continued to decline and in 1976 the contract of employment was amended to a two-day working week. Mrs Clemens went along with this arrangement under protest, supplementing her earnings with unemployment benefit. When the guarantee payment provisions came into operation in 1977 unemployment benefit could no longer be claimed and she was advised to claim a guarantee payment. The industrial tribunal refused the claim arguing that, although the unilateral variation constituted a breach of contract, Mrs Clemens had accepted the variation, albeit under protest, and because the employers were no longer obliged to supply work the days could no longer be regarded as days on which she was normally required to work.

Drake and Bercusson argue that the approach taken by the tribunals in these cases reflects a 'managerial perspective' and amounts to the insertion of extra words into section 12 of the Employment Protection (Consolidation) Act 1978 in that the industrial tribunals are asking the question 'Was the employee normally required to work "by the employer" rather than in accordance with his contract of employment?' Thus the industrial tribunals have given the employee a difficult choice. The employee can either accept the proposed changes in the working hours; terminate the contract of employment, bringing a claim of unfair dismissal on the basis that there has been a constructive dismissal; or refuse to accept the change and sue the employer for breach of contract.[29] Section 14(3) of the Employment Protection (Consolidation) Act 1978 expressly provides that where a contract has been varied to allow for short-time working this variation does not affect the *calculation* of guarantee payments. The payments are to be calculated by reference to the last day on which the original contract was in force. Thus it could be argued that *entitlement* to a guarantee payment should similarly be unaffected.

A middle ground was found by the industrial tribunal in *Bulsara and Others* v. *C. Barker and Co. Ltd.*[30] Here a bus strike forced the employers to close their factory for one day. This was in agreement with the union, and the employees attempted to claim a guarantee payment for the lost day. The employer refused the request, arguing that the contracts of employment had been varied so that the employees were not obliged to work on that day. The industrial tribunal disagreed with this interpretation:

> We consider that cogent evidence is needed to substantiate that in the instant case the workforce had agreed to vary their contracts of employment so that they would not be required to work and would forgo their rights to guarantee pay. It may be that a large number of the workforce resigned themselves to the situation that on the following Monday there would be no work and no pay for them but that is far from saying that they agreed with their employers to vary the terms of employment which would deprive them of their rights under recent employment protection legislation.

Days on which an employee is absent from work because of illness or during a holiday period cannot be compensated for by a guarantee payment. Thus in *York and Reynolds* v. *College Hosiery Co. Ltd.*[31] it was the employer's practice to provide work for employees who wished to work during the annual holiday fortnight when the factory would normally be shut. In 1977 the applicant asked for work during the annual holiday but for four days the employers were unable to provide work and the employees claimed a guarantee payment. The industrial tribunal refused the claim arguing that the 'workless day' has to be one where, in normal circumstances, the employer can insist that the employee should attend for work and the employee can insist that the employer provide work under the terms of the contract of employment. In this instance the employer had no right to insist that the employees attend work and the employees could not insist that work be provided. The arrangement was merely designed to minimize the loss of earnings for those employees who chose to take their holiday at a different time of year.

This aspect of compulsion is important for determining whether or not an employee is eligible for a guarantee payment. In *Mailway (Southern) Ltd.* v. *Willsher*[32] the fact that the employee had the option of attending for work denied the possibility of her being entitled to a guarantee payment when a lay-off occurred, despite the fact that from September 1974 to March 1977 she had worked on average for more than 16 hours per week.

In contrast, a guarantee payment was allowed in *Miller* v. *Harry Thornton (Lollies) Ltd.*,[33] where the employer allowed employees (most of whom were married women with children) to choose the hours of work most convenient for them. After agreeing to suitable hours they were then expected to attend for work on any day when they were called upon unless they were sick or had previously been granted leave of absence. The management had a discretion to vary the total number of hours according to the demand for the firm's products and to lay-off employees at any time when it was impossible to manufacture. The applicant had worked to these conditions for five years. During the 12 months before the lay-off the customary hours of work had been from 8.30 a.m. to 4 p.m. for five days per week. On 6 and 7 September the applicant had been laid off because of threatened power cuts. The employer had refused her claim for a guarantee payment on the grounds that the applicant was a casual worker with no normal working hours. The industrial tribunal was able to distinguish the *Willsher* decision on the grounds that, although the applicant was referred to as a casual worker having no written fixed hours, the industrial tribunal was entitled to look at the way the parties had contemplated that the contract would work out in practice. If the contemplated result was a pattern of so many hours per week then it could be said there were normal working hours even though those hours may be varied from time to time by mutual consent. The industrial tribunal was able to conclude that the employees were compelled to attend work if called and if it had not been for the anticipated power cuts the employees would normally have been required to work in accordance with their contracts.

Not only must the employees be normally required to work on the workless days but they must also have 'normal working hours' on that day.[34] Thus if employees' hours vary from day to day they will not be entitled to a guarantee payment. This in effect is an additional category of workers excluded from the statutory scheme since the provision excludes casual workers from the guarantee payment provisions unless the industrial tribunal can find that the employees were expected to, and did in fact, work fixed hours agreed between the parties. Section 14(2)(b) of the Employment Protection (Consolidation) Act 1978 does allow employees' hours to vary from week to week without disqualifying them from eligibility for a guarantee payment.

Reason for the Workless Day

Section 12(1)(a) of the Employment Protection (Consolidation) Act 1978 states that the workless day must be due to a diminution in the employer's requirements for work of the kind which the employee is employed to do. These provisions resemble the description of lay-off used in the definition of a redundancy-lay-off in section 81(2)(b) of the Employment Protection (Consolidation) Act 1978, which was discussed in the previous chapter. While the interpretation of this section might be used by analogy it is clear that the situations are not identical. Under section 12 the lay-off is intended to be temporary and section 12(1)(b) allows for wider circumstances affecting the employer's business to be taken into account. This would cover such events as equipment failures, power cuts and natural disasters. In *Newbrooks and Sweet* v. *Saigal*,[35] however, a guarantee payment was allowed where a lay-off was the consequence of the employer's illness because he was unable to supervise the work. In contrast, a lay-off caused by an employer who wished to close his factories on Jewish holidays was held not to be an 'occurrence' which affected the working of the factory but was an event which affected the employer personally. Thus the employees were not entitled to a guarantee payment.[36]

EXCLUSIONS

The Employment Protection (Consolidation) Act 1978 (as amended by the Employment Act 1981) identifies three situations where an employee may be excluded from receiving statutory guarantee pay for a workless day. These are where the workless day is in consequence of industrial action involving employees of the employer or an associated employer,[37] where the employee has unreasonably refused an offer of alternative employment which is suitable in all the circumstances,[38] or where the employee has not complied with reasonable requirements imposed by the employer with a view to ensuring that her services are available.[39]

Industrial Action

The original wording of section 13(1) Employment Protection (Consolidation) Act 1978 excluded the right to a guarantee payment if the lack of work was due to a 'trade dispute'. Drake and Bercusson noted that the disqualification for the guarantee payment was even wider and more arbitrary than the 'trade dispute qualification' for social security benefits because under these an employee could escape disqualification if she could prove she had nothing to do with the dispute.[40] The interpretation of a 'trade dispute' for guarantee payment purposes was to have been in accordance with section 29 of the Trade Union and Labour Relations Act 1974, but the subsequent interpretations have been varied. Drake and Bercusson cite the Ulster workers' strike of May 1977 as being a *political* dispute not a 'trade dispute' within the meaning of section 29 of the Trade Union and Labour Relations Act 1974, enabling the workers laid off as a consequence to claim a guarantee payment. This might be compared with *Ibbett* v. *Birds Eye Foods*,[41] where a strike against the introduction of tachographs in lorries (which surely must be a dispute about the terms and conditions of employment) was held to disqualify the laid-off employees from claiming a guarantee payment. Other decisions have given even wider interpretations. For example, in *Garvey* v. *J. and J. Maybank (Oldham) Ltd.*,[42] a dispute over guarantee payments arose out of the road haulage strike of 1979. The respondent waste paper merchants relied upon outside contractors and their own lorry drivers to bring in supplies. Initially the strike only affected the outside contractors but subsequently the firm's own drivers were prevented from crossing a picket line to bring in the supplies. As a result the applicant and about 50 other employees were laid off. The employers refused the request for a guarantee payment, arguing that the refusal of the firm's own lorry drivers to cross picket lines constituted a breach of contract. This brought the dispute within section 29(1)(d) of the Trade Union and Labour Relations Act 1974, which includes a 'matter of discipline' as being a 'trade dispute'. Although the firm's lorry drivers were not involved in the national dispute they had disobeyed orders in not crossing the picket line. Since the applicant was laid off as a result of this 'trade dispute' between the respondents and their own drivers he was not entitled to a guarantee payment.

This wide approach is seen in *Thomson* v. *Priest (Lindley) Ltd.*[43] Here the lay-off was due to a combination of factors, *inter alia* the cancellation of orders, collapse of a major customer and shortage of essential materials. These factors were aggravated by a strike at the factory of an associated employer. It was argued that the strike by itself would not have caused the lay-off since the lay-off was the consequence of a number of economic factors. The industrial tribunal rejected this argument, adopting a position that the strike did not have to be the *sole* factor causing the lay-off. If an affirmative answer can be given to the question 'But for the trade dispute would there have been a lay-off?' then the employees would be disqualified from claiming a guarantee payment.

The industrial action must involve employees of the employer (or of an associated employer). In *Newman* v. *Edward Hanson Ltd.*[44] the employers supplied contract labour to the British Steel Corporation. Their employees were laid off during the national steel strike and were denied a guarantee payment. On application to an industrial tribunal it was decided that the concept of involvement must imply some sort of participation: it was not enough that the workforce was merely affected by the strike. Since the employees were not participating in the dispute they were entitled to guarantee payments. A refusal to cross picket lines will amount to involvement, as is shown in the case of *McMonagle* v. *Cementation Mining Co.*[45] Here the National Coal Board sub-contractors who were members of the National Union of Mineworkers refused to cross picket lines. Although they were not physically participating in the strike they were held to be involved in it. In contrast, guarantee payments were allowed in a situation where the employer suspended work because of a strike on a customer's premises which involved the customer's employees but not his own. Here the industrial tribunal held that this was an 'occurrence' affecting the normal working of the business.[46]

The words 'trade dispute' were replaced by an even wider definition of industrial disputes by paragraph 15 of Schedule 3 to the Employment Act 1982, which now includes a 'strike, lock-out, or other industrial action'. The words 'industrial action' have been interpreted by the Court of Appeal under section 62 of the Employment Protection (Consolidation) Act 1978.[47] This section excludes an industrial tribunal's jurisdiction to consider the reasonableness of a dismissal where the employee is taking part in a strike or other industrial action. There was a dispute over wages and as a consequence the employees concertedly refused to work voluntary overtime and the employer dismissed the applicant. The Court of Appeal argued that the words 'industrial action' should be given their 'ordinary and natural' meaning and a discretion should be given to the industrial tribunals to determine whether the action, although not amounting to a breach of contract, is being used as a bargaining weapon to apply pressure on an employer. Such a wide interpretation may have implications for guarantee payments. For example, if employees are laid off due to shortages of materials as a result of action not in breach of contract, such as a ban on voluntary overtime by other employees of their own or of an associated employer, then it could be possible for an employer to legitimately refuse a request for a guarantee payment.

Unreasonable Refusal of an Offer of Alternative Employment

Section 13(4)(a) of the Employment Protection (Consolidation) Act 1978 provides that an employee shall not be eligible for a guarantee payment if:

> . . . his employer has offered to provide alternative work for that day which is suitable in all the circumstances whether or not work which the employee is under his contract to perform and the employee has unreasonably refused that offer.

If the employer finds work for the employees which they are bound to perform under the contract of employment, the guarantee payment provisions are not applicable. A refusal to carry out the work will amount to a breach of contract and may also be a matter to be dealt with under disciplinary rules. Most collectively bargained guaranteed week provisions make guarantee pay contingent upon the acceptance of some flexibility over alternative working arrangements. Prolonged alternative working arrangements, however, open up the possibility that the employee may be seen to have consented to a permanent variation of their contracts of employment, which in turn may have repercussions for other employment protection rights.

The use of the past tense (the 'employer has offered') would imply that any offers of alternative work must be made *before* the workless day. This was the interpretation given in *Newbrooks and Sweet* v. *Saigal*,[48] where the two applicants had gone into work to inform their employer they would be making a claim for a guarantee payment. The industrial tribunal decided that they were not unreasonable in rejecting the employer's offer of alternative work made on that day. This should not be construed as a general rule, however, since each case will turn upon its own particular circumstances.

Further interpretation of section 13(4)(a) has emerged from the industrial tribunal decision in *North* v. *Pavleigh Ltd.*,[49] where it was held that an offer to an employee to work on a different day from the workless day does not constitute an offer of alternative work. Employees may of course choose to work the alternative arrangements, but they may also claim the statutory guarantee payment for the workless day. The offer and acceptance of alternative work does not extinguish the employer's liability to make guarantee payments; liability may still arise if there is a subsequent lay-off. In *Lincoln* v. *Dunling*[50] a term of the contract of employment of a lorry driver stated that if no driving work was available the employer should try to find alternative work which the employee was obliged to accept. Mr Lincoln's lorry broke down and alternative work was provided for one week but then he was laid off. The employer refused the request for a guarantee payment, arguing that his statutory liability had been discharged during the week alternative work had been provided. The industrial tribunal rejected this argument in finding that the workless days occurred *after* the week in which the alternative work had been provided.[51]

In approaching the question of whether an employee is disqualified from receiving a guarantee payment, two tests have been applied to section 13(2)(a). First, there is an objective test: is the alternative work suitable? Then a subjective test applies: was the employee's conduct reasonable in refusing the offer? The first test looks at the nature of the alternative work. Factors such as hours, skill, status, opportunity to earn bonus payments, all play an important role, together with the length of time the employee was expected to carry out the alternative work. Presumably to allow flexibility, the Employment Protection (Consolidation) Act 1978 does not lay down the criteria to be employed in assessing the suitability of the employment and this allows employers to respond to a work shortage in a way best suited to their employment and the particular reasons for the lay-off. Similar wording to section 13(2)(a) is used in section 82(5) of the Employment Protection (Consolidation) Act 1978 which deals with offers of alternative work in a redundancy situation but the two situations are not analogous and the industrial tribunals have resisted applying similar interpretations to both sections. Thus in *Duckenfield* v. *G.W. Thornton Ltd.*[52] an industrial tribunal recognized that the two sections had the same kind of meaning but the wording under the guarantee payment provisions should be construed more widely since they contemplate a 'temporary or partial' redundancy rather than a permanent situation:

> The probability is that [during a temporary lay-off] an employee can be required to co-operate by working in a number of jobs which on a more long-term point of view would be regarded as distinctly unsuitable.

Where a lay-off is temporary an industrial tribunal has recognized that it may be in the interests of employer and employee that the offer of alternative work is accepted in order to keep the business viable or to alleviate the problems causing the lay-off. In *Purdy* v. *Willowbrook International Ltd.*[53] the applicant normally worked as a coach trimmer. He had previously been transferred to work in the finishing shop when his normal work was unavailable. This alternative work was of an equivalent type and skill with an opportunity to earn similar bonuses as in his normal work. During one shortage of normal work the applicant declined the offer of alternative work, preferring instead to make a claim for a guarantee payment. The claim was rejected, one of the reasons being that if the applicant had accepted the alternative work there was no reason to suppose it would be a permanent move and indeed by speeding up production it would have hastened the resumption of full-time working in the applicant's normal work.

The second test, the reasonableness of the refusal, depends very much upon the employee's personal circumstances. In *Purdy* v. *Willowbrook International Ltd.* the industrial tribunal was influenced by the fact that the applicant had previously undertaken the alternative employment and was conversant with the work and conditions in the finishing shop. This interpretation is problematic since by accepting the offer of alternative employment once, it becomes difficult for an employee to decline future offers without good cause, thus exposing herself to the situation that repeated spells of alternative employment imply consent to the variation of the normal contract of employment.

Further examples of the operation of the second test are seen in *Duckenfield* v. *G.W. Thornton Ltd.*, where the refusal to undertake work in a grinding shop as opposed to the normal work in the press department was held to be a reasonable refusal of the alternative work when supported by the fact that the applicant had received medical advice to avoid working in a dusty atmosphere. This did not entitle him to refuse a second offer of alternative work in the inspection department since this work was not covered by the medical advice. Similarly in *Roberts and Howells* v. *Firth Cleveland Engineering Ltd.*,[54] Roberts refused an offer of alternative work involving shovelling because he considered such work was beneath him as a skilled man. The industrial tribunal rejected his application for a guarantee payment since there was no alternative work available and Roberts was unreasonable in refusing the offer. Howells, on the other had, had refused the alternative work because it might have been in the paint shop and he was suffering from bronchitis. The industrial tribunal found that the work would not have been in the paint shop and that Howells was unreasonable to refuse the alternative work without first discovering its location. In contrast, a woman was awarded a guarantee payment when there was a shortage of her normal packing work and she was unable to work at hoeing because of a bad back.[55]

Imposing Reasonable Requirements to Ensure the Employee's Services are Available

Section 13(4)(b) of the Employment Protection (Consolidation) Act 1978 allows the employer to impose some requirements for an employee to be available for work in the event of a temporary work shortage. Failure to comply with these requirements will disentitle the employee from a guarantee payment. It is difficult to generalize as to what are 'reasonable requirements' to impose upon the employee; much will depend upon established industrial practice and also the reasons for the lay-off. Some employers may insist upon the employee reporting for work while other employers may be satisfied with the employee telephoning in. This section is likely to be most problematic where there is no established practice or an emergency confronts the employer. The industrial tribunal in *Meadows* v. *Faithfull Overalls Ltd.*[56] has given some indication as to how this section should be approached. The employees arrived at work one morning to discover that the oil supply had run out and there was no heating in the factory. This had happened on previous occasions and then the employees had waited in the canteen, warmed by hot tea. On one occasion it was not until three o'clock in the afternoon that the factory reached the statutory minimum temperature and the employees could undertake work. This time the factory manager asked the workforce to wait in the canteen as his supplier had promised the oil would arrive by 9.30 a.m. This request was extended to 9.45 a.m. and it was made clear to the employees that they would not be paid if they went home. When the oil did not arrive at 9.45 a.m. the workforce voted to leave the factory. In fact the oil did arrive shortly afterwards. The employees' claim for a guarantee payment was rejected by the industrial tribunal. The correct way to approach the reasonableness of the employer's request to stay in the factory was:

> ... a consideration of the evidence concerning the state of mind of the employers at the material time and some guide towards the reasonableness or otherwise of any requirements made by the employer may be found in the evidence about the information communicated by the employer to the workforce.

Here the management had passed on the information from the oil supplier and there was good reason to believe that its arrival was imminent. It was reasonable, therefore, for the employees to stay on the factory premises to ensure that work could resume as soon as the minimum working temperature was reached. The difficulty with this approach is that it looks at the question of reasonableness purely from management's point of view rather than as between the parties. This approach is seen also in *Bufton* v. *Hall and Son*[57] concerning a rejection of a guarantee payment in a similar situation. Here there was no heating oil on a Monday and the employees were sent home and told to come back on the Tuesday afternoon. On the Tuesday morning the employees held a meeting and concluded that it was unlikely that the heating would be working by the afternoon and therefore none of the employees came into work in the afternoon. The industrial tribunal found that they had not complied with a requirement that was reasonable from the employer's point of view.

A further illustration of the interpretation of the section can be found in *Holding* v. *Paul Clements Transport Services Ltd.*,[58] where an HGV driver had a loose arrangement that he would telephone in to work on Fridays to see what work was available. During one week when his lorry was being repaired he did not telephone in to work. He then obtained another job but claimed guarantee payments from the old employer for the week he had not worked. The industrial tribunal found that there was work available for at least three days of that week and that there was an implied requirement imposed by the employer that the employee should present himself for work or, at least enquire whether work was available. Since the employee had done nothing he was disentitled from claiming a guarantee payment.

CALCULATION OF A GUARANTEE PAYMENT

Guarantee payments are calculated in accordance with section 14 of the Employment Protection (Consolidation) Act 1978, subject to the limits imposed by section 15 of that Act. A guarantee payment is calculated by multiplying the number of working hours on the workless day by the guaranteed hourly rate. The hourly rate is calculated as a normal week's pay divided by the number of normal working hours in the week. If the hours vary from week to week the average number of weekly hours is taken over the preceding 12-week period ending with the last complete week before the day in respect of which the guarantee payment is payable. If the employee has not been employed for a sufficient number of weeks to calculate this average, the number of hours in a week the employee could expect to work in accordance with the contract of employment may be taken, and an employer may look at the average number of hours worked by an employee in comparable employment in an attempt to calculate this figure.

If the employee's contract has been varied or replaced with a new one during a period of short-time working, the number of hours should be calculated in accordance with the original contract.

Section 15 of the Employment Protection (Consolidation) Act 1978 limits the number of days for which guarantee payments can be claimed to a maximum of five workless days in any three-month period. Originally section 15(2) stated that this maximum was to apply to fixed quarters (beginning on 1 February, 1 May, 1 August, and 1 November). Given the close connection between guarantee payments and subsequent claims for social security benefits these fixed quarters were deliberately chosen for the administrative convenience of supplementary benefits offices who traditionally have increased workloads around Easter, Summer and Christmas vacations when students and temporary or seasonal workers would swell the numbers of those looking for work.

The substitution of the rolling three-month period for the fixed quarters was a direct result of the road haulage strike of 1979, when some workers who were laid off received two sets of guarantee payments in quick succession when the lay-offs straddled two fixed quarters. These payments, although far below the supplementary benefit allowance, were described as a 'windfall' by the Conservative government and this was perceived as too much of a financial burden for small employers to bear.[59] Paradoxically, however, the new provisions are likely to cause a greater administrative burden to employers, who must now keep much more detailed records of each employee's lay-off periods.

The amount of guarantee payment is subject to a daily maximum. From 1 April 1989 this figure is £11.85.[60] Although the maximum is revised annually, the sums are not very large and the increases have not keep pace with inflation. Also, although employees who are laid off for less than three days for every three months are better off than before 1977, those laid off for longer periods would have been better off receiving social security benefits.

Finally, section 16(2) Employment Protection (Consolidation) Act 1978 provides for the mutual set-off of any statutory guarantee payments and any contractual pay (which will probably be of a greater amount) due under a guaranteed week agreement or any contractual provision.

CONTRACTING OUT OF THE STATUTORY PROVISIONS

Section 18 of the Employment Protection (Consolidation) Act 1978 provides that a collective agreement or wages order providing for guarantee payments may be exempted from the statutory obligation on application of all the parties to the agreement to the Secretary of State.[61] Since employees may choose the more advantageous rights Rubenstein predicted that section 18 would be under-utilized.[62] Contrary to these predictions, the exemption provisions of section 18 have been utilized more frequently than other areas which allow for the possibility of contracting-out of the employment protection legislation.[63] This probably reflects the relatively advanced development of collectively bargained guaranteed week agreements by 1978. At the time of writing 23 exemption orders have been granted and these are listed in Appendix B. Some examples of the exempted agreements are to be found in Appendix C. The impact of the Temporary Short-time Working Compensation Scheme may have had an effect upon the development of collective bargaining since it is quite notable that, after a rush of applications for exemptions under section 18 in 1977–8, the number of applications decreased after the introduction of the scheme in 1979. The closure of the scheme in March 1984 has not stimulated collective bargaining in order to contract out of the statutory scheme of guarantee payments.

Section 18 of the Employment Protection (Consolidation) Act 1978 should be contextualized within the general framework of employment protection legislation developed in the seventies. This legislation encouraged and provided space for the continuation of collective bargaining with the proviso that the 'floor of rights' established in the legislation was maintained on a comparable basis. The rationale of section 18 is to allow scope for individual employers and trade unions to make their own arrangements for guarantee payments that are better suited to the specific circumstances of their own employment or industry. For this reason it is not a condition of exemption that the terms of the collective agreement or wages order do not contain provisions less favourable than the statutory guarantees. Presumably a trade union would not agree to an exemption if this were not the case, and it is left to the discretion of the Secretary of State to assess the relative disadvantage of some terms over the advantages of the more favourable terms found in the collective agreement. It is a condition of exemption, however, that there is a mechanism to deal with any disputes over guarantee payments. Most of the exempted agreements provide for an initial voluntary conciliation process before a claim is made to an industrial tribunal, and the majority of the exempted agreements have utilized the existing grievance procedures by adapting their terms to allow either an appeal to the Advisory Conciliation and Arbitration Service (ACAS) as a final stage of the normal procedure, or by allowing an appeal to an industrial tribunal at any stage in the proceedings. Bourn argues that the presentation of a claim to an industrial tribunal is the more favoured clause since it protects the rights and position of non-union employees.[64] Exemption Orders Nos. 10, 13 and 15 provide that the only remedy for disputes over guarantee payments is to be obtained from an industrial tribunal. In contrast, Exemption Orders Nos. 1 and 3 provide that disputes may at the *option of the claimant* be referred to ACAS and/or an industrial tribunal in the event of no decision by the Joint Civil Engineering/Building Industry Board. On the other hand, Exemption Order No. 12 provides for ACAS to appoint an arbitrator in the event of no decision emerging from the voluntary procedure specified in the order.

Many of the substantive terms of the exempted agreements differ from the statutory terms. Many agreements also contain restrictions as to when the guarantee payments are payable. For example, in Exemption Order No. 9 no guarantee is payable where the lay-off is due to the refusal of *another* employee to carry out work temporarily assigned to him. Whereas Exemption Order No. 18 disentitles an employee from a guarantee payment where the plant is idle through avoidable absenteeism or the failure of any employee to take reasonable action to keep the plant working. Lay-offs as a result of strike action of the employees of the firm or any associated firms figure prominently in the exclusion clauses. Exemption Orders Nos. 4 and 12 have a wide suspension clause operative when the lay-off is caused by industrial action by any employees within the industry or covered by the relevant national agreement. In contrast, Exemption Orders Nos. 5 and 9 have narrower clauses, suspending the payment only when the industrial action is within the department or the factory where the lay-off occurs.

Often the Exemption Orders are adapted to the particular industry's needs; for example, in Exemption Orders Nos. 1, 2 and 3 relating to the civil engineering, demolition, and building industries, particular account is taken of lay-offs due to bad weather.

An Exemption Order made under section 18 may be revoked or varied by the Secretary of State without an application from the parties to the collective agreement. This allows for a flexible response where there is a change in circumstances; for example, when the statutory limits are improved or where there is a change in the pattern of short-time working.

ENFORCEMENT OF GUARANTEE PAYMENTS

If an employer fails to make a statutory guarantee payment an employee may initiate a complaint to an industrial tribunal within three months of the day for which the guarantee payment is claimed.[65] The industrial tribunal may waive this limitation period if it considers that it was not reasonably practicable for the complaint to be presented within the three-month period; for example, where a dispute has arisen over eligibility for a payment under a guaranteed week agreement or eligibility for unemployment benefit.

The original Employment Protection Bill contained what were described by Rubenstein as 'draconian' enforcement provisions.[66] Clause 27 proposed that an employer would be obliged to inform an employee within two days of a lay-off whether or not she was going to make a guarantee payment. A failure to inform the employee would have rendered the employer liable to make a guarantee payment even if the employee had exhausted her entitlement. This would have placed a heavy administrative burden upon the employer to monitor each employee's short-time working, thus counteracting the aim of making the administration of guarantee payments relatively simple by using fixed quarters to calculate entitlement. The change from fixed quarters to rolling quarters together with the use of the Temporary Short-time Working Compensation Scheme has reversed this situation and employers are now obliged to keep more complex records of short-time working anyway if they wish to avoid litigation.

THE INTERACTION OF STATUTORY GUARANTEE PAYMENTS AND UNEMPLOYMENT BENEFIT

Social Security Regulations

The introduction of statutory guarantee payments entailed an amendment to the unemployment benefit regulations disentitling employees from receiving unemployment benefit on days they were eligible for a statutory guarantee payment.[67] Before the introduction of statutory guarantee payments, workers who were laid off were able to claim social security payments although unemployment benefit was only available *after* the first three days of lay-off and the earnings-related supplement was only payable after six consecutive days of unemployment. Hepple, Partington and Simpson[68] pointed out that while those employees laid off for three days in any fixed quarter were better off, as they received compensation for the initial spell of unemployment, workers laid off for between five and eight days could be at a disadvantage as unemployment benefit is not payable during this period. They do acknowledge that a number of factors are relevant in this calculation, for example, the size of the family, availability of income tax rebates. The abolition of the earnings related supplement (as from 3 January 1982) has decreased the advantages of unemployment benefit for employees laid off for longer periods.

Employees may also find themselves in financial difficulties if the employer disputes a claim for a statutory guarantee payment. If the employee tries to claim unemployment benefit the adjudication officer must deal with the claim within 14 days.[69] The adjudication officer can check the situation with the employer and if the officer decides that the employee is eligible for a guarantee payment unemployment benefit will be refused until eight days have elapsed.[70] The employee may fall back upon income support and must either appeal against the adjudication officer's decision within 28 days and/or bring a claim for a guarantee payment to an industrial tribunal within three months of the day for which guarantee pay is claimed. Procedures exist to allow the Department of Social Security to recoup any social security benefits that have been paid when the employee was eligible for compensation under the employment protection provisions.[71] These claims could also be complicated by the interaction of collective guaranteed week agreements and the availability of the Temporary Short-time Working Compensation Scheme when it existed.

These procedures are complex and confusing and, not surprisingly, given the small amounts of money involved, few employees have risked legal costs in litigating over these issues. We have little indication, therefore, of how many employees are denied both unemployment benefit and guarantee payments for the initial days of a lay-off.

Two cases show that if the employee does choose to litigate the process is fairly lengthy, thus supporting the view put forward by Drake and Bercusson that the legal provisions seem better designed for the protection of the National Insurance Fund than the protection of workers.[72] The circumstances in *Robinson v. Claxton and Garland (Teesside) Ltd.*[73] were unusual in that the case was concerned with the hiatus caused when an exemption order granted under section 18 Employment Protection (Consolidation) Act 1978 came into effect on 2 February 1977 one day after the statutory guarantee payment provisions came into force. The applicant was laid off from 17 January 1977 and had received one week's guarantee pay under a collective agreement. He was then advised to claim unemployment benefit as the lay-off was expected to last for some time. Unemployment benefit was paid until 31 January 1977 but then ceased when the guarantee payment provisions came into effect on 1 February 1977. It took more than seven weeks before the industrial tribunal confirmed that the employer was liable to make a guarantee payment for 1 February 1977.

In another case, *Clemens* v. *Peter Richards Ltd.*,[74] the Department of Health and Social Security (as it was then named) had made a mistake and 14 weeks after the worker had been denied unemployment benefit the industrial tribunal decided she was not entitled to a guarantee payment.

Turning to more general issues, the fact that the contract of employment is still subsisting while an employee is claiming unemployment benefit after guarantee payments have been exhausted, gives rise to several conceptual and administrative problems. Ogus and Barendt identify five special rules that are applied to employees claiming unemployment benefit while short-time working is in existence.[75] These are the 'subsidiary employment rule', the 'full extent normal' rule, the 'normal idle day' rule, the 'holiday' rule, and the rules relating to days compensated by guarantee payments, employment subsidies or guaranteed work agreements.

THE 'SUBSIDIARY EMPLOYMENT RULE'

Since 1982 the government has promoted a policy of allowing social security claimants to undertake voluntary and community work or subsidiary part-time work provided that this work is low paid and does not conflict with the requirement of being available for full-time employment. A claimant may claim unemployment benefit provided she can satisfy three conditions.[76] First, that her earnings do not exceed more than £2 per day. Second, that she is available for full-time employment. Finally, if the subsidiary work is the employed earner's employment it must be charity work or must not be the claimant's usual main occupation. The latter condition was imposed in 1955[77] to prevent an employer dismissing an employee and then re-engaging her at a nominal wage.

THE 'FULL EXTENT NORMAL' RULE

This rule is designed to check that the employee in question has in fact worked less hours than is normal in her current employment.[78] This rule originally developed in relation to situations where an employee was put on short-time working. Thus it was fairly easy to establish what was the 'normal' working arrangement, although of course where the employment was irregular special tests were developed. The adjudication officer may look at the claimant's record for the period of 12 months immediately preceding the claim to determine what are the normal hours, but no account is taken of any short-time working due to adverse industrial conditions.[79] If the claimant's employment was irregular or casual then the 12 months' reference period is not applicable.[80]

The issues have become more complicated since the 'full extent normal' rule has been used increasingly in the situation where a contract for full-time employment has been terminated and the claimant has been unable to find full-time work but is working part time and asking for unemployment benefit to supplement the part-time wages. The Commissioners have utilized a number of other tests in order to interpret the 'full extent normal' rule. In addition to the '12-months before' rule, the 'stop gap' was propounded in decision CU/518/49. This was the situation when an applicant who was unemployed took up temporary, part-time work as a 'stop gap' when looking for full employment. In R(U) 3/86 (T) it was suggested that account should be taken of current economic and social conditions so that in periods of high unemployment it would be more readily accepted that part-time work was being undertaken as a stop-gap exercise. The part-time hours were not considered the normal hours of work. Another test was the '50 per cent test' explained in decision R(U)/14/59. This was the situation where the applicant had worked less than 50 per cent of the days of the week in which unemployment benefit was claimed. If the claimant had worked as much as 50 per cent of the relevant days it would not have been shown that in the normal course of events she would not have worked on the day in question.

The Court of Appeal and the House of Lords have now had the opportunity of reviewing the tests adopted by the Commissioners. In *Riley* v. *Chief Adjudication Officer*[81] Slade LJ made an attempt to reconcile the different approaches by stressing the importance of the personal circumstances of the claimant. The past employment record was relevant, but only for the purposes of shedding light on what was normal for the claimant at the relevant week of the claim. To this end the 'one year before test' provided a 'practical but not inviolable approach'.[82] In contrast, the 'stop gap' test may assist in establishing the normal pattern of work as at the relevant week, but it should be applied 'only with circumspection'.[83] Slade LJ then went on to add a new dimension to the inquiry when he argued that:

> [T]he officer or tribunal concerned should try to look into the future in order to decide how permanent or transitory the present pattern of work is likely to be.[84]

This additional requirement is regarded as impractical by Ogus and Barendt.[85] As Buck[86] points out, the adjudication officer can only make a rough and impressionistic judgment since the criteria for determining the likelihood of securing full-time employment are far more wide-ranging than those envisaged by the adjudication officers in the case law. Even if such an inquiry was practical Buck[87] argues that it is wrong in principle:

> Why should the fortunate claimant who is deemed likely to return to (full-time) work in the future be awarded unemployment benefit for the remaining days of unemployment in the week while his not so fortunate friend also working part time but without such immediate prospect of a return to full-time work, is disallowed from claiming?

The House of Lords has now held that the tests employed by the Commissioners were only guidelines. In *Chief Adjudication Officer* v. *Brunt and Another*[88] The House of Lords disallowed a claim for unemployment benefit by an applicant employed part-time (for two-and-a half days per week) under (what was then) a Manpower Services Commission Community Programme scheme. Here, it was argued that in deciding if a person was employed to 'the full extent normal' when taking voluntary part-time work after a period of full employment followed by a period of unemployment, consideration must be given, together with other relevant facts, to the whole period which has elapsed since the worker ceased to be employed full time. Lord Templeman delivered the only judgment and, while he clearly regarded the application of these guidelines as unsatisfactory, he made no attempt to deal with the difficulties of interpretation that have emerged with the application of the rule.[89]

THE 'NORMAL IDLE DAY' RULE

This rule deals with the anomaly that unemployment benefit is paid on the basis of a six-day working week whereas most people work less than this each week. Thus in 1957 a rule was introduced disentitling a claimant from unemployment benefit on any days she would not normally work unless she was unemployed on all the other days of the week (except Sunday or its substitute). An example of the operation of this rule is provided by Bourn:

> If a person would normally only work on Monday, Tuesday and Wednesday he cannot claim benefit for Thursday, Friday or Saturday unless he is not working on any day that week. If his employment were interrupted on, say, a Tuesday, he could claim benefit for the Tuesday but not for the other days of the week on which he would not normally work.

The 'normal idle day' rule does not apply to employees whose employment has terminated[90] or who have no normal working week such as casual workers.[91]

THE 'HOLIDAY' RULE

The holiday rule disentitles an employee from receiving unemployment benefit on days when there is a recognized or customary holiday in connection with the employment while the contract of employment is subsisting.[92]

OTHER PAYMENTS

Finally, special rules have been drawn up over time to disentitle an employee from receiving unemployment benefit while in receipt of statutory guarantee payments,[93] payments under the Temporary Short-time Working Compensation Scheme or other subsidies made under the Employment Subsidies Act 1978,[94] or a payment under the contract of employment as a result of a guaranteed week agreement.[95]

Any other payments are covered by the general rules developed by the Commissioners. In particular the legal consequences of any agreement will be examined to see if the employee is entitled to payments from the employer on the day of the alleged unemployment.

GENERAL ISSUES ARISING FROM THE USE OF STATUTORY GUARANTEE PAYMENTS

Once it is established that a claimant on short-time working is entitled to claim unemployment benefit it is not necessary for her to register weekly with the unemployment benefit office provided that the Secretary of State is satisfied that the award and payment of unemployment benefit can be controlled adequately.[96] The policy behind this change is to reduce the high costs of administering unemployment benefit for those employees on short-time working.[97]

The rules governing the interaction of guarantee payments and unemployment benefit have been criticized extensively. Words such as 'awkward and ill-fitting'[98] and 'poorly thought through'[99] prevail in the literature. Bercusson and Drake add even more trenchant criticism:

The right to guarantee payments turns out in practice to be another exercise, albeit particularly galling, whereby under the guise of protecting workers, the State effectively harasses them. Workers are deprived of the National Insurance Unemployment Benefits they were previously entitled to .... This is accomplished through the interworking of these provisions with those contained in various social security regulations. The result will be to increase workers' problems, not alleviate them.

As we have seen, the rules relating to eligibility for unemployment benefit for employees on short-time working are complex because underlying the concept of unemployment benefit is the idea that a person is unemployed and seeking work whereas the regulations governing short-time working imply that there is a subsisting contract of employment and that employers should bear the risk of initial and temporary spells of short-time working.[100] As short-time working has increased these policy rules have been stretched to their limit.

The statutory guarantee payment provisions may be insignificant in financial terms when compared with the more sophisticated and financially advantageous collectively bargained guaranteed week agreements. Statutory guarantee payments have received scant attention in the basic texts on employment law and doubts have been cast upon their value in improving the welfare of individual employees given the complexity of the arrangements.[101] Others, such as Hepple, Partington and Simpson, have criticized the policy by which the risk of initial spells of short-time working is transferred on to individual employers. Although the use of the Temporary Short-time Working Compensation Scheme did transfer part of this burden on to the state, it can be argued that the complexity of short-time working compensation was even further increased by this measure.

Nevertheless, it was argued earlier in this chapter that the main role of statutory guarantee payments was the part they played in establishing the foundation of the 'floor of rights' in relation to the employment contract especially for the low paid and least unionized workers. For these workers coverage by collective guaranteed week agreements is non-existent. Furthermore, in the absence of statutory guarantee payments these employees would be in danger of a change of status to that of 'casual workers' if employers were able to lay-off at will without the obligation to provide financial compensation. If these aims are to continue to be fulfilled the statutory guarantee payment provisions must be increased and extended or the unemployment benefit regulations amended to complement the statutory guarantee payment provisions to cover times of prolonged periods of short-time working. In contrast to this proposal the Engineering Employers' Federation, with the support of other members of the Confederation of British Industry, attempted to widen the powers of employers to lay-off workers without pay by including amendments to the Employment Bill 1981, but these amendments were lost in the guillotining of the Bill.[102]

The rationale of transferring the financial burden of the initial spell of short-time working away from the National Insurance Fund to individual employers has also been subject to critical comment by Hepple *et al*. One issue stemming from this transfer is that the effective incidence of these measures is unclear. For while evidence suggests that employers generally can pass on most of the National Insurance contributions in the form of lower wages or higher prices,[103] whether individual employers facing an unequal incidence of claims for guarantee payments can do so is less clear.

There is little evidence available as to how the 'floor of rights', including statutory guarantee payments, affects the behaviour of individual employers. In particular, how do employers react in considering optimal employment adjustment in the face of unexpected reductions in product demand? Daniel and Stilgoe[104] argued, on the basis of survey data, that the various aspects of the employment protection legislation had had little effect. A more rigorous test of the proposition that employment protection legislation has affected the employers' adjustment of labour input would need to use time series analysis to analyse these adjustments before and after the introduction of the legislation. Preliminary evidence provided by Disney and Szyszczak[105] shows that, pooling cross-section and time-series data, there is evidence of significant differences in hours and employment elasticities before and after the extension of the employment protection legislation to a greater number of workers under the Employment Protection Act 1975. It seems likely, therefore, that statutory guarantee payments, as part of this 'floor of rights', play a part in stabilizing labour demand and thereby underpinning the employment contract.

THE SHORT-TIME WORKING FUND

As the economic recession deepened in the 1970s neither side of industry was appeased by the state's attempts to regulate short-time working through statutory guarantee payments. The Department of Employment canvassed the idea of restructuring the financing of short-time working by establishing a Short-time Working Fund.[106] It was envisaged that this Fund would comprise two tiers: one temporary, one permanent. The permanent tier would have required employers to provide employees on short-time working with compensation amounting to 75 per cent of gross normal pay for each day of work lost, with a maximum limit of one week's continuous lay-off. The payments would have been taxable and recipients ineligible for unemployment benefit. An

upper limit of payment was envisaged – set at £110 – in line with the weekly
pay limits set for the calculation of redundancy payments and unfair dismissal
awards. A minimum figure of £7.25 was also envisaged to ensure that no full-
time worker received less than the statutory guarantee pay provisions (or full
normal pay in the unlikely event that this figure was lower). Compensation
would not have been payable if employees were put on an indefinite lay-off or
were laid off because of an industrial dispute. The Short-time Working Fund
was to be financed by equal contributions from employers and the state.
Employers were to receive a 50 per cent rebate of any compensation paid
under the permanent tier with an additional amount, set initially at 6.75 per
cent. Half the rebate would come from the Redundancy and Employment
Fund created from the Redundancy and Maternity Fund, and half the rebate
would come from money provided by Parliament.

The temporary tier of the Fund was to come into operation at high periods of
unemployment. The temporary scheme could apply to the whole of Britain or
to specified areas. Then the Fund would refund all the costs of short-time
working, provided that employers could satisfy the Department of Employment that short-time working had been adopted as an alternative to redundancy, that the firm would remain solvent, and that there were good prospects
of returning to normal working. The Consultative Document limited payments to 12 months, but this period was extended to 18 months in the Short-
time Working Bill 1979. Provision was made in the White Papers on the
government's expenditure plans to cover the schemes. £200 million was
estimated for 1979/80, £425 million in 1980/81 and £460 million a year
thereafter for the subsidy schemes.[107] As Partington points out, however, the
criteria for triggering the temporary tier were vague,[108] and a lot of discretion
was left to the Department of Employment to determine eligibility. Equally a
temporary measure would be unlikely to deal with large and permanent
increases in unemployment. Despite these weaknesses the Department of
Employment proposals formed the basis of the Short-time Working Bill
presented to Parliament in March 1979.[109] The Bill was lost in the dissolution
of Parliament for the General Election of May 1979.

As events turned out, no restructuring of short-time compensation was
implemented. Instead Britain saw the arrival and departure of a series of *ad hoc*
interventions in the labour market. Some of these interventions, such as the
Temporary Employment Subsidy and the Temporary Short-time Compensation Scheme, were designed to prevent redundancies; others, such as Job
Release, Early Retirement or Youth Training Schemes, were designed to
create flexibility in the labour market and alleviate unemployment through
the creation of new jobs. Section 1 of the Employment Subsidies Act 1978
facilitated the introduction of these schemes, implemented through brief
pamphlets and unpublished administrative rules and administered by civil
servants' discretion. The era of 'leaflet law' was in full swing.[110]

THE TEMPORARY SHORT-TIME WORKING COMPENSATION SCHEME

The Temporary Employment Subsidy

Before looking at the Temporary Short-time Working Compensation Scheme it is perhaps useful to compare its predecessor, the Temporary Employment Subsidy.[111] This subsidy came into operation on 18 August 1975 and closed for applications on 31 March 1979. Provided employers were prepared to defer impending redundancies affecting ten or more workers the employer could claim a subsidy of £20 per week for each full-time job maintained. In many respects, and in contrast to its successor the Temporary Short-time Working Compensation Scheme, the Temporary Employment Subsidy achieved some success at averting redundancies while allowing employers to continue to produce or manufacture goods. The scheme was criticized particularly by France and Ireland, who argued that the scheme was contrary to the European Economic Community competition rules on state aids since unemployment was being displaced by virtue of the alleged unfair advantage British industry was gaining.[112] The EC Commission investigated the complaint and the British government was ordered to withdraw the subsidy.

The Employment Subsidies Act 1978

As an interim measure the Temporary Short-time Working Compensation Scheme came into operation on 1 April 1979 and closed for applications on 31 March 1984. The legal basis of the scheme was section 1(1) of the Employment Subsidies Act 1978. This Act was rushed through Parliament between February and March 1978, the alleged reason for the urgency being the pressure from the EC Commission to amend the Temporary Employment Subsidy. Section 1(1) of the Employment Subsidies Act granted the Secretary of State a wide discretion:

> The Secretary of State may, if in his opinion unemployment in Great Britain continues at a high level, with Treasury approval, set up schemes for making payments to employers which will enable them to retain persons in employment who would or might otherwise become unemployed, to take on new employees and generally to maintain or enlarge their labour force.

The limitations of the Employment and Training Act 1973 had already obliged the government to ask Parliament for additional powers to establish the Temporary Employment Subsidy, and the deepening recession was used to justify the use of wide discretionary powers in an enabling Act. Albert Booth, the Secretary of State of Employment, argued for the necessity of a 'flexible' power so that employment schemes could be reviewed and adapted according to economic circumstances without 'undue delay'.[113] In addition to increasing the Secretary of State's power, the necessity for making legislation 'tidier' and easily understood was argued. To legitimate these proposals the legislation was viewed as merely temporary, and after 1979 the Employment Subsidies Act 1978 could only be renewed for 18 months at a time with Treasury and Parliamentary approval. This was achieved through the use of statutory instruments introduced under the affirmative resolution procedure.

Section 1(1) of the Employment Subsidies Act 1978 grants a wide discretion to the Secretary of State to establish schemes to alleviate unemployment. There are some constraints upon this discretion, however, in that before a scheme is introduced unemployment must be at a high level. This is deliberately vague and clearly the government did not want to be fettered by any trigger mechanisms. During the Committee stage of the Bill attempts were made to give the phrase greater precision in terms of widening the reference to include high regional unemployment or unemployment as a result of a temporary recession, but these amendments were withdrawn. Two significant amendments were introduced at the Committee stage.[114] The first was an obligation to consult 'with such organizations, including those representing employers and workers respectively, as are appropriate'.[115] The second constraint is more significant in that Treasury approval is necessary for new employment schemes and section 2(1) provides that the Secretary of State shall not:

(a) set up any new scheme whose expected cost exceeds £10 million a year; or (b) alter or extend any existing scheme ... not so far costing more than £10 million a year in such a way that the expected cost of the scheme as altered exceeds that amount unless he has previously been authorized to do so by a Resolution of the House of Commons.

Section 2(3) grants an exception to this requirement:

where the Secretary of State is satisfied that compliance would involve unacceptable delay in the taking of urgent essential measures against unemployment; but if he proceeds without a Resolution of the House he shall lay before the House a statement of the action he has taken and his reasons for so proceeding.

How the Temporary Short-time Working Compensation Scheme Worked

The Temporary Short-time Working Compensation Scheme resembled the temporary tier proposals put forward in the Department of Employment Consultative Document.[116] While the Temporary Employment Subsidy subsidized jobs to continue producing output, the Temporary Short-time Working Compensation Scheme subsidized short-time working. Compensation was payable (at the discretion of the Secretary of State) to employers who agreed to withdraw a redundancy notice issued under the redundancy consultation provisions of section 100 of the Employment Protection Act 1975. Instead of employees targeted for a redundancy being put on short-time working, the short-time working could be rotated throughout the workforce. Originally employees on short-time working had to be paid at least 75 per cent of their normal pay for each day without work, provided that they had carried out a normal day's work after a maximum of seven consecutive days without work. The employer was reimbursed the short-time payments, related National Insurance contributions and holiday pay credits. Compensation could be paid for a maximum of 12 months.[117] These rules changed over time; for example, the reimbursement of holiday credits was abolished and the duration of support was reduced to six months as the scheme was phased out.[118]

The Procedural Rules Relating to the Subsidy

In order to apply for the subsidy the proposed redundancy had to be notified to the Department of Employment on form 'HR1' as required by sections 99 and 100 of the Employment Protection Act 1975. To ensure uniformity of treatment the subsidy was administered on a regional (as opposed to local) basis. The employer was asked to fill in form 'TST1' which asked for information on how many people were to be made redundant and why, how many would be required to work short-time to avoid redundancies, and what pattern of short-time working would be used. The employer had to supply a copy of the latest available audited accounts and a copy of the management accounts for the current financial year. The form was jointly signed by management or the employer and any recognized trade union or employee representative. The information required to substantiate that a redundancy was imminent varied. The Department of Employment Leaflet PL 692 'Temporary Short-time Working Compensation Scheme' gave examples of relevant information such as levels of business on a monthly basis over the previous 12 months and an earlier comparable period, details of expected business over the next 12 months, current and previous stock levels. However, each applicant received a letter listing the specific information required.

A fairly rigid set of instructions was sent from Department of Employment headquarters to each regional office explaining how the scheme was to be administered.[119] The subsidy was overseen by a Senior Regional Officer, and once the application was received it was checked by clerical staff who sorted out any queries. The firm was given assistance with its application, and the observations of Ganz[120] in relation to applications under the Industry Act 1972, seem applicable to employment subsidies:

> The firm negotiates with the Department and will often amend its application to make it acceptable. These procedures are completely informal and contain no legal safeguards but they have received little criticism.

The application was then passed on to a Visiting Officer, who checked the paperwork and then made a visit to the firm to verify the facts. This involved looking at staffing levels, future orders and what stocks the company was holding. The services of a professional accountant were available to assess the financial information.

The Visiting Officer then made a recommendation to the Senior Regional Officer and if there were any doubts the application was referred to head-quarters. If the application was refused there was no formal appeal procedure and, it seems, no internal guidelines as to how the case would be reviewed. Each application was decided according to its own facts. The number of rejected applications was in fact very small (about 2 per cent) and usually the rejections were because the applications did not satisfy the requirements of a genuine threat of redundancy.[121]

Applicants whose cases were rejected used different methods to challenge the decision. Some appealed directly to the Department of Employment headquarters, others wrote to the Secretary of State or the Parliamentary Under-Secretary. Others resorted to their Member of Parliament, and the Parliamentary Commissioner for Administration was approached and investigated at least four complaints. This lack of a formal appeals procedure was commented upon by Barney Hayhoe in the debate on the Resolution proposing the subsidy,[122] but his question as to whether an aggrieved employer could have an adverse decision reconsidered was not answered. No provision was made for an appeal to an independent tribunal. It could be argued that provisions for an appeal in such circumstances would substitute the tribunal's decision for that of a Minister, but equally it could be argued that such reasoning confuses issues about the *merits* of a case with the application of legal procedural safeguards such as accountability, fairness, due process and the rules of natural justice.

If the application for the subsidy was approved, the subsidy was paid in arrears although the Minister of State had discretion to backdate the subsidy if short-time working had already commenced,[123] or if the employers were experiencing severe cash-flow problems.[124] Results from our interviews and surveys on the Short-time Working Project showed that for many firms this was a major problem and many suffered a cash-flow crisis. The employer could choose how to implement short-time working, the only requirement being that there had to be at least one normal day's working after a period of seven consecutive days without work. All employees who qualified for statutory guarantee payments were eligible for Temporary Short-time Working Compensation Scheme payments and the scheme was extended to employees who had less than four weeks' service with the firm. The employer was allowed to rotate short-time working throughout the workforce but records had to be maintained so that workers on short-time could be identified. The Department of Employment's administrative rules provided that at least two prepayment visits had to be made by a Department of Employment officer. After receiving the subsidy for 13 weeks the employer was sent a form to fill in, to report upon the current position. Shortly before the end of the 26-week period a final visit was made to check that the scheme had been operating correctly. Oddly enough, the employer did not have to show that there was a realistic possibility that full-time working would resume after the 26-week period and the Department of Employment did not ask the employer what she intended to do after the subsidy ended. Given that the purpose of the scheme was to *avert* redundancies surprisingly little check was made upon the efficacy of the Temporary Short-time Working Compensation Scheme. Although the subsidy was withdrawn if any jobs were declared redundant when the subsidy application was being considered, no sanctions were imposed if redundancies were declared after the subsidy had ended. Such sanctions were considered impractical in the light of the fact that redundancies could occur as a result of several factors outside the employer's control.

The efficacy of the scheme has in fact been subject to little scrutiny. The Parliamentary Accounts Committee evaluated Special Employment Measures in the light of their effect upon unemployment (that is, the net cost per person taken off the unemployment register) and rebuked the Department of Employment for not assessing effectively the impact of the Temporary Short-time Working Compensation Scheme in averting redundancies.[125] The Department of Employment undertook a survey of the scheme but this has not been made publicly available, although a series of reports on the operation of the scheme were published in the *Employment Gazette*.[126]

The Impact of the Temporary Short-time Working Compensation Scheme

The Temporary Short-time Working Compensation Scheme has been one of the most important special employment measures for adult workers. An estimated one million jobs threatened with redundancy were covered by the scheme and gross spending on supporting these jobs has cost over one billion pounds (1983/4 cash prices). Over three million employees were placed on short-time working in order to avert these redundancies. Despite these impressive figures, investigations into the operation of the scheme carried out on the University of Kent Short-time Working Project revealed many limitations of the scheme.

First, the scheme was only temporary in nature and in fact succeeded only in *postponing* rather than averting redundancies.[127] Secondly, the industrial distribution of the subsidy was very narrow; in particular, manufacturing industry used the scheme disproportionately.[128] Almost 96 per cent of subsidized jobs threatened with redundancy were found in this sector compared with just under 30 per cent of employees in employment. Some industries made extensive use of the scheme; for example, in metal manufacture, textiles, clothing and footwear over one-quarter of the labour force had received Temporary Short-time Working Compensation Scheme support. Outside manufacturing only the construction industry had more than 1 per cent of their employees covered by the subsidy. Small firms were excluded from the subsidy by virtue of the fact that at least ten jobs had to be threatened in order to qualify for the scheme and it is unlikely, therefore, that a small firm would remain viable after losing so many jobs. This was a peculiar omission since the government had pinned its hopes of economic recovery on the small business but made such businesses ineligible to receive the temporary subsidy. The Confederation of British Industry and Members of Parliament appealed to the government to extend the subsidy to small firms but these pleas were ignored. Another limitation of the subsidy is linked closely to explicit contract theory, discussed earlier in Chapter 1. The effects of the subsidy seem to have resulted in allowing firms to retain skilled workers. Unlike statutory guarantee payments or the flat-rate Temporary Employment Subsidy, unskilled workers (among whom unemployment was high) were less likely to be covered by the subsidy.

The Legal Control of Special Employment Measures

Special Employment Measures have been utilized by successive governments throughout the 1970s and in restricted forms in the early 1980s as a means of combating high and rising unemployment. The effect of these measures on the employment relationship is significant, yet few of the leading texts on employment law acknowledge this. Only Davies and Freedland discuss the implications of Special Employment Measures in their perceptive analysis of the role of law to control the size and quality of the labour market.[129] But even Davies and Freedland's analysis is limited. First, like other authors of employment texts, they fail to integrate the effect of Special Employment Measures into their general account of modern labour law. Secondly, working within the confines of a labour law text, they are unable to capture the highly complex constitutional implications of Special Employment Measures, not only at the level of the relationship between the firm and the state, but also the increasing constitutional significance of the relationship between the state and private industry and the role of law in the implementation of economic policy. Although Special Employment Measures have not been used as extensively in the late eighties they have continued to play an important role in the regulation of the youth labour market and in training.

An early and perceptive analysis of some of these issues is seen in Frank's 1950 book *The New Industrial Law*,[130] in which he attempts to integrate the themes of traditional labour law (master and servant law) with the wider issues of law relating to industry in general, particularly the regulation of economic aspects of planning. In many respects, given the historical development of labour law away from the marginal aspect of commercial law to a subject in its own right, it is somewhat of a paradox to argue for its integration back into the regulation of industry.[131] However, the shortcomings of labour law as a distinct discipline are now beginning to be addressed. The pressing need for an analysis of the interaction of labour law and social security measures is revealed in this chapter.[132] Freedland,[133] influenced by the Continental classification of a 'droit social', has also argued for a more expansive analysis of Special Employment Measures. This analysis would need to be integrated into a wider picture of industrial and social provisions which affect the employment relationship and a person's relationship with the labour market.[134]

Many of the issues raised by the regulation of the labour market have been recognized by lawyers. As long ago as 1974 Daintith revealed the inadequacies of traditional legal techniques to describe and control the increasing involvement of the state in directing economic policy through law:

> The public law framework for economic policy is so loose and flexible as to be hardly worthy of being called a framework at all. With no substantive guidelines for policy whether in the shape of constitutional guarantees of individual rights or of legislative statements of economic objectives or instruments, and with the institutional constraint of Parliament de-natured, public law seems called upon to play an exclusively instrumental role in relation to economic policy.[135]

At the individual employment level, the use of the Temporary Short-time Working Compensation Scheme had an impact upon eligibility for statutory guarantee payments, the suspension of guaranteed week agreements and the variation of individual contracts of employment. Most trade unions and employees were given little option but to accept the changes and thus amendments were made with few legal safeguards. This is probably because the consultation periods of the Employment Protection Act 1975 were too short for any meaningful consultation about various alternative courses of action to redundancy. Thus the Temporary Short-time Working Compensation Scheme appeared an attractive proposition to both management (in terms of costs) and to unions (in terms of jobs). Embracing unions in this way perhaps served to legitimate management's perspective of the situation and developed a notion of consensus: management and unions were working together to avert redundancy.

The constitutional significance of Special Employment Measures is equally as problematic. Lawyers have differed in their analysis of these constitutional changes.[136] Special Employment Measures fit easily into the tendency discerned by Baldwin and Houghton that there is:

> . . . a retreat from primary legislation in favour of government by informal rules. Each time a government confronts a difficult regulatory task, it seems to come up with a new device: a code of practice, guidance note, circular, approved code, outline scheme, statement of advice, departmental circular – the list goes on.[137]

Special Employment Measures can be seen also as part of a tendency on the part of the state to intervene and direct economic affairs although one could argue that such an analysis is at odds with the dominant theme of 'Thatcherism' – that of deregulation. Yet much of what has happened within the last ten years of the Conservative administration is merely a continuation of a tendency developed under earlier periods. Equally, the political rhetoric of 'non-intervention' may provide a useful device to mask the directive role that modern governments utilize in order to achieve political and economic ends.

In order to explain this process, which results in a blurring of the economic and political spheres of life, a useful analysis is offered by Prosser.[138] In looking at the more general aspect of how power is exercised in the modern state he has utilized the term coined by Poggi as seeing the modern process of allocating power as part of the 'compenetration' of the state and civil society.[139] This view argues that the state gradually encroaches into traditional areas of life normally confined to the 'private' sphere and outside the regulation of law. Thus the distinction between orthodox 'public' and 'private' spheres of law, central to the nineteenth century Diceyian constitutional theory, is lost to the lawyer of the 1980s or 1990s. The mapping of 'public' and 'private' spheres of life, once regarded as unproblematic, becomes in fact a highly complex exercise.

The theme of the 'public/private' distinction in labour law has been addressed by the Critical Legal Studies Movement in the United States[140] and some of the issues regarding the regulation of the employment relationship within the context of issues of controlling 'private' economic power are beginning to permeate British academic writing. Collins, in arguing that the concept of private bureaucratic power has played little part in the history of liberal democratic thought argues that:

> The rigid but elusive distinction between public and private law collapses legal problems into issues of protection of the citizen's rights against the state and the protection of their economic interests from harm by each other.[141]

Collins has pursued this theme in relation to an analysis of the role of the contract of employment in regulating the power relations of the employment relationship. In recognizing the need to control the growth in economic power of large corporations he draws parallels between the power of the employer and the power of the modern state. By seeing the need to regulate employers' and capital's power in the same way as administrative lawyers have attempted to subject the powers of the state to legal control a different perspective is drawn upon the nature of labour law:

> Legal reasoning has been slow to respond to these fundamental adjustments in legal orientation. The dead weight of tradition in the common law accounts in part for the survival of the simple contractual account of the employment relation. More fundamentally, however, the rigid distinction between public and private law has inhibited the development of a more radical perspective within labour law which requires the power of employers to be justified by more appeals to agreements in market transactions. Once managerial power is likened to government power, old questions concerning the absence of democracy and respect for civil liberties in the workplace begin to press upon us with renewed intensity.[142]

But this thesis, of recognizing the blurring between the 'public' and 'private' forms of power and how it is utilized, is by no means novel. Ganz, in particular, has alerted lawyers' attention to the need to analyse earlier interventions in the 'private' sphere such as the Industry Acts 1972–5, and Daintith has also been influential in attempting to theorize the role of law and economic policy.[143] This analysis has not been extended, however, to a discussion of the role of Special Employment Measures. Surprisingly, even in Ganz's most recent book, *Quasi-Legislation: Recent Developments in Secondary Legislation*,[144] the areas of administrative law making in the field of labour law, including 'leaflet law', are not even mentioned.[145] Similarly, Collins, in a more recent article, contrasts the different approaches to labour law as an academic subject.[146] While arguing against the adoption of an 'economistic' approach to the study of labour law in order to analyse the role of law as a tool for *regulating* the labour market, Collins offers little guidance on how he would incorporate his ideas of labour lawyers providing a *normative* aspect to the power relations engendered by the state's intervention in the labour market and the *individual* employment relationship. In particular his discussion excludes any attempt to analyse the effects of over ten years of Special Employment Measures and ameliorative social security schemes into both collective and individual aspects of 'traditional' labour law.

In addition to these wide theoretical problems more specific legal issues emerge. A central element of the administration of Special Employment Measures is the use of discretionary powers to introduce and administer the various schemes. In the Temporary Short-time Working Compensation Scheme discretion existed at many levels. First, the discretion vested in the Secretary of State to decide that a measure was necessary. Secondly, the choice of the measure. Thirdly, the discretion given to the Department of Employment to devise and administer the schemes. Fourthly, the discretion of the employer to apply for and utilize the subsidy. It would seem that the exercise of the discretion remained unchecked at a legal level.

Equally it was not only the parties who were directly involved in the receipt of the subsidy whose 'legal' interests were inadequately protected. Competitors, both at home and abroad, may have had a legal interest in challenging the use of discretionary measures to ensure that competition was not distorted by the use of such subsidies. While the provisions relating to the control of state aids in the Treaty of Rome 1957 provide a system of review, these provisions may only be used by the EC Commission. Members of Parliament through questions in Parliament, the Parliamentary Commissioner for Administration,[147] and the Public Accounts Committee provided some form of external review of the operation of the Temporary Short-time Working Compensation Scheme, but with the exception of the limited powers of the Parliamentary Commissioner for Administration none of these procedures provided a forum for the airing of individual grievances over the exercise of the discretionary powers or for asserting individual legal rights.

While labour lawyers have paid little attention to the practical and day-to-day impact of Special Employment Measures on legal rights and legal relationships, lawyers engaged in research in the area of public law[148] have paid attention to the issue of discretion in modern government, stimulated by the debate generated by the work of Davis in America.[149] The tenet of Davis's thesis was the realistic assumption that in the modern state discretion should not, or indeed could not, be abolished but rather the interests of individual justice would be better served if there was greater confining, structuring and checking of the use of unnecessary discretion. Davis's work has had the greatest impact upon the study of discretion in social welfare legislation, the focus being upon the relationship between individuals and administrative officers, primarily at the point of delivery of a social service. But, as Baldwin and Houghton point out, views differ as to the purpose of informal administrative rules,[150] and while Britain has experienced nearly a decade of debate on the relative merits of the use of discretion and the structuring of the use of discretion it could be argued that the narrow focus of this debate has obscured the complexity of discretionary powers. In particular, by concentrating upon the individual relationship of recipient and administrative officer the debate on the use of discretion has isolated from scrutiny the operation of individual discretionary action from collective interests and the wider political context in which it operates. These limitations are identified by Baldwin and Horne, who point out that discretion may embrace wider factors such as the discretion whether or not to make a rule, or a policy.[151] Furthermore, discretion may be exercised by a wider variety of actors than administrative officials. A further weakness in the debate over the use of discretion is that the focus upon *individual* rights and justice ignores the wider interests which may arise from the operation of a discretionary policy.[152] Applying these points to the operation of the Temporary Short-time Working Compensation Scheme, the impact of the scheme upon collective bargaining over guaranteed week agreements and redundancy schemes is an obvious area where wider consequences were felt. Equally, employers and employees outside the manufacturing sector who did not benefit from the scheme and competitors at home and abroad were all interested parties. At a more general level, the role of employment subsidies to cushion the impact of redundancies may have changed perceptions about job loss and the role of the state to provide a 'welfare' role in making money available to ailing, rather than developing, industry are examples of how legal principles might be used to structure the use of discretion by government.

Lawyers and sociologists have argued for the need for law to intervene and control what is seen as 'government largesse' arising out of the New Deal legislation in the United States and the rise of the Welfare State in Britain.[153] The focus has been to turn attention to the new forms and structures of legal power and control in society and how that power is legitimized. Other than the pioneering work by Freedland, little attempt has been made to bring Special Employment Measures into this debate, and yet the constitutional significance of these forms of state intervention is just as important as other forms of state encroachment into the 'private' sphere. In particular, it could be argued that the use of discretionary and informal administrative procedures allows the state to encroach into the private employment relationship in an informal and subtle way, often using the private sphere to mediate government policies. This is seen particularly in the regulation of training and the use of 'ameliorative' social security/labour market regulation measures in the late eighties.

Recently calls have been made for a more radical and critical approach to public law to provide a framework which identifies the complexity of public power and its regulation but also exposes the legitimation techniques whereby that power is exercised and accepted.[154] This needs to be added to Collins' attempts to map out the future direction of Labour Law as a discrete academic discipline. The value of an integrated approach for an analysis of Special Employment Measures is revealed in the above description of the Temporary Short-time Working Compensation Scheme. Since the scheme operated outside the realm of traditional employment law, traditional legal techniques and evaluations could not adequately explain the role or significance of the scheme on the individual employment relationship, collective labour relations or the wider implications it had for welfare/social policy or the regulation and restructuring of the labour market.

CONCLUSION

This chapter has revealed that in the post-1975 era the state has taken a more interventionist role in regulating partial unemployment. First, by introducing compulsory guarantee payment provisions, and secondly by subsidizing partial unemployment through employment subsidies. Thus, until 1984, a number of complex schemes were in operation regulating partial unemployment. With the closing of the Temporary Short-time Working Compensation Scheme in March 1984 a significant form of compensation for partial unemployment ended but there followed no radical restructuring or rationalization of the regulation of partial unemployment. The next chapter, therefore, looks at different ways in which partial unemployment is regulated in other industrialized states and considers different ways in which partial unemployment might be regulated in the future.

NOTES

1. See Davies, P. and Freedland, M., *Labour Law: Texts and Materials*, (London, Weidenfeld and Nicolson, 2nd edn, 1984) at p. 347.
2. Report of Standing Committee F on the Employment Protection Bill, 11th Sitting, 17 June 1975.
3. Order for Second Reading on Employment Protection Bill 1975, House of Commons Papers, col. 69, Vol. 891, 28 April 1975.
4. Standing Committee F, Employment Protection Bill, col. 551, June 1975.
5. *Ibid.* col. 553.
6. *Ibid.* col. 557. James Prior quotes a figure of £80 million, Report of Standing Committee F on the Employment Protection Bill, 11th Sitting, col. 551, 17 June 1975.
7. 'The Impact of Employment Protection Laws', *Policy Studies*, Vol. XLIV, No. 577 (London, June 1978).

8. Clifton, R. and Tatton-Brown, C., *The Impact of Employment Legislation on Small Firms*, (Department of Employment Research Paper No. 6, July 1979).

9. Section 148(2) Employment Protection (Consolidation) Act 1978.

10. Richards, J. and Szyszczak, E., 'Guarantee Pay and Unemployment Benefit: Criticisms and Evidence', Working Paper No. 18 Short-time Working Project 1983–5, (Canterbury, University of Kent, May 1985).

11. Section 13(1) Employment Protection (Consolidation) Act 1978. This was changed from a qualifying period of four weeks by para 1 of Schedule 2 to the Employment Act 1982.

12. Schedule 13 paragraph 3 Employment Protection (Consolidation) Act 1978. Employees working under a contract of employment which normally involves working for between eight and 16 hours a week may be eligible for a guarantee payment if they have worked under such a contract for a continuous period of at least five years, or if they ceased working under a contract of employment involving at least 16 hours work per week within 26 weeks before a claim, Schedule 13 paragraph 6 of the Employment Protection (Consolidation) Act 1978.

13. *Mailway (Southern) Ltd.* v. *Willsher* [1978] IRLR 322.

14. Section 138(3) Employment Protection (Consolidation) Act 1978.

15. Section 141(2) Employment Protection (Consolidation) Act 1978.

16. Section 144(2) Employment Protection (Consolidation) Act 1978.

17. Section 146(2) Employment Protection (Consolidation) Act 1978.

18. Section 145(2) Employment Protection (Consolidation) Act 1978.

19. See *Sowden* v. *J. and A.P. Nichols* Unreported COIT 694/81 where the applicant worked for nine weeks before being laid off. Since there was no evidence of a fixed-term contract or a task contract he was entitled to a guarantee payment. Cf. with *Vanson* v. *Osborne* Unreported COIT 674/153 where the applicant worked for eight weeks as a potato picker before being laid off. It was shown that there was a well-known custom that pickers were hired to pick a particular crop and this employment lasted about eight weeks. The guarantee payment was denied therefore.

20. Section 16(1) Employment Protection (Consolidation) Act 1978.

21. Section 16(2) Employment Protection (Consolidation) Act 1978.

22. [1977] IRLR 416.

23. [1978] IRLR 53.

24. *O'Kelly* v. *Trusthouse Forte Plc* [1983] ICR 728.

25. [1984] IRLR 240.

26. *Christopher Neame Ltd.* v. *White* Unreported 461/79 (EAT).

27. [1977] IRLR 414.

28. [1977] IRLR 332.

29. These issues are discussed in Chapter 3.

30. Unreported COIT 8133/79 (5 June 1979).

31. [1978] IRLR 53.

32. [1978] IRLR 322.

33. [1978] IRLR 430.

34. Section 14(1) Employment Protection (Consolidation) Act 1978.

35. Unreported COIT 689/154.

36. *North* v. *Pavleigh Ltd.* [1977] IRLR 461.

37. Section 13(3) Employment Protection (Consolidation) Act 1978.

38. Section 13(4)(a) Employment Protection (Consolidation) Act 1978.

39. Section 13(4)(b) Employment Protection (Consolidation) Act 1978.

40. *The Employment Acts 1974–80: With Commentary* (London, Sweet and Maxwell, 1981). The reference to the social security disqualification is to Section 19(1) Social Security Act 1975. Cf. *Presho* v. *Department of Health and Social Security* [1984] IRLR 74.

41. Unreported COIT 831/131 (1978).

42. [1979] IRLR 408.

43. [1978] IRLR 99.

44. Unreported COIT 1035/223.

45. Unreported COIT 1586/68.

46. *Peplow* v. *Bennett Swiftline (Birmingham) Ltd.* Unreported COIT 1324/30.

47. *Faust* v. *Power Packing Casemakers Ltd.* [1983] IRLR 117.

48. Unreported COIT 689/154.

49. [1977] IRLR 461.
50. Unreported COIT 7986/77 (3 May 1977).
51. Cf. the situation in *Cartwright* v. *G. Clancy Ltd*. [1983] IRLR 355.
52. Unreported COIT 1048/77 (6 July 1977).
53. [1977] IRLR 388.
54. Unreported COIT 1774/33.
55. *Lakeland* v. *North Creake Produce Co. Ltd*. Unreported COIT 963/54.
56. [1977] IRLR 330.
57. Unreported COIT 905/27.
58. Unreported COIT 1786/71.
59. See Lewis, R. and Simpson, B., *Striking a Balance? Employment Law after the 1980 Act*, (Oxford, Martin Robertson, 1981) at p. 42.
60. The Employment Protection (Variation of Limits) Order 1989 SI 1989/526. See Appendix A.
61. Section 140 of the Employment Protection (Consolidation) Act 1978 renders void any other attempt to contract out of the guarantee payment provisions. See, for example, *Shaw and Earnshaw* v. *Trendsetter Furniture Ltd*. Unreported COIT 692/168 where a union-management agreement that employees would not present guarantee payment claims was held void under section 140.
62. *A Practical Guide to the Employment Protection Act 1975*, (London, Institute of Personnel Management and Industrial Relations Review and Report, 1975) at p. 25.
63. These are redundancy payments (section 96 Employment Protection (Consolidation) Act 1978); the handling of redundancy situations (section 107 Employment Protection (Consolidation) Act 1978), and unfair dismissal (section 65 Employment Protection (Consolidation) Act 1978). See Bourn, C.J., 'Statutory Exemptions for Collective Agreements', 8 *Industrial Law Journal*, pp. 85–9 (1979); Davies, P. and Freedland, M., *Labour Law: Text and Materials*, (London, Weidenfeld and Nicolson, 2nd edn, 1984) pp. 262–7.
64. *Ibid*.
65. Section 17(1) Employment Protection (Consolidation) Act 1978.
66. *Op. cit.* note 62 at p. 24.
67. SI 1975/564 as amended by SI 1976/323 and SI 1976/677.
68. 'The Employment Protection Act and Unemployment Benefit: Protection for Whom?', 6 *Industrial Law Journal*, pp. 54–8 (1977).
69. See Ogus and Barendt *op. cit.* Chapter 16 for a full discussion of the adjudication process.
70. This is calculated as five days guarantee pay and the three waiting days for unemployment benefit.
71. The Employment Protection (Recoupment of Unemployment and Supplementary Benefit) Regulations 1977. SI 674/1977 (as amended by SI 1980/1608; SI 1984/458; SI 1988/419).
72. *Op. cit.* note 40.
73. [1977] IRLR 159.
74. [1977] IRLR 332.
75. *The Law of Social Security*, (London, Butterworths, 3rd edn, 1988) at pp. 79 ff.
76. SI 1983/1598, Regulation 7(1)(g). Crewing or launching a lifeboat and performing part-time duties with the fire brigade are exempted.
77. SI 1955/143.
78. Regulation 7(1)(e) SI 1983/1598.
79. CU 518/49. SI 1983/1598, Regulation 7(1)(e).
80. SI 1983/1598, Regulation 7(2).
81. [1988] 1 All ER 457.
82. *Ibid*. at p. 465.
83. *Ibid*. at p. 464.
84. *Ibid*. at p. 464.
85. *Op. cit.* at p. 82.
86. *Op. cit.* at pp. 31–2.
87. 'Unemployment Benefit: The "Full Extent Normal" Rule', *Journal of Social Welfare Law*, pp. 23–36 (1987).
88. [1988] 2 WLR 511.

89. Buck, T., 'Part-time Workers and Unemployment Benefit', 52 *Modern Law Review*, pp. 93–104 (1988) at p. 102 argues that the brevity of the House of Lords' ruling is due to anticipated amending legislation, although as Buck and Ogus and Barendt (*op. cit.* note 75 at p. 83) point out, governments are not always swift to respond to judicial decisions in the area of social security law.

90. SI 1983/1598 Regulation 19(2).

91. *Ibid.* Regulation 19(3)(a).

92. *Ibid.* Regulation 7(1)(h).

93. SI 1983/1598 Regulation 7(1)(1). *Supra* note 64.

94. SI 1983/1598 Regulation 7(1)(1).

95. Section 17(1)(a) Social Security Act 1975. See R(U) 21/56; R(U) 2/58; R(U) 15/61; R(U) 1/76.

96. SI 1982/1344.

97. See *Social Security Advisory Committee Report on the Draft Regulations*, Cmnd 8667, and the Rayner Report on Payment of Benefits to Unemployed People 1981.

98. Bourn, C.J., *Redundancy: Law and Practice*, (London, Butterworths, 1983) at p. 241.

99. Hepple *et al. op. cit.* note 68 at p. 56.

100. Report on Very Short Spells of Unemployment, Cmnd 9609 (1955).

101. See Drake and Bercusson *op. cit.*

102. See *IDS Study 235*, 'The Guaranteed Week', (February 1981).

103. Beach, C.M. and Balfour, F.S., 'Estimated Payroll Tax Incidence and Aggregate Demand for Labour in the United Kingdom', 50 *Economica*, pp. 35–48 (1983).

104. *Op. cit.* note 7.

105. 'Protective Legislation and Part-time Employment in Britain', 22 *British Journal of Industrial Relations*, pp. 78–100 (1984).

106. Department of Employment, *Compensation for Short-time Working: Consultative Document*, (London, 1978).

107. The Government's Expenditure Plans 1978–79 to 1981–82, Cmnd 7049 (1978).

108. 'Compensation for Short-time Working: New Government Proposals', 7 *Industrial Law Journal*, pp. 187–90 (1978).

109. 964 HC Deb, 21 March 1979, 1499–1500; HC Bill 1978–9 [116].

110. Freedland, M.R., 'Leaflet Law: The Temporary Short-time Working Compensation Scheme', 9 *Industrial Law Journal*, pp. 254–8 (1980); 'Labour Law and Leaflet Law: The Youth Training Scheme of 1983', 12 *Industrial Law Journal*, pp. 220–35 (1983).

111. For full details see Deakin, B.M. and Pratten, C.F., *Effects of the Temporary Employment Subsidy*, (Cambridge, Cambridge University Press, 1982).

112. See EC Commission, 5th Report on Competition Policy at p. 91 ff (Brussels, April 1976), 7th Report on Competition Policy at p. 165 (Brussels, April 1978), 8th Report on Competition Policy at p. 161 ff (Brussels, April 1979), 9th Report on Competition Policy at pp. 119 ff (Brussels, April 1980); European Parliament, Debate on Employment Subsidies, OJ No. 226, Debates of the European Parliament 1977–8, Report of Proceedings from 13–17 February 1978, (16.2.78); Question by Mr Power, OJ No. 225/210, Debates of the European Parliament 1977–8, Report of the Proceedings for the week 16–20 January 1978; Question by Mr Bangemann, OJ No. 228/170; Written Question by Mr Ryan to the EC Commission, OJ C 199/22 (21.8.78); Taylor, R., 'EEC Job Subsidies', *New Society*, 2 February 1978 p. 256; 'Jobs for Some of the Boys', *The Economist*, 45, 14 January 1978.

113. 944 Hansard, 20 February 1978, cols 1097–1173.

114. The original Bill was presented to Parliament on 8 February 1978. 943 Hansard, col. 1452; Amended HCB 1977–8 76.

115. Section 1(3) Employment Subsidies Act 1978.

116. *Supra* note 106.

117. The details of the scheme can be found in Department of Employment Leaflet PL 692: Department of Employment, 'Temporary Short-time Working Compensation Scheme', 88 *Employment Gazette*, pp. 478–81 (May 1980); Freedland, M.R. *op.cit.* note 110.

118. For details see Szyszczak, E., 'Employment Protection and Social Security', in Lewis, R. (ed), *Labour Law in Britain*, (Oxford, Basil Blackwell, 1986) at p. 377.

119. The following account is based upon interviews conducted by the author at the Depart-

ment of Employment and case studies carried out on the Short-time Working Project 1983–5 at the University of Kent.

120. *Government and Industry*, (Abingdon, Oxon., Professional Books, 1977) at pp. 32–3.

121. 'Using Government Subsidies to Offset Redundancies', *Industrial Relations Review and Report 233*, pp. 2–6 (October 1980).

122. 964 Hansard, 21 March 1979, col. 1637.

123. DE Leaflet PL 692 'Temporary Short-time Working Compensation Scheme'.

124. 964 Hansard, 21 March 1979, col. 1630.

125. House of Commons, Fourth Report from the Committee of Public Accounts Session 1983–4, Department of Employment Manpower Services Commission Special Employment Measures, 7 November 1983 (HC 1982–3, 235-i and 235-ii), (London, HMSO).

126. 'The Development of Special Employment Measures', 87 *Employment Gazette*, 478–81 (November 1979); 'Temporary Short-time Working Compensation Scheme', 88 *Employment Gazette*, 478–81 (May 1980); 'Special Employment Measures', 90 *Employment Gazette*, 470–72 (November 1982).

127. See Metcalf, D. and Richards, J., 'Subsidised Worksharing, Redundancies and Employment Adjustment: A Study of the Temporary Short-time Working Compensation Scheme', Working Paper No. 22, Short-time Working Project, (Canterbury, University of Kent, September 1985); Metcalf, D., 'Employment Subsidies and Redundancy', in Blundell, R. and Walker, I. (eds) *Unemployment, Search and Labour Supply*, (Cambridge, Cambridge University Press, 1986).

128. Richards, J., 'Explaining the distribution of the Temporary Short-time Working Compensation Scheme', Working Paper No. 4 (revised), Short-time Working Project 1983–5, (Canterbury, University of Kent, September 1984).

129. *Labour Law: Cases and Materials*, (London, Weidenfeld and Nicolson, 1984) Chapter 1. For an earlier critique of the limitations of existing labour law/labour market analysis see the Editors' Introduction to *Kahn-Freund's Labour and the Law* (London, Stevens, 3rd edn, 1983).

130. (London, The Thames Bank Publishing Co. Ltd.)

131. For the history of the development of labour law as a distinct subject see Hepple, B., 'Labour Law and Social Security in Great Britain', in Rood, M.G. *et al.* (eds) *Fifty Years of Labour Law and Social Security*, (Deventer, The Netherlands, Kluwer, 1986).

132. For a wider discussion see Szyszczak, E., 'Employment Protection and Social Security', in Lewis, R. (ed) *Labour Law in Britain*, (Oxford, Basil Blackwell, 1986).

133. 'Leaflet Law: The Temporary Short-time Working Compensation Scheme', 9 *Industrial Law Journal*, pp. 254–8 (1980).

134. For a much earlier critical account of the limitations of 'industrial law' which has been built up in a 'haphazard and piecemeal fashion according to the exigencies of the situation' see Robson, W.A., 'Industrial Law', 51 *Law Quarterly Review*, pp. 195–210 (1935).

135. 'Public Law and Economic Policy', *Journal of Business Law*, pp. 9–22 (1974) at p. 17.

136. See the exchange between Loughlin, M., 'Tinkering with the Constitution', 51 *Modern Law Review*, pp. 531–48 (1988), and Harden, I. and Lewis, N., 'The Noble Lie: A Rejoinder', 51 *Modern Law Review*, pp. 812–16 (1988).

137. 'Circular Arguments: The Status and Legitimacy of Administrative Rules', *Public Law*, pp. 239–84 (1986).

138. 'Towards a Critical Public Law', 9 *Journal of Law and Society*, pp. 1–19 (1982).

139. *The Development of the Modern State: A Sociological Introduction*, (London, Hutchinson, 1978) Chapter 6.

140. The greatest exponent of this thesis is probably Klare, K. in 'The Public/Private Distinction in Labour Law', 130 *University of Pennsylvania Law Review*, pp. 1358–1422 (1982).

141. 'Market Power, Bureaucratic Power, and the Contract of Employment', 15 *Industrial Law Journal*, pp. 1–14 (1986) at p. 14.

142. *Ibid.* at p. 14.

143. *Op. cit.*; 'Regulation by Contract: The New Prerogative', 32 *Current Legal Problems*, pp. 41–59 (1979). See also Winkler, J., 'Law, State and Economy: The Industry Acts in Context', 2 *British Journal of Law and Society*, pp. 103–28 (1975).

144. (London, Sweet and Maxwell, 1987).

145. See the book review by Freedland, M.R., *Legal Studies*, pp. 229–34 (1988). In fact only Freedland, better known as a labour lawyer than as a constitutional or administrative law expert,

has alerted lawyers' attention to the need to examine the role of delegated legislation (or what he terms 'leaflet law') and its effect on the *individual* employment relationship. Administrative law specialists have tended to single out for special attention only the delegated legislation relating to picketing or the administration of Health and Safety at Work measures in the employment law field.

146. 'Labour Law as a Vocation', 105 *Law Quarterly Review*, pp. 468–84 (1989).

147. See for example, Case C591/81 *Mishandling of Application for Assistance under the TSTWCS* PCA, First Report, Session 1982–3 (1982) Vol. 4, p. 21.

148. See 'Discretion in Making Legal Decisions', A Colloquium Sponsored by the Centre for Socio-Legal Studies, Oxford University and The Frances Lewis Law Center, School of Law, Washington and Lee University, 43 *Washington and Lee Law Review*, pp. 1161–1311 (1986).

149. *Discretionary Justice: A Preliminary Inquiry* (Baton Rouge, Louisiana State University Press, 1969). Cf. Baldwin, R. and Hawkins, K., 'Discretionary Justice: Davis Reconsidered', *Public Law*, pp. 570–99 (1984). See also Fulbrook, J., *Administrative Justice and the Unemployed*, (London, Mansell, 1978).

150. 'Circular Arguments: The Status and Legitimacy of Administrative Rules', *Public Law*, pp. 239–84 (1986).

151. 'Expectations in a Joyless Landscape', 49 *Modern Law Review*, pp. 685–711 (1986).

152. For a discussion of the problems of persuading the courts to stop seeing issues from the point of view of individual interests see McAuslan, P., 'Administrative Law, Collective Consumption and Judicial Policy', 46 *Modern Law Review*, pp. 1–20 (1983).

153. See Reich, C., 'The New Property', 73 *Yale Law Journal*, pp. 731–87 (1964). ·

154. See Prosser, T., 'Towards a Critical Public Law', 9 *Journal of Law and Society*, pp. 1–19 (1982).

6

New Ways of Adapting to Work Shortages

Partial unemployment is prevalent throughout industrialized societies and, as Chapter 1 outlined, it may occur at any time and result from a wide variety of factors, not being confined merely to periods of trade depression. The preceding chapters have described the historical factors which have given rise to the *ad hoc* responses to partial unemployment in Britain. Before suggesting ways in which the existing plethora of measures and policies could be rationalized it is worth an excursion around a few industrialized states to see how they have responded to the issue of partial unemployment and to see whether Britain has anything to learn from these experiences. This chapter then goes on to consider two topical policies, 'worksharing' and 'labour market flexibility'; both policies have been considered as a means of responding to work shortages in the United States and Europe.

OTHER SCHEMES TO REGULATE PARTIAL UNEMPLOYMENT

Definitions of and Compensation for Partial Unemployment

While partial unemployment is recognized more explicitly in other European states, there is a wide divergence of definitions of the concept.[1]

The Federal Republic of Germany was one of the earliest European states to acknowledge the need for the state to regulate partial unemployment. Unemployment Insurance was established in the 1870s and in 1927 the Unemployment Insurance system was modified to allow groups of workers subject to a planned reduced working programme to collect *pro-rata* compensation benefits.[2] This system of short-time working, known as 'Kurzarbeitergeld–Kug', has been modified over time to adapt to changing economic circumstances, and short-time working compensation is in fact only one of a series of employment programmes administered by the Federal Employment Institute (FEI).

The legal basis of the Short-time Working Compensation Scheme is found in the Employment Promotion Act 1969. This Act prescribes three goals of short-time working compensation: first, to preserve training and experience in firm-specific skills and thus to avoid lay-off and re-hiring costs; second, to protect workers' 'property' interest in their jobs and to reduce income loss arising from full unemployment; and third, to provide economic stability. The Employment Promotion Act 1969 is flexible in the establishment of guidelines for the administration of short-time working compensation while providing safe-guards for workers in terms of the temporary nature of the measures and the duty to inform workers of the programme. Roughly two-thirds of the workers' normal wage is paid through the scheme. The FEI also organizes vacancy referral (employment exchanges), the Unemployment Insurance scheme, vocational counselling and training and other forms of job subsidy.

In Italy compensation for a temporary reduction in working time is available where work cannot be carried out because of economic difficulties.[3] This definition embraces a shortage of orders within the firm or a situation of extreme gravity affecting an entire sector of the economy. The employer may claim compensation from the Cassa Integrazione Guadagni (Earnings Integration Fund) provided the employer informs the relevant trade unions in advance and either notifies the regional social security authorities (under the 'ordinary' scheme for problems concerning a single firm) or obtains a Labour Ministry declaration that a situation of extreme gravity exists (under the 'extraordinary' scheme which applies to difficult economic conditions in an entire sector). The Cassa Integrazione Guadagni pays allowances up to a maximum figure each month for hours not worked with up to 40 hourly payments in a week. Allowances are payable for up to one year under the 'ordinary' scheme, and under the 'extraordinary' scheme for up to two years (or indeed practically indefinitely in the case of reorganizations of the firm, even though employees may not have been dismissed for economic reasons).

The Cassa Integrazione Guadagni originally applied to northern Italy and was extended to the whole of the country in 1945. Over time it has provided some flexibility in adapting to changing economic crises although the recession of the seventies revealed the limitations of the legal regulation of the Fund. Originally the function of the Cassa Integrazione Guadagni was to allow for cyclical flexibility in the labour costs of industrial employers. Particularly during the recession of the 1970s and 1980s the Italian government responded to trade union demands to adapt the Fund to provide wage guarantees and to recognize the protection of property rights in jobs. The Cassa Integrazione Guadagni has had some success, particularly since the expansion of its functions in the 1970s: labour turnover has been reduced by 50 per cent.[4] Now the Cassa Integrazione Guadagni has adopted a supplementary or 'shadow' role to the unemployment compensation scheme offering higher benefits. This has brought criticisms of subsidizing labour hoarding; for instance, Emerson gives the example of Fiat announcing in March 1986 the re-employment of 6,000 workers who had been laid off for almost six years.[5] Thus a large number of workers may be inactive for long periods and may resort to the 'underground economy' as well as receiving lay-off compensation.

In contrast to these two special schemes, other European states have utilized the general unemployment benefit system to regulate and compensate for partial unemployment. In Belgium unemployment benefit is payable for whole days lost because of a work shortage and there are no waiting days. The qualification rules relating to eligibility vary with age, family status, gross earnings and period of insured employment.[6] The regional employment office must be notified in advance that lay-offs will occur and the unemployment benefit system makes specific provision for short-time working where there is a work shortage for economic reasons for either up to four continuous weeks, or for less than three working days in a week, or for one week without work in every two weeks for up to three months. Full-time working must resume at the end of each of these periods. An alternative definition of partial unemployment, which does not require the resumption of full-time working within a given period, is that work may be lost for at least three working days per week, one week in every two weeks. Employees are disqualified from unemployment benefit if the partial unemployment is caused by a strike in which they are participating or from which they may derive a benefit.

Luxembourg provides compensation for partial unemployment where there has been a shortfall in orders coupled with a significant diminution in labour requirements which arise from the economic climate, and a return to normal working must be anticipated within a reasonable time. The reduction in hours must not exceed half the working time per month for each employee. Provided that the working time reduction has been authorized by the employment authorities each month in advance all workers 'regularly employed' are entitled to compensation. The first eight hours of short-time working each month are paid by the employer; the state pays 80 per cent of gross hourly earnings for the remaining hours not worked. The payments are made through the Unemployment Insurance Fund but are a distinct part of the Fund. The days of short-time working are regarded as days worked for unemployment benefit purposes. There is a ceiling for the state payments which must not exceed 250 per cent of the adult statutory minimum monthly wage.

In the Republic of Ireland partial unemployment is defined in a complicated way. Employees can be 'partly idle' for three complete days in a consecutive six-day period resulting in a reduction by at least half of their normal total hours or earnings. Alternatively, they may be 'wholly idle' during a week because of a work shortage. Employees must be told that the lay-off is temporary before they may claim unemployment benefit. Again unemployment benefit is not available if the work shortage is caused by a strike in which the employees are participating. In addition, a lump-sum redundancy payment may be claimed where the employee is 'wholly idle' for four consecutive weeks.

Vaguer definitions of partial unemployment are found in the Netherlands and Spain. In the Netherlands employees may claim unemployment benefit where work cannot be carried out because of economic difficulties. There are no waiting days and unemployment benefit is set at 80 per cent of normal gross earnings and is payable for up to six weeks where working time is temporarily reduced. The local Labour Inspectorate must grant an authorization,[7] and permission for the payment of unemployment benefit for short-time working is given sparingly.[8] In Spain compensation is payable in the form of unemployment benefit when there is a temporary reduction in working time where technological, economic or *force majeure* circumstances prevent normal work from being carried out. Again local employment offices must authorize the temporary nature of the payment.

Unemployment benefit is administered differently in Sweden, where the Labour Market Board operates a job guarantee system.[9] This policy puts emphasis on retraining as a means of adapting to work shortages. Unemployment benefit is available for ten months and the Labour Market Board ensures that all unemployed people receive a job offer or a place on a training scheme before their unemployment benefit runs out. Unemployed people who turn down offers of jobs or training lose their entitlement to unemployment benefit.

In contrast, France has placed more emphasis upon working time restructuring by adopting early retirement schemes and introducing a shorter working week of 39 hours (instead of the previous norm of 40 hours).[10] Provision for compensation for lost working time is specifically decreed to be negotiated through collective agreements and is not subject to legal regulation except for the fact that no worker may be paid below the level of the statutory minimum wage.[11] Any reduction in working time below the statutory norm may be compensated if it is caused by the economic situation, shortages of raw materials or a situation of an 'exceptional nature'. Compensation for partial unemployment takes two forms: a basic 'specific allowance' paid, following local employment authority notification, to all employees except those laid off because of an industrial dispute in their undertaking and 'supplementary compensation' payable to all employees eligible for the specific allowance. The 'specific allowance' is set at an hourly rate and 'supplementary compensation' is calculated so that the total payment is set at 50 per cent of gross hourly earnings. The two payments are made concurrently and up to 600 hours of reduced time per year are compensated. If no work is carried out after four consecutive weeks standard unemployment benefit is payable.

In contrast to Western Europe, where short-time working (and by implication worksharing) is the dominant response to work shortages, a system of total lay-off with the possibility of recall when trade improves has emerged in the United States. Workers who are laid off may receive unemployment benefit. While evidence suggests that many laid-off workers do eventually return to the same employer, labour hoarding occurs and some workers spend years out of the labour market and are unable to develop their skills or gain experience. Younger, less experienced or less skilled workers or members of minority groups may try to seek work elsewhere. During the 1970s and 1980s a certain interest in worksharing was stimulated by the success of such measures in Germany and Canada.[12] California was the first state to introduce legislation to facilitate worksharing in 1978 in order to mitigate public sector employment problems. Worksharing was compensated through the Unemployment Insurance system. Other states,[13] beset by economic recession, followed this example. Arizona implemented a short-time compensation (STC) programme in January 1982, followed by Oregon in July 1982. Later STC programmes were implemented in Washington (August 1983), Florida (January 1984), Illinois and Maryland (July 1984). Arkansas and Texas implemented schemes in 1985. In 1975 the New York City Commission on Human Relations issued guidelines requiring employers to consider worksharing as an alternative to lay-offs, but an STC programme was not introduced until 1986, at the same time as Louisiana and Vermont enacted programmes. Since STC programmes reduce temporary lay-offs Congress facilitated the introduction of such unemployment benefit compensation schemes by enacting section 194 of the Tax Equity and Fiscal Responsibility Act (PL 97-248) in 1982. This Act suggested a number of ways in which the Federal states could implement STC programmes and also commissioned a study to monitor the impact of lay-offs and STC schemes.[14]

Although there is a wide geographic coverage of states facilitating worksharing compensated through the unemployment benefit scheme, evidence suggests that STC programmes have not been utilized a great deal by individual employers.[15] The study commissioned under the Tax Equity and Fiscal Responsibility Act 1982 could not give any concrete conclusions as to why fewer than 1 per cent of all employers utilized STC programmes. Lack of information about such programmes and the unsuitability of the programmes for certain industries were two possible reasons put forward to explain the low level of participation in STC schemes.

The Financing of Compensation for Partial Unemployment

One of the arguments made earlier in this book, in Chapters 4 and 5, was that the British system of financing the compensation of partial unemployment did not utilize the available resources consistently. The unemployment benefit system is financed from employer, employee and state contributions while collectively guaranteed week agreements and statutory guarantee payments are paid directly by the employer. Redundancy payments are paid by the employer but she could claim a rebate from the Redundancy Fund. This rebate was progressively reduced and finally abolished for large firms in the Wages Act 1986. Section 17 of the Employment Act 1989 implements the total abolition of redundancy rebates. The employer paid employees directly under the Temporary Short-time Working Compensation Scheme but was able to claim reimbursment from the Department of Employment.

Most European countries finance their unemployment benefit system through contributions made by employers, employees and the state, but the amounts and ratios of the contribution vary from country to country. In the United States unemployment benefits are financed almost exclusively by payroll taxes charged to employers. The use of unemployment benefit to compensate laid-off workers is experience-rated; that is, the more use the firm has made of unemployment benefits in the past, the higher the rate of payroll taxes. It is often argued, however, that the benefits received by the firm in being able to retain skilled workers far exceed the amount of maximum payroll taxes charged and that firms who utilize the system extensively should incur greater penalties through the tax system.[16]

In Germany compensation is paid directly by the employer, who reclaims the amount from the Federal Employment Institute. The short-time working compensation is financed by a contribution of 4.6 per cent of wages divided equally between worker and employer, and the state meets any deficit by a loan raised from taxation. The fund was in surplus until 1975, when a heavy increase in partial unemployment led to a deficit.

In Italy the Cassa Integrazione Guadagni is run by the National Pensions Institute and pays allowances either through the social security authorities (when workers have been laid off for a long time) or through the employer. The fund is financed by employers, who contribute a percentage of their wage bills to the central fund. Firms with up to 50 employees contribute 1.9% of their wage bill; firms with more than 50 employees contribute 2.2% of their wage bill. These contribution rates are increased on the basis of 4 per cent and 8 per cent respectively of allowances received for the Cassa Integrazione Guadagni in respect of workers receiving payments under the 'ordinary' scheme.

Most European schemes and the United States one have followed a fairly conservative approach to financing short-time working compensation either through special funds or through the general social security system. The recession of the 1970s provided the impetus for academics, policy makers and politicians to consider alternative methods of regulating and compensating partial unemployment, and the rest of this chapter considers two topical and controversial policies that have been discussed in recent years. The issue of worksharing has hardly been considered and yet, historically, as Chapter 4 shows, there is evidence of customary worksharing arrangements in certain industries. In contrast, the issue of 'labour market flexibility' has been a central policy issue of the present Conservative government in Britain.

WORKSHARING

During the recession of the 1970s an interest emerged in some academic and political circles in the idea of redistributing among a greater number of people what was argued to be a fixed amount of available work. The debate embraced many policies, for example the use of flexitime, shorter working weeks, early retirement and worksharing.[17] Worksharing is the temporary reduction of work hours of a group of workers on a recognized programme designed to distribute the available work among the members of the group to prevent lay-offs or redundancies.[18] Worksharing would appear to be a flexible way of responding to a work shortage since a scheme of worksharing can be implemented in a number of ways. The viability of this depends upon the nature of the workforce and the type of industry in question. For example, there can be a reduction in the number of hours worked each day or a reduction in the number of days worked per week or a rotation system of weeks at work and weeks off work, or a mixture of these schedules. Employees are compensated for some or all of the shortfall in their earnings from either specific employment funds or unemployment insurance funds. Both Britain and the United States have experienced systems of worksharing in the past and both countries have tried tentative worksharing programmes in recent years. However, the modern application of worksharing has subsidized employers' continuing duty to pay wages for reductions in working time. Yet in both countries there is a reluctance to accept wholeheartedly the concept of worksharing as a means of responding to partial unemployment.

This reluctance may stem from two factors. In Britain worksharing was often implemented with the consent of workers and trade unions and was often compensated through trade union, occupational or general social security schemes.[19] This system of worksharing fell into disuse with the growth of collective guaranteed week agreements in the post-1945 period in industries where there was strong collective bargaining. The growth of the statutory scheme of employment protection rights may have resulted in a different kind of 'worksharing'. Because of the need to satisfy certain continuous service qualifications in order to qualify for rights to redundancy payments and unfair dismissal protection, employers may have been able to adapt to fluctuations in supply and demand in the labour market by using the employees who fell outside the scope of employment protection as a 'flexible' workforce.[20]

In contrast, the system of worksharing experienced by the United States was imposed upon workers and unions who were not compensated for the resultant loss of earnings.[21] President Hoover actively encouraged worksharing as a means of responding to the General Depression of the twenties in order to avoid an activist Federal fiscal policy, and to forestall the introduction of a national public social security system. Thus workers, often existing at poverty level wages anyway, bore the consequences of the worksharing. While it was argued that worksharing did save jobs and maintained productivity[22] the policy of worksharing left a legacy of bitter memories. 'Spread the misery' and 'Communism in its worst form – the equal sharing of poverty' were just two of the descriptions of the practice.[23] Worksharing fell into disuse after the passage of the Social Security Act 1935 implemented a comprehensive unemployment insurance programme, and the Wagner Act 1935 provided trade unions with a framework in which to negotiate seniority systems and challenge the imposition of unilateral worksharing. However, trade union membership has not been as extensive as that in Britain.

A second factor is that the use of seniority protection clauses ('Last In, First Out' or, in the United States, 'Last Hired, First Fired') has been a dominant form of administering lay-offs and redundancies in Britain, and more especially, in the United States, for most of this century. Seniority emerged as an important aspect of collective bargaining in the railroad and printing industries of the United States at the turn of this century.[24] In exchange for the right to manage, employers accepted trade unions' preference for lay-offs to be conducted in reverse order of seniority. Seniority protection is also found in non-unionized sectors of industry and the public sector as an accepted method of allocating work shortages.[25]

Seniority has advantages for employers in that it allows the firm to retain the older, more experienced members of the workforce, members on whom time and money has been invested in firm-specific training. Lay-offs of inexperienced employees may be implemented with lower employment protection costs (for example, dismissal or redundancy compensation (in Britain) where the costs are related to seniority). In America, since lay-offs are experienced-rated, it is less expensive for the employer to fire outright than to retain inexperienced workers on a lay-off schedule. Also, the overall amount of payroll taxes for employers would be lower since fewer employees remain on the payroll.

There are disadvantages, however, in using seniority lay-offs. The loss of younger or less experienced workers may create skill shortages when work picks up, resulting in rehiring costs. Experience in a job may not always equal greater productivity since junior workers may be paid less than their marginal product and employers may want to retain them. Also, younger workers are eventually likely to gain more experience and be more productive while older workers will become less productive. The indiscriminate firing of workers may change the mix of skills within the firm, resulting in the retraining of older employees who may not be so adaptable and thus losing the advantages to be gained from protecting seniority. In recent years some workers have used the legal process to challenge lay-off and firing procedures under the unfair dismissal and anti-discrimination law of Britain and the Civil Rights Act 1964 in the United States. Unions, too, may suffer disadvantages in the use of seniority protection clauses. They may find they are faced by claims from members and non-members of the union arguing against the unfairness of the selection procedures. Overall, their membership (and consequently the union subscriptions) may decline as a result of workforce reductions.

During the recession of the seventies doubts were cast upon the utility of implementing lay-offs according to seniority. Management wanted a greater freedom to make selective lay-offs of less productive workers[26] and within the civil rights movement in the United States attention was turned towards worksharing as an alternative way of regulating work shortages. Inspired by the success of worksharing schemes in Germany a new debate emerged in the United States in the seventies as to the effectiveness of worksharing. The debate has both an economic and a civil rights perspective.

Worksharing: The Economic Perspective

From an employee perspective, worksharing has advantages in that it offers a means of protecting particular industries or local communities from total job loss while allowing workers to retain job-specific skills.[27] Thus continuity of employment is maintained as well as continued protection of fringe benefits attached to work. In the report of STC programmes commissioned under the Tax Equity and Fiscal Responsibility Act 1982 (discussed earlier in this chapter) practically all employers retained health and retirement benefits for workers who were placed on reduced hours even though state laws did not require that such benefits be maintained. This continuity is important for many women and minority workers who are recent entrants to the labour market, and it may allow some families to preserve two incomes. Another advantage of worksharing is that it provides an opportunity for older workers to experience increased leisure with only a marginal decrease in pay, thus developing a 'taste'[28] for retirement. Employers can see advantages in that worksharing precludes or reduces hiring and training costs if business picks up by allowing the firm to retain its investment in skilled labour. However, while firms participating in STC programmes in the United States saved on hiring and training costs, for some firms these savings were counter-balanced by the higher fringe benefits costs involved in STC participation. Equally the costs of severance pay and early retirement schemes are reduced. The implementation of worksharing may maintain morale among the workforce by reinforcing group loyalties and strengthening employee loyalty to the firm. The production process can be maintained and there is some evidence of increased productivity through worksharing during temporary depressions.[29] Finally, the employer is given greater flexibility in responding to adverse economic conditions. From the government's point of view the cost of public welfare and social insurance benefits, job search programmes and other 'social' costs of large-scale unemployment (such as ill-health) are reduced.

There are disadvantages, too. For employees, part of their normal income is lost unless worksharing is subsidized by the state through unemployment insurance or employment subsidies. Employers may incur administrative costs in the organization of worksharing schedules. This was an important factor emerging from the STC study commissioned in the United States, although it was argued that administrative costs may decline over time as experience with STC programmes accumulates. Aspects of the 'pay package', particularly fringe benefits and medical insurance, may not be subsidized by the state scheme. In the United States employers may be penalized by surcharges for drawing too heavily on the Unemployment Insurance Fund to subsidize worksharing. Similarly the state may pick up the burden of financing worksharing if payments from the National Insurance or employment subsidy funds are not balanced by an increase in taxes.

Worksharing: A Civil Rights Perspective

In recent years the established practices of reducing workforces according to seniority systems have been challenged from a civil rights perspective in the United States. Two central issues have emerged. First, the question of whether there is a legal duty to minimize job loss according to fair employment practices; and secondly, whether there is a legal duty to implement worksharing as a means of protecting women and minorities from unemployment.

The argument runs as follows. Older workers, women and minorities may have a legal ground to challenge a lay-off procedure on the basis that the proposed choice of workers for a lay-off affects a disproportionately high number of workers from a particular group. Many women and minorities cannot wait to be recalled and take up new jobs with no seniority, and thus remain permanently vulnerable in the labour market. Ruth and Arthur Blumrosen argued that the application of seniority rules in a lay-off had a disproportionate impact upon workers who had only recently entered the labour market under the affirmative action programmes of the civil rights legislation of the 1960s.[30] In order to maintain the gains made through affirmative action it was argued that lay-offs should be conducted so as to maintain the same percentage of minority groups and women in the workforce. The Blumrosens also maintained that a true civil rights perspective should not ask the question of *how* to undertake the lay-off but instead attention should be focused upon the more difficult question of 'is a lay-off necessary?' The Blumrosens asserted that in the event of a work shortage the employer had a legal duty to attempt to reduce work hours without adopting a system that produced a disparate impact upon a particular group of workers.

Two legal barriers prevent an automatic implementation of this interpretation of the legislation. The first problem is that section 703(h) of the Civil Rights Act 1964 allows an employer to justify a bona fide seniority-based lay-off. This has been interpreted to mean that the lay-off must not be based on race or sex discrimination and that all workers must be treated alike.[31] While accepting the point that decisions of arbitrators have protected seniority systems of lay-off, Ruth Blumrosen argued that such decisions did not prevent the employer from adopting worksharing as an alternative to lay-off procedures.[32] By so doing, however, the possibility of the union or senior white employees bringing a claim against the employer could not be ruled out.[33]

The proponents of a wider civil liberties perspective have received a serious setback after the ruling of the Supreme Court in *Memphis Firefighters* v. *Stotts*.[34] This was an action brought by black firefighters hired under a consent decree established to rectify past racial discrimination in hiring. The firefighters argued that the application of a seniority-based lay-off in response to a projected budget deficit had a disproportionate impact upon the recently hired or promoted black firefighters and thus jeopardized the recent gains made by them in the labour market. In upholding that the lay-off satisfied the bona fide defence of section 703(h) of the Civil Rights Act 1964, the Supreme Court applied its earlier ruling of *International Brotherhood of Teamsters* v. *US*,[35] that competitive seniority could only be awarded if the applicant could prove that he had been victim of past discrimination which had prevented him from acquiring the requisite seniority to retain his job.[36] Spiegelman argues that the effects of *Stotts* may have far-reaching consequences for all remedial actions attempting to counter the effects of past discrimination:

> Since a quota by definition is a remedy which goes only to persons who are *not* actual and direct victims, the interpretation of section 706(g) in *Stotts* potentially denies to courts all power to order quotas.[37]

A second limitation in applying the civil liberties perspective to lay-off is that, as a defence, the employer may argue that the seniority system satisfies a 'business necessity'. This defence has received a more stringent interpretation than the interpretation given to the equivalent defence in Britain since the reasons put forward by the employer must be 'job related'.[38] Ruth Blumrosen has argued, however, that the employer may be required to consider and assess the probable impact of alternative methods of coping with the work shortages.[39]

Evidence exists in the United States that black workers run a greater risk of being laid off than white workers and similar arguments can be made in relation to redundancy and unemployment among black and ethnic minorities in Britain.[40] For example, while only 11 per cent of white males are recorded as unemployed, 16 per cent of West Indian males and 18 per cent of Indian,

Pakistani and Bangladeshi males are recorded as economically inactive in *Social Trends 1987*.[41] One of the issues addressed in the review of STC programmes in the United States was the extent to which STC programmes protected and preserved the jobs of workers with special emphasis on newly hired employees, minorities and women. The results were disappointing (from the perspective of STC as part of an affirmative action strategy) in that it was found that the patterns of employment and lay-off were quite similar between STC participating firms and non-participating firms. It was acknowledged that the data available was perhaps not precise enough, but the study draws the conclusion that, from the evidence available, STC programmes do not have any major affirmative action advantages. One interesting feature of the study, however, is the fact that when investigating lay-offs prior to STC use it was found that women and minorities did not appear to be affected disproportionately. Thus STC schemes tended to be used by employers who were already not discriminating in lay-off selection criteria and the impact of the scheme did not vary their behaviour.

To date the issue of tackling discriminatory redundancy and lay-off procedures has not attracted a wide legal discussion in Britain. The issues have been aired only in relation to sex discrimination. This is interesting since economic evidence from the United States shows that in fact women workers are less likely to be laid off than male workers with the same tenure, experience and in the same occupation or industry.[42] This finding may be explained by the fact that women often occupy jobs that are less sensitive to fluctuations in demand or that they undertake work that is part of the overhead labour necessary to keep the firm operating when production is cut. Another explanation is that firms may prefer to fire outright rather than lay-off that part of the workforce with lower job tenure and less employment protection. Women are most likely to fall into this category and it is in relation to redundancy and dismissal that litigation has arisen.

In Britain the civil rights approach to questioning the legality of redundancy and lay-off procedures has been piecemeal. Studies have been undertaken on the effect of redundancy processes upon women,[43] the disparate effects the operation of the redundancy compensation system may have upon women,[44] and the extent of legal protection against unfair dismissal on the grounds of sex discrimination.[45] The Equal Opportunities Commission has also conducted a Formal Investigation into the implementation of redundancies at British Steel Corporation.[46]

Although Britain does not have a 'bona fide' seniority protection defence enshrined in the Sex Discrimination Act 1975, the practice of 'Last In, First Out' ('LIFO') selection for redundancy was not regarded as discriminatory since in the Committee discussion of the Sex Discrimination Bill John Fraser used 'LIFO' as an example of a policy that was 'justifiable'.[47] This view was reiterated by the Employment Appeal Tribunal in *Clarke and Powell* v. *Eley*

(IMI) Kynoch Ltd.[48] The practice of 'LIFO' has been protected on the grounds that an employer may argue in defence to a claim of sex discrimination that the operation of 'LIFO' was justifiable. The tribunals have been reluctant to accept challenges to seniority systems. For example, 'LIFO' was accepted as a customary practice in the textile industry in *Kaur and Begum* v. *Firth Brothers (Shepley) Ltd.*[49] Here women were made redundant and not offered retraining on the same terms as male employees because to do so would have led to an infringement of the protective legislation: the Factories Act 1961. The women unsuccessfully argued that the employer could have obtained an Exemption Order from the Factories Inspectorate. The industrial tribunal held that there was no evidence as to how easy it would have been to obtain such an Exemption Order. In contrast, in *Green* v. *E. Cookson and Sons Ltd., Exhibition Bakery*,[50] an industrial tribunal accepted that the operation of 'LIFO' resulted in indirect discrimination. Again the employer tried to argue as a defence that to retain the women in employment after a reorganization of working time would have contravened the Factories Act 1961. Here the industrial tribunal held that the employer should have applied for an Exemption Order and would probably have been granted one. Mrs Green was successful in a claim for sex discrimination and unfair dismissal. The tribunal recommended that the employer seek an Exemption Order and, if it was granted, to re-employ Mrs Green.[51]

The use of the protective legislation as a defence to lay-offs and dismissals will probably be less relevant in future. Section 7 of the Sex Discrimination Act 1986 began a process of repealing protection legislation in order to conform with European Community equality legislation.[52] This process is continued in the Employment Act 1989 which narrows down the scope of section 51 of the Sex Discrimination Act 1975.

Another defence that may be available to the employer is that the reorganization of the workforce resulting in discriminatory redundancy selection may be justified because the work that remains must be undertaken by either a man or a woman: a 'genuine occupational qualification' defence under section 7(2) of the Sex Discrimination Act 1975. In *Timex Corporation* v. *Mr C. Hodgson*[53] the customary use of 'LIFO' was abandoned (with the consent of the trade union) in favour of retaining a female employee with less service than Mr Hodgson, who was made redundant. The employers argued that it was necessary to retain at least one female supervisor in the factory and the Employment Appeal Tribunal accepted that the 'genuine occupational qualification' defence could be argued in relation to such a redundancy selection procedure.

Recent years have seen challenges to redundancy selection procedures whereby employers (sometimes with the collusion of trade unions) have attempted to apply criteria other than a seniority system in the hope of dismissing workers with less employment protection rights, in particular the selection of part-time workers (who are mainly women) before the application of agreed or customary seniority procedures. Although it has been accepted that indirect sex discrimination may occur if such procedures are used,[54] attempts to tackle redundancy arising from segregation in employment have failed. For example, in *Cox* v. *Kraft Foods Ltd*.[55] the employers argued that male employees were retained because they possessed wide skills and experience. Redundancies were made only from the production and cleaning departments, which employed only female employees. The Employment Appeal Tribunal held that the dismissal was fair because the employer had justified the retention of the male employees on the grounds of their 'greater versatility'.[56] Equally the Employment Appeal Tribunal has not been very sensitive to the allegation that indirect *marital* discrimination may occur if part-time workers are selected for redundancy before full-time workers.[57]

In contrast, a Scottish industrial tribunal in *Allan and Others* v. *Leyland Vehicles*[58] found that discrimination had occurred in an agreed 'LIFO' redundancy selection procedure where part-time service was ignored. All the employees who had worked part-time were women and it was held that 'special circumstances' would be necessary to show that such an unlawful discriminatory dismissal was a fair dismissal.

The first case taken by the *Women's Legal Defence Fund* explores the scope of discrimination in allocating short-time working. Following the national 'salmonella in eggs' scare in 1988/89 an East Anglian firm rearing chickens for egg producers found itself in financial difficulties and cut costs by reducing a day's work (and just less than the equivalent of pay) for all four of its female employees. The male employees were not affected by these cuts. At the time of writing a claim of sex discrimination has been brought under sections 1 and 6 of the Sex Discrimination Act 1975 and an unfair dismissal complaint has been lodged on the ground that the reduction in pay amounts to a constructive dismissal.[59]

Another limiting factor to the claim for indirect discrimination is that the defence to such claims has been given a broad interpretation by the British courts and tribunals. The application of the European Court of Justice ruling in *Bilka-Kaufhaus GmbH* v. *Weber von Hartz*[60] at first sight has tightened up the interpretation of the defence of justifiability found in the Sex Discrimination Act 1975. The national court must apply a threefold test: the policy must be based on objectively justified factors unrelated to any discrimination on grounds of sex, the means chosen for achieving the objective must correspond to a real need on the part of the undertaking and be appropriate with a view to achieving the said objective and be necessary to that end. While the employer must now satisfy these criteria she may raise economic factors as a means of justifying discriminatory dismissals and lay-offs and the Employment Appeal Tribunal has also included 'administrative efficiency' as a valid defence to a sex discrimination claim.[61]

Challenges to seniority systems have been brought also in Australia under

Anti-Discrimination legislation modelled upon the British legislation. In *Najdovska and Others* v. *Australian Iron and Steel Pty Ltd.*[62] 34 women lodged complaints alleging discrimination by their employer in relation to the allocation of job vacancies for women, threat of 'retrenchment' and actual 'retrenchment'.[63] The substance of the sex discrimination complaints was that when the women had applied for jobs as ironworkers they were placed upon a waiting list and in some cases were waiting for more than three years before being employed. Men in similar positions were employed without a waiting period. When the employer announced 'retrenchments' a system of 'Last In, First Out' was utilized to select workers.[64] The women complained that this method of selection discriminated against women employees since they had to wait much longer than men to obtain their jobs and therefore had less comparative seniority with the result that the selection criteria had a greater impact upon women workers. This point was backed up with statistics showing employment patterns within the Australian Iron and Steel company between 1 June 1977 and April 1980. These statistics revealed that only 1.35 per cent of all ironworkers recruited during this period were women. Evidence was also adduced alleging sexist attitudes by senior company officers and sex segregation in job classification. Both the New South Wales Equal Opportunity Tribunal and the New South Wales Court of Appeal[65] upheld the complaint of discrimination, arguing that, while the concept of 'Last In, First Out' might appear facially neutral it operated in this case to the disadvantage of women by continuing the effects of past discrimination.

As a result of these legal developments it would seem, in principle, that there is scope to bring worksharing ideas into a legal civil liberties discourse in Britain and that procedures exist for challenging established industrial relations practices in relation to lay-off and short-time working selection procedures. The major stumbling block is how far the courts and tribunals will continue to abstain from questioning managerial discretion in the application of the defences to unfair dismissal and sex discrimination claims. Equally the debate within the United States would offer some legal basis for introducing at least a discussion of how to avoid extending the inequalities that already exist in female and minority groups' access to, and participation in, the labour market to the handling of work shortages. While the limitations and advantages as well as the various meanings attached to worksharing are still being debated at an economic level in the United States, Britain is perhaps missing an opportunity of discussing the alternatives to large-scale lay-off and redundancy by not engaging, in any committed way, the possibility of using worksharing. Up until now worksharing in the form of employment subsidies has only been utilized as a response to crises.

LABOUR MARKET FLEXIBILITY

Another way of adapting to work shortages is to reduce the rigidities of the labour market created by the use of explicit contracts. If 'employment protection' emerged as a theme of the 1970s, 'labour market flexibility' has become the concern of the 1980s. Recent years have seen an increased interest in the use of labour market flexibility as a way of responding to the economic recession of the 1970s and early 1980s.[66] 'Flexibility' in fact has various meanings. As the Advisory Conciliation and Arbitration Service (ACAS) points out:

> Part time working, sub contracting, shift working and attempts to break down demarcation between trades have been a feature of the British economy for many years. ... Nevertheless in recent years it has been suggested that new types of flexibility are arising and that all kinds are being introduced on a much greater scale than before.

Controversy surrounds the use of the strategy, however, in terms of definitions and ultimate goals. 'Flexibility' is seen by employers as a means of reducing the fixed costs of labour and making an efficient use of labour resources to adapt to technological as well as market changes. Trade unions and employees would argue that 'flexibility' is a means whereby management and capital can *transfer* some, or all, of the risks of the market on to the employees.

Looking first at defining the issue of what is 'flexibility', we see that in fact the idea of 'flexibility' is a multi-dimensional concept. Labour economists, for example, have focused attention upon wage flexibility, meaning the extent to which wage levels are able to respond to shifts in supply and demand in the labour market. This concept has both a dimension of labour market structure, as the composition of employment changes, and a dimension of aggregate employment: in particular as to whether the severity of the rise in unemployment in the post-1979 recession was caused by a lack of wage flexibility.[67] In Chapter 3 we discussed the difficulties encountered by employers in adjusting wages and imposing wage cuts under the contract of employment when no particular method of allowing for such flexibility has been specifically incorporated into the contract.

Other specific aspects of 'flexibility' include geographical flexibility. This may be the attempts by employers to use the idea of implied terms to introduce mobility within the firm so that employees can be used in a flexible way across different work sites[68] or it may be the willingness (voluntary or otherwise) of employees to travel greater distances to alternative work.[69] The need for this often occurs when a firm relocates or streamlines its operations and workers are prepared to accept commuting, rather than a redundancy payment with little prospect of alternative work.

Labour law has only recently focused attention upon the composition of the labour market.[70] Legal commentators have recognized the complexity of the legal regulation of the employment relationship and have attempted to move away from the simple distinctions drawn in labour law between what is described as a 'core' of full-time permanent employees who enjoy the advantages of collective bargaining as well as the statutory 'floor of rights' guarantees, and a 'periphery' of what are described as 'marginal' or 'vulnerable' workers.[71] Davies and Freedland, for example, provide a perceptive analysis of the use of (or rather the lack of) statutory and common law restraints upon employers in *constituting* the employment relationship.[72] Other attempts have been made to integrate the interaction of the social security and the tax systems in explaining constraints upon employers and inducements for workers to participate in the labour market and how these constraints affect the size and composition of the labour market.[73]

Other industrial relations specialists have focused attention upon 'functional' and 'numerical' flexibility. Functional flexibility is the growth of flexible job descriptions resulting in multi-skilling and reduced demarcations between different categories of worker.[74] Pollert argues that this form of managerial concern with labour market flexibility is not new but was a central element of productivity bargaining in the 1960s and 1970s.[75] This form of 'flexibility' has accompanied the need to adapt quickly to new technology and with the growth of employment protection rights employers would seem to be concerned to draw up contracts of employment allowing for job flexibility rather than constantly varying the contracts of employment and running the risk of constructive dismissal or breach of contract claims.[76] This form of 'flexibility' is particularly useful for dealing with work shortages since it allows for the transfer of workers to different jobs in the event of a temporary dislocation of production. The concept of multi-skilling has also brought with it a parallel concept of harmonization of terms and conditions of employment, in particular the extension of uniform facilities at work and access to fringe benefits.

In contrast, numerical flexibility is the use of so-called 'peripheral' workers to adjust to fluctuations in demand. These workers can be hired and fired with little cost to the employer. Statistical evidence suggests that the number of 'flexible' workers is growing rapidly. For example, Hakim argues that this 'group' of workers comprises about one-third of the total workforce[77] and the ACAS survey reports the extension of 'flexible' working to all sectors of industry.[78] There are variations in terms of the geographical distribution of the flexible workforce and in the form of the ''peripheral' work. Part-time working tends to be the main form of such work, followed by self-employment, sub-contracting and temporary work. Also the sex composition of the 'peripheral' workforce varies according to occupation and sector of industry. This growth in the 'periphery' is not isolated to Britain but is in evidence elsewhere

in Western Europe and the United States.[79] Workforce composition projec-
tions indicate that the number of peripheral workers will continue to grow.[80]

Differences of opinion surround the debates over the aims of 'labour market
flexibility'. Pollert[81] argues that labour market segmentation should be seen as
part of a historically longer process rather than as a new managerial strategy.
She argues that in many respects the presentation of 'flexibility' as a panacea
for the employment problems generated by the recession is conceptually and
practically flawed in that it fails to take on board the need of firms to retain
skills or to train workers as well as the wider concerns of international
competition such as the need to adapt to changing economic conditions,
product organization, marketing or industrial relations practices generally.
These issues are seen in the experience of the American multinational Ford
Motor Company where the response to the recession in the late 1970s and
early 1980s was to lay-off workers. This policy was adapted in 1982 to
incorporate an Employee Development and Training Programme (EDTP)
funded by a 'five-cents-per-hour-worked' contribution from the firm to re-
train laid-off workers. The EDTP was able to progress from managing lay-offs
to training the employed workforce to allow workers to learn broader skills.[82]
In general, however, the United States is still painted as an 'employment at
will' economy, despite attempts to increase protection from dismissal by
unionized labour.[83]

Essentially it can be argued that a dominant feature of 'labour market
flexibility' is the transfer of the risks of the market away from employers and on
to employees. As Chapter 1 argued, minimum employment relationships are
not an easy solution to work shortages and the idea of providing employment
protection and compensation for partial employment reveals the acknowledgment by employers of maintaining formal employment relationships particularly for skilled workers, rather than operating with minimal employment
relationships. Despite the reservations drawn by Pollert, she admits that
'flexibility' has become an attractive concept, supported by the Conservative
government, the Confederation of British Industry, and the Institute of
Directors. The concept has gained in political and economic credence particularly when coupled with the other 'buzz words' of the 1980s such as 'enterprise
culture' and 'deregulation', promoted by the government.[84]

One aspect of this approach to the 'regeneration' of British industry which
has not been thought through in any coherent fashion is the attitudes which
should be taken towards the regulation of training, in particular the maintenance of acquired skills and the adaptation of traditional skills to new forms of
technology. During the recession of the 1970s and early 1980s training as a key
policy issue was abandoned as firms and the government concentrated upon
the more immediate issue of day-to-day economic survival. In many respects
Britain has been unfortunate in that demographic trends have run counter to
industrial needs. Although there was a surge of young people entering the

labour market at the height of the recession their numbers dwindled as the recession eased out, leaving industry with chronic skill shortages. One immediate effect of this demographic change is that the government has quietly dropped many of its earlier plans to 'deregulate' the labour market by decreasing the protection afforded to part-time workers,[85] and within the private sector of industry we see greater emphasis upon tapping the resources of married women and parents who would normally have difficulty re-entering the labour market after carrying out domestic commitments. Suddenly, parental leave, career breaks and childcare facilities have become important items of personnel policy. In 1989 (and perhaps rather belatedly) the Department of Employment released a White Paper entitled *Employment for the 1990s*.[86] This outlined the government's proposals to replace the skill shortages now found in the labour market. In fact the White Paper is rather thin on policy. It echoes much of the current Conservative government policy for the labour market, in particular pinning hopes on the 'privatization' of training. To date the Manpower Services Commission has been abolished and was replaced by the Training Commission. This Commission was ineffective since the Trades Union Congress refused to participate in its operations and section 18 of the Employment Act 1989 abolished the Training Commission, transferring its powers to the Secretary of State. In March 1989 a £3 billion training scheme was launched establishing Training and Enterprise Councils (TEC). These are to be employer-led, where business people will oversee spending on national training programmes and assess local labour markets and skill needs.

In addition to these domestic developments the European Community has focused supra-national attention on issues of labour market flexibility. The 'adaption of working time' project is designed to combat large-scale and long-term unemployment.[87] Within the supra-national forum there is perhaps more space to air the problems of utilizing 'labour market flexibility' as the answer to work shortages. In between presenting detailed policy documents, the EC Commission has initiated a series of proposals[88] to regulate temporary work,[89] voluntary part-time work[90] and flexible retirement.[91] These proposals would protect and enhance the status of traditionally vulnerable forms of work: the aim being to encourage workers to move from full-time secure employment to this kind of working thus creating more employment opportunities. In addition a more radical and controversial proposal has been to create a Community Charter of Fundamental Social Rights.[92] Various civil liberties and equal opportunities organizations have welcomed these proposals as an extension to existing employment protection legislation. Even the Trades Union Congress has eschewed the traditional 'left-wing' hostility to the European Community and given its support to the extensions to employment protection rights by the European Community.[93] The success of the equality legislation has perhaps driven home the value of directly enforceable European Community rights within the national labour market.[94] The member states of the European Community, on the other hand, far from embracing these attempts to adapt working time, have given the provisions a cool reception. Most of the blame for failing to agree to these proposals has been directed at the use of the veto by the United Kingdom government when the proposals have been put before the Council of Ministers. Equally the United Kingdom is not slow to challenge the legal basis of measures it does not support but which may have been enacted at the Community level.[95] The United Kingdom government has signalled its preference to leave such matters of internal labour market regulation to the member states' discretion. At the internal level this is seen in the so-called 'step by step' approach of dismantling the collective and individual employment law protection developed in the 1970s. The United Kingdom government has argued that, far from creating 'flexibility', the provisions will increase fixed labour costs and create more rigidity in the labour market. Little empirical evidence has been adduced for these assertions.[96]

It remains to be seen, therefore, whether 'labour market flexibility' can contribute to the regulation of partial unemployment caused by work shortages. Although the idea may allow employers to adjust easily to variations in demand, the problem with the concept is that it fails to recognize the employer's role in compensating for partial unemployment. Since many of the 'peripheral workforce' may also be without public or private forms of social security[97] to provide compensation when work is unavailable, as a long-term solution such forms of 'flexibility' are unlikely to be attractive in social policy terms.

An important factor which may influence the viability of this solution is what happens to the international economy and the political situation in the European Community. The Single European Act 1986 and the approach of '1992' may force political and economic developments upon the British labour market. The need for 'flexibility' in order to remain competitive may be at odds with the problem of 'social dumping'. If Britain adopts a deregulated, flexible labour market while other European Community states tighten up their employment laws European Community firms and other multinationals may be attracted by the low labour costs of the United Kingdom, which undoubtedly will distort competition. In those circumstances it will not be long before either the United Kingdom government or the EC Commission realize the need to tighten up the regulation of the British labour market.[98]

NOTES

1. Material in this section is taken from Industrial Relations Services, 'International Short-time and Lay-offs'. *European Industrial Relations Review*, No. 111, pp. 15–19 (April 1983); Grais, B.,

Lay-off and Short-time in Selected OECD Countries, (Paris, OECD, 1983); MaCoy, R. and Morand, M.J., *Short-time Compensation: A Formula for Work-Sharing*, (New York, Pergamon Press, 1984).

2. Meisel, H., 'The Pioneers: STC in the Federal Republic of Germany', in MaCoy and Morand *ibid.*

3. For full details see D'Harmant, A.F. and Brunetta, R., 'The Cassa Integrazione Guadagni', 1 *Labour*, pp. 15–56, (1987).

4. D'Apice, C. and Del Boca, A., 'The Impact of Social Policies on Income Distribution and the Labour Market in Italy', 14 *Journal of Social Policy*, pp. 385–401 (1985).

5. 'Regulation or Deregulation of the Labour Market', 32 *European Economic Review*, pp. 775–817 (1988) at p. 793.

6. Industrial Relations Services, 'International Unemployment Benefits in 12 Countries', *European Industrial Relations Review* 105, pp. 12–19 (October 1982).

7. Note that for the retail trade authorization must come from the labour relations department of the Social Affairs Ministry.

8. Department of Employment, *Consultative Document on Compensation for Short-time Working*, (London, April 1978).

9. Jackman, R. and others, *A Job Guarantee for Long-term Unemployed People*, (London, Employment Institute 1986), Chapter 4.

10. See Hart, R.A., *Shorter Working Time: A Dilemma for Collective Bargaining*, (Paris, OECD, 1984).

11. Two surveys give details of collective agreements negotiated in the public and private sector: Industrial Relations Services, 'France: Working Time Law Reform', *European Industrial Relations Review 97*, pp. 16–20 (February 1982); 'France: Bargaining on Reduced Working Time', *European Industrial Relations Review* 105, pp. 21–3 (October 1982). These agreements are called 'solidarity contracts'. A similar experiment has been tried in Belgium; see Hart, R.A., *Working Time and Employment*, (London, Allen and Unwin, 1987) at p. 10.

12. See Meisel *op. cit.* note 2; Reid, F. and Meltz, N.M., 'Canada's STC: A Comparison with the California Version', in MaCoy and Morand *op. cit.* note 1.

13. Cf. the situation in Arizona where the impetus for worksharing came from the large firm of Motorola, St Louis, R., 'Arizona, Motorola, and STC', in MaCoy and Morand *op. cit.* note 1.

14. A summary of this study can be found in US Department of Labor *Short-time Compensation: A Handbook of Basic Source Material*, (Washington, Unemployment Insurance Service Occasional Paper 87–2, 1987). Section 194 is reproduced in Appendix D.

15. See Chapter XX 'Work Sharing: New Experiences', in Dennis, B.D. (ed) *Industrial Relations Research Association Series, Proceedings of the 38th Annual Meeting December 28–30 1985*, (New York, 1986). Comprehensive material can also be found in US Department of Labor *Short-time Compensation: A Handbook of Basic Source Material*, (Washington, Unemployment Insurance Service Occasional Paper 87–2 1987).

16. Hamermesh, D.S. and Rees, A.R., *The Economics of Work and Pay*, (New York, Harper and Row, 4th edn, 1988) at p. 219 ff.

17. For a discussion of these policies see Hart, R.A. *op. cit.* note 10.

18. See Mesa, J.M., *Short-time Working as an Alternative to Lay-off: The Case of Canada and California*, (Geneva, ILO, 1982).

19. See chapter 4.

20. See Szyszczak, E., 'Employment Protection and Social Security', in Lewis, R. (ed) *Labour Law in Britain*, (Oxford, Basil Blackwell, 1986); O'Donovan, K. and Szyszczak, E., '*Equality and Sex Discrimination Law*, (Oxford, Basil Blackwell, 1988) Chapter 6; Dickens, L., 'Falling through the Net: Employment Change and Worker Protection', 19 *Industrial Relations Journal*, pp. 139–53 (1988). Cf. Hakim, C., 'Employment Rights: A Comparison of Part-time and Full-time Employees', 18 *Industrial Law Journal*, pp. 69–83 (1989) and Disney, R. and Szyszczak, E.M., 'Part-time Work: Reply to Catherine Hakim', 18 *Industrial Law Journal*, pp. 223–8 (1989).

21. Bernstein, I., *The Lean Years: A History of the American Workers 1920–33*, (Boston, Houghton Mifflin, 1960).

22. Hoover, H., *The Memoirs of Herbert Hoover: Vol. 3, The Great Depression*, (New York, Macmillan, 1952) at p. 45.

23. Bernstein, *op. cit.* note 21 at p. 478.

24. Gersuny, C., 'Origins of Seniority Provisions in Collective Bargaining', 37 *Labor Law*

Journal, pp. 518–24 (1982); Perlman, S., *A History of Trade Unionism in the US*, (New York, Macmillan, 1922).

25. Seniority may also be used with other policies, such as two-tier wage discrimination as a method of segregating workforces or creating dual labour markets. Inferior treatment of new or younger workers can lead to employment discrimination in two ways. First, by eliminating or delaying the possibility of lower-tier employees from attaining the same advantageous terms of employment as upper-tier employees. Secondly, a lower-tier employee will achieve less in terms of employment protection rights at each level of seniority than an upper-tier counterpart under the former employment structure.

26. See the debate on the importance of seniority: Turnbull, P., 'The Economic Theory of Trade Union Behaviour: A Critique', 26 *British Journal of Industrial Relations*, pp. 99–118 (1988); Disney, R. and Gospel, H., 'The Seniority Model of Trade Union Behaviour: A (Partial) Defence', 27 *British Journal of Industrial Relations*, pp. 179–95 (1989). See also ACAS, *Redundancy Arrangements: The 1986 ACAS Survey*, (London, ACAS Occasional Paper 37, 1987). For comparison with the United States see Gersuny, C., 'Erosion of Seniority Rights in the US Labor Force', 12 *Labor Studies Journal*, pp. 62–75 (1987).

27. The arguments discussed in this section are taken from Nemirow, M., 'Short-time Compensation: Some Policy Considerations', in MaCoy and Morand *op. cit.* note 1; Briggs, S., 'Allocating Available Work in a Union Environment: Layoffs vs. Work Sharing', 38 *Labor Law Journal*, pp. 650–7 (1987).

28. This is an economist's term for the idea of a preference.

29. See Nemirow, M., 'Short-time Compensation: Some Policy Considerations', in MaCoy, R. and Morand, M.J. *op. cit.* note 1.

30. 'The Duty to Plan for Fair Employment Revisited: Work Sharing in Hard Times', 28 *Rutgers Law Review*, pp. 1082–1106 (1975). See also, *inter alia*, Summers, C.W. and Love, M.C., 'Work Sharing as an Alternative to Lay-offs by Seniority: Title VII Remedies in Recession', 124 *University of Pennsylvania Law Review*, pp. 893–941 (1976); Tilly, C., 'Title VII, Seniority Discrimination, and the Incumbent Negro', 80 *Harvard Law Review*, pp. 1260–83 (1967); Anon., 'Last Hired, First Fired Layoffs and Title VII', 88 *Harvard Law Review*, pp. 1544–70 (1975); US Commission on Civil Rights, *Last Hired, First Fired*, (Washington, 1977); Burstein, P., *Discrimination, Jobs, and Politics*, (Chicago and London, The University of Chicago Press, 1985).

31. *International Brotherhood of Teamsters* v. *US* 431 US 324 (1977).

32. 'Worksharing, STC, and Affirmative Action', in MaCoy and Morand *op. cit.* note 1.

33. *Vulcan Pioneers* v. *New Jersey Department of Civil Service* 34 FEP Cases 1239 DNJ (1984). Reviewed and reversed 35 FEP 25 (1985) after the decision in *Memphis Firefighters* v. *Stotts* 104 Supreme Court 2576 (1984). In Britain unions have sought to protect customary redundancy and lay-off procedures using section 59 of the Employment Protection (Consolidation) Act 1978, which states that a dismissal is automatically unfair if an employee is selected for redundancy in contravention of a customary arrangement. The Employment Appeal Tribunal in *Suflex* v. *Thomas and Others* [1987] IRLR 435 held that 'LIFO', subject to certain exceptions, could amount to a 'customary arrangement' even if it was subject to some discretionary application by management provided it was followed with some certainty. In contrast, a redundancy selection process calling for volunteers first before the application of 'LIFO' was held not to be a customary arrangement by the Court of Appeal in *Rogers and Others* v. *Vosper Thornycroft (UK) Ltd.* [1989] IRLR 82 since the call for volunteers was part of the sifting process and not part of a selection process. An example of how an employer may be protected from a complaint of unlawful discrimination can be found in section 37AA of the Fair Employment Act 1976. The employer must be able to show that the redundancy selection procedure was agreed with a trade union, was adopted in pursuance of affirmative action and not framed by pursuance to a religious belief.

34. 104 Supreme Court 2576 (1984).

35. 431 US 324 (1977).

36. For an intensive critique of this decision see Fallon, R.H. and Weiler, P.C., '*Firefighters* v. *Stotts*: Conflicting Models of Racial Justice', *Supreme Court Review*, pp. 1–68 (1984).

37. 'Court-Ordered Hiring Quotas after *Stotts*: A Narrative on the Role of the Moralities of the Web and the Ladder in Employment Discrimination Doctrine', 20 *Harvard Civil Rights – Civil Liberties Law Review*, pp. 339–424 (1985).

38. *Griggs* v. *Duke Power Company* 401 US 424 (1971).

39. *Op. cit.* note 30.

40. Cf. Cornfield, D.B., 'Ethnic Inequality in Layoff Chances: The Impact of Unionisation on Layoff Procedure', in Lee, R.R. (ed) *Redundancy Layoffs and Plant Closures*, (London, Croom Helm, 1987).

41. (London, HMSO) Table 4.4. at p. 71.

42. See Blau, F. and Kahn, L., 'Causes and Consequences of Layoffs', 19 *Economic Inquiry*, pp. 270–96 (1981).

43. See Coyle, A. *Redundant Women*, (London, Women's Press, 1984), 'An Investigation into the Long Term Impact of Redundancy and Unemployment amongst Women', *EOC Research Bulletin*, No. 8, pp. 68–84 (1983–4); Callender, C., 'Women and the Redundancy Process: A Case Study', in Lee, R.R. (ed) *Redundancy, Layoffs and Plant Closures*, (London, Croom Helm, 1987).

44. Callender, C., 'Gender Inequality and Social Policy: Women and the Redundancy Payments Scheme', 14 *Journal of Social Policy*, pp. 189–213 (1985).

45. Earnshaw, J., *Sex Discrimination and Dismissal: A Review of Recent Case Law*, (University of Manchester, Department of Management Sciences, Occasional Paper No. 8505, 1985).

46. Equal Opportunities Commission, *Formal Investigation Report: British Steel Corporation*, (Manchester, 1981). For a discussion of the limitations of the Formal Investigation powers see Appleby, G. and Ellis, E., 'Formal Investigations: The Commission for Racial Equality and the Equal Opportunities Commission as Law Enforcement Agencies', *Public Law*, pp. 236–76 (1984).

47. Standing Committee B, col. 71, 24 April 1975.

48. [1982] IRLR 482.

49. EOC, *Towards Equality: Casebook of Decisions (1976–81)* p. 98.

50. *Ibid.* p. 61.

51. The employer did in fact obtain an Exemption Order but at a subsequent hearing the tribunal refused to order Mrs Green's re-engagement since her relations with the employer had become so difficult. Instead she was awarded compensation for unfair dismissal amounting to £1, 396.39.

52. *Protective Legislation for Women in the Member States of the European Community* COM (87) 105, 20 March 1987. See Case 222/84, *Johnston* v. *Chief Constable of Royal Ulster Constabulary* [1985] ECR 1651; Case 312/86 *Re Protection of Women: EC Commission* v. *France* [1989] 1 CMLR 408.

53. [1981] IRLR 530.

54. *Clarke and Powell* v. *Eley (IMI) Kynoch Ltd.* [1982] IRLR 482; for comment see Sedley, S., 'Pin Money: A Test Case on Discrimination against Part-time Workers', in Wallington, P. (ed) *Civil Liberties 1984*, (Oxford, Martin Robertson, 1984). See also *Allan and Others* v. *Leyland Vehicles Ltd.* Unreported SCOIT 3897/82, where only full-time service counted towards the implementation of a 'LIFO' redundancy. All the part-time workers were women and some women who had transferred from part-time to full-time work were dismissed because of 'short' service qualifications. The Scottish tribunal held that the selection criteria were discriminatory and could not be justified.

55. Unreported EAT 281/82.

56. See also *David Gold and Son (Holdings) Ltd.* v. *Mrs Noble and Others* [1980] IRLR 253.

57. *Kidd* v. *DRG (UK) Ltd.* [1985] IRLR 190.

58. Unreported SCOIT 3897/82.

59. Women's Legal Defence Fund, *Between Equals* Issue 1, Summer 1989.

60. Case 170/84, [1986] 2 CMLR 701.

61. *Greater Glasgow Health Board* v. *Carey* [1987] IRLR 484. Cf. *Hampson* v. *Department of Education and Science* [1989] IRLR 69.

62. (1985) EOC 92–140.

63. 'Retrenchment' would be the equivalent of a dismissal under British law.

64. This is known as 'reverse gate seniority' in Australia.

65. (1988) EOC 92-223.

66. See OECD, *Flexibility in the Labour Market: The Current Debate*, (OECD, Paris, 1986).

67. Department of Employment, *Employment: The Challenge for the Nation*, Cmnd 9474 (London, HMSO 1985); Metcalf, D., 'Labour Market Flexibility and Jobs: A Survey of Evidence from OECD Countries with Special Reference to Great Britain and Europe', Discussion Paper No. 254, (London, Centre For Labour Economics, London School of Economics, 1986).

68. See the discussion of *Courtaulds Northern Spinning Ltd.* v. *Sibson and the TGWU* [1988] ICR 451 in Chapter 3.

69. Hogarth, T., 'Long Distance Weekly Commuting', 8 *Policy Studies*, pp. 27–43 (1987).

70. For the most far-ranging analysis see Chapter 1 of Davies, P. and Freedland, M., *Labour Law: Text and Materials*, (London, Weidenfeld and Nicolson, 1984).

71. See, *inter alia*, Leighton, P. and Painter, R. (eds), 'Vulnerable Workers in the UK Labour Market: Some Challenges for Labour Law', 9 *Employee Relations* (Special Edition, 1987); Szyszczak, E., 'Employment Protection and Social Security', in Lewis, R. (ed) *Labour Law in Britain*, (Oxford, Basil Blackwell, 1986); Deakin, S., 'Labour Law and the Developing Employment Relationship in the UK', 10 *Cambridge Journal of Economics*, pp. 225–46 (1986); Hepple, B., 'Restructuring Employment Rights', 15 *Industrial Law Journal*, pp. 69–83 (1986); Hakim, C., 'Trends in the Flexible Workforce', 95 *Employment Gazette*, pp. 549–60 (November 1987); Disney, R. and Szyszczak, E.M., 'Part-time Work: Reply to Catherine Hakim' 18 *Industrial Law Journal*, pp. 223–8 (1989).

72. Chapter 1 of *Labour Law: Text and Materials*, (London, Weidenfeld and Nicolson, 2nd edn, 1984).

73. Disney, R. and Szyszczak, E.M. (1984), 'Protective Legislation and Part-time Employment in Britain', 22 *British Journal of Industrial Relations*, pp. 78–100 (1984); Disney, R. and Szyszczak, E.M. (1989) *op. cit.* note 71; Szyszczak, E. (1986) *op. cit.* note 71.

74. For a recent survey see 'Flexible Working', *IDS Study 407* (April 1988); ACAS *Labour Flexibility in Britain: The 1987 ACAS Survey*, (London, ACAS 1988).

75. 'The "Flexible Firm": A Model in Search of Reality (or a Policy in Search of a Practice?)', Warwick Papers in Industrial Relations No. 19 (Coventry, Industrial Relations Research Unit, School of Industrial and Business Studies, University of Warwick, December 1987).

76. See the discussion in Chapter 3. Of course there are costs involved in defending such claims but employers should not feel unduly worried by the outcome of recent litigation in this area; see *Cresswell* v. *Board of Inland Revenue* [1984] IRLR 190 and *MacPherson* v. *London Borough of Lambeth* [1988] IRLR 470.

77. *Op. cit.* note 71.

78. *Op. cit* note 74.

79. Cordova, E., 'From Full-time Wage Employment to Atypical Employment: A Major Shift in the Evolution of Labour Relations', 125 *International Labour Review*, pp. 641–57 (1986); Vranken, M., 'De-regulating the Employment Relationship: Current Trends in Europe', 7 *Comparative Labor Law*, pp. 143–65 (1986); Wise, D.C., Bernstein, A. and Cuneo, A.Z., 'Part-time Workers: Rising Numbers, Rising Discord', *Business Week*, pp. 62–3 (1 April 1985); Emerson, M., 'Regulation or Deregulation of the Labour Market', 32 *European Economic Review*, pp. 775–817 (1988).

80. See Hakim *op. cit.* note 71.

81. *Op. cit.* note 71.

82. Source: Leadbeater, C. and Lloyd, J., *In Search of Work*, (Harmondsworth, Penguin Books, 1987) at p. 135.

83. Cf. Hakim *op. cit.* note 71 and Stieber, J., 'Most US Workers Still May Be Fired under the Employment-At-Will Doctrine', 107 *Monthly Labor Review*, pp. 34–8 (1984) with Hoerr, J., Glaberson, W.G., Moskowitz, D.B., Cahan, V., Pollock, M.A. and Tasini, J., 'Beyond Unions', *Business Weekly*, pp. 72–7 (8 July 1985).

84. See, *inter alia*, Department of Employment, *Employment: The Challenge for the Nation*, Cmnd 9474 (London, HMSO 1985); Department of Trade and Industry, *Burdens on Business: Report of a Scrutiny of Administrative and Legislative Requirements*, (London, HMSO 1985); *Building Businesses, Not Barriers*, Cmnd 9794 (1986) *Releasing Enterprise*, Cm 512 (1988); *Removing Barriers to Employment*, Cm 655 (1989).

85. These ideas were put forward in *Building Businesses, Not Barriers*, Cmnd 9794 (1986).

86. Cm 540.

87. Council Resolution OJ C 2/1980 (4 January 1980); European Parliament Resolution OJ C 260/1981 (17 September 1981); OJ C 290/83 (26 October 1983).

88. See Hepple, B., 'The Crisis in EEC Labour Law', 16 *Industrial Law Journal*, pp. 69–83 (1986); Hepple, B. and Byre, A., 'EEC Labour Law in the United Kingdom', 18 *Industrial Law Journal*, pp. 129–43 (1989); Brewster, C. and Teague, P., *European Social Policy: Its Impact on the UK*, (London, IPM, 1989).

89. OJ C 128/82 (19 May 1982).

90. OJ C 62/82 (12 March 1982), amended OJ C 18/83 (22 January 1983).

91. OJ C 357/82 (10 December 1982).

92. COM (89) 248 final, Brussels, 30 May 1989; Action Programme, COM (89) 568 final, Brussels.

93. See *Maximising the Benefits, Minimising the Costs*, (London, TUC, 1988).

94. For a general discussion of the effects of European law in Britain see McCrudden, C. (ed) *Women, Employment and European Equality Legislation*, (London, Eclipse, 1988), and for Eire see Curtin, D., *Irish Employment Equality Law*, (Dublin, Round Hall Press, 1989).

95. See, for example, Case 56/88, *Re Vocational Training Programme: United Kingdom* v. *EC Council* [1989] 3 CMLR 789.

96. For comment see Disney, R. and Szyszczak, E.M., 'Protective Legislation and Part-time Employment in Britain', 22 *British Journal of Industrial Relations*, pp. 78–100 (1984).

97. A twin policy of labour market regulation has been the so-called 'privatization' of certain forms of social security provision, previously administered by the state, such as sick pay, maternity pay and pension provision. The transfer of the administration of these forms of social security has led to a much closer connection between a specific job and availability of such forms of income guarantee. Arguably one could say that it may have increased employers' *administrative* costs and perhaps led to increased rigidities in the labour market since occupational benefits have become firm-specific.

98. See Deakin, S., 'Towards a Social Europe: Social Policy and Reform Strategies after the Single European Act', 35 *Low Pay Review*, pp. 12–17 (Winter 1988/9).

7

Conclusion

The aim of this book has been to isolate and describe from a British perspective the legal regulation of an economic problem experienced in most industrialized societies: partial unemployment. What emerges from the discussion is that Britain has adopted a complex and, at times, inefficient response to the problems posed by partial unemployment. This is due largely to the particular historical development of the contract model as a way of regulating the employment relationship at a formal legal level. In some respects the common law has displayed a remarkable flexibility in adapting the contract model to accommodate changing social expectations and economic fluctuations.[1] Although this flexibility can sometimes be stretched to cover prolonged work shortages or to respond to unforeseen and unexpected dislocations in production, this response is not always favourable to employees, who seek certainty and continuity of pay. Furthermore, the interaction with basic contractual principles of collective bargaining and statutory employment protection rights, which are contingent upon a continuous employment relationship, has resulted in a complex system of regulation. One consequence, illustrated by the case law throughout the book, is that employers and employees often respond to work shortages in a practical and informal manner which may have adverse consequences for employment protection guarantees.

Despite the recurrence of economic recessions, the state response has been tentative and temporary. The result is a web of overlapping schemes to regulate and compensate for partial unemployment. These schemes do not utilize the available resources efficiently and do not provide an even distribution of employment protection and financial compensation for all sectors of the workforce. These limitations of the British regulation of partial unemployment raise the question of whether the present system could be improved to respond more equitably and efficiently to work shortages in the future.

Looking first at the existing schemes, certain modifications could be made to increase their efficiency and decrease their complexity. Statutory guarantee payments, for example, are a useful means whereby employers can respond to a temporary crisis and, as argued in Chapter 5, they play an important part in underpinning the contract of employment for many vulnerable workers. To provide adequate financial protection for such workers, however, the amount and duration of statutory guarantee payments would need to be improved and the interaction with the social security system dovetailed. Alternatively, collective bargaining might be extended to embrace workers presently outside the scope of the more generous collective guaranteed week agreements. Given the original fears surrounding the introduction of statutory guarantee payments, the decline in coverage by collective agreements in recent years and the current political and economic climate, it is unlikely that employers or the present government would agree to such an extension of basic employment rights, arguing that the increased costs would lead to rigidities in the labour market.

Chapter 4 made a case for the redundancy-lay-off provisions to be retained since they provide lump-sum financial compensation and give a worker some bargaining power against an employer implementing a prolonged lay-off. They are important from a different perspective in that they prevent the employer from evading the statutory redundancy payment obligations. The complex legal procedures and the need to terminate the employment relationship have made this an unattractive remedy for employees. Equally, this form of regulation has few advantages for employers, who would prefer to retain an interest in skilled labour and who must now bear the full cost of redundancy compensation. To remedy these deficiencies, the procedures regulating redundancy-lay-off could be simplified and employers could once again be reimbursed some or all of the cost of the redundancy compensation from a Redundancy Fund. To prevent abuse of such a system and to answer the criticisms of cross-subsidization, a careful inquiry could be made by the Department of Employment as to the reasons for the redundancy and, as with the United States' lay-off system, payments from the Fund could be experience-rated. This would lead to high transaction costs.

Within academic circles in the United States and political circles in Western Europe, worksharing has emerged as an attractive proposition, both from a civil liberties perspective and an economic perspective. Worksharing does not fit easily into the British industrial relations environment and yet the concept raises some policy issues at present unarticulated in Britain. These are the issues as to how far seniority systems should be protected, how far there should be a duty upon employers to avoid unemployment, and whether available work should be shared out not only between workers who have jobs but also those workers who do not. We have seen that Britain has experienced voluntary and informal worksharing in the past. Sometimes this was compensated through trade union, public or occupational unemployment benefit systems, sometimes it went uncompensated and workers shared the loss of income. Chapter 5 argued that Britain's experiment of state-regulated worksharing under the Temporary Short-time Working Compensation Scheme was not entirely successful. The measures were temporary, they did not have a wide industrial distribution and were not efficient in terms of their projected aim of averting redundancies. This was probably because the subsidy was granted mainly to the declining manufacturing sector of industry and was inextricably linked to an imminent redundancy situation. A permanent scheme of work-sharing would need to be more widespread involving intervention at an earlier stage. Such a scheme would, of course, need safeguards against the abuse of employment subsidies; that is, a method of administration to check that the subsidy was necessary and that the behaviour of the firm was changed by the subsidy. Presumably the Department of Employment would be asked to take a greater involvement in the management of individual firms, to date a role which it has refused to undertake in any significant way. Ideally a new scheme would engage trade unions and other employee representatives in consultation processes on how to respond to proposals for worksharing to a greater degree than the present redundancy consultation procedures allow.[2] It may be that the adoption of a Charter of Fundamental Social Rights by the European Community will facilitate a greater role for employees and trade unions in the economic decision making process of the firm.

The major drawback of retaining the general social security scheme to regulate and compensate for partial unemployment is that the scheme is not designed for the situation of partial unemployment. In particular, it is not easy to avoid collusion between employer and employee to maximize payments through the use of the social security system rather than payments through the firm, as in the inter-war period described in Chapter 4. This could be remedied by establishing a separate social security scheme for partial unemployment which provided the necessary flexibility for employers and employees to adapt to their particular work shortage. The problems raised by abuse of the system and cross-subsidization arguments could again be met by experience-rating remedies: employers who drew excessively on the scheme would be penalized through higher National Insurance contributions. Given the current climate of 'privatization' of social security and the attempts to reduce public expenditure in this area it is unlikely that the present government would seriously consider additional social security schemes. An alternative course of action, however, might be to follow the example of statutory sick pay and statutory maternity pay and transfer the *administration* of social security for partial unemployment to employers.[3] Such a system was implemented in the 'Three-Day Week' crisis of 1974.

The problem with approaching the regulation of partial unemployment in this manner is the question of whether this is merely a stop-gap solution. For it does not tackle the underlying weakness of the British approach to partial unemployment – the duplication and the complexity arising from the interaction of so many forms of regulation which leaves many workers without financial or employment protection during protracted work shortages. There are, therefore, many attractions in the establishment of one specific partial unemployment scheme. This is reinforced by the relatively successful use of such schemes in Italy and Germany.

The idea of a Short-time Working Fund was canvassed in 1978 but the proposals have been forgotten.[4] The establishment and administration of such a Fund would not be simple: flexibility would be one of the key elements since one of the difficulties of the Cassa Integrazione Guadagni is the rigidity of legal definitions and regulations in responding to different economic situations. The criticisms of the use of discretion in the Temporary Short-time Working Compensation Scheme in Chapter 5 have alerted lawyers to the need to combine flexibility with the control of discretionary powers by those who administer and those who utilize such a scheme. Equally the old problems of labour hoarding, abuse and cross-subsidization would need to be tackled. If such a Fund were financed by contributions from all employers and employees the same criticisms that were levelled against the use of the social security scheme to finance partial unemployment would remain. It may be that separate systems of funding are necessary to cover specific regions or certain industrial sectors or the use of experience-rating is brought into play, perhaps with some concessions to isolate excessive claims that are made by employers claiming that the work ·shortages are due to factors outside their control. Equally the issue of whether contributions to the Fund should be compulsory raises problems. Certain employers might wish to 'contract-out' of such a Fund, arguing that short-time working is not a risk they feel prone to or that they wish to negotiate a collective agreement more suitable to their particular experience of partial unemployment. While Bourn argues that in general the exemption provisions of the Employment Protection (Consolidation) Act 1978 were relatively under-used, they do provide a precedent for dealing with this particular argument.[5] Indeed, it is interesting to note the number of guaranteed week agreements exempted under section 18 of the Employment Protection (Consolidation) Act 1978 discussed in Chapter 5. A disadvantage of retaining contracting-out provisions is that it would continue the number and complexity of partial unemployment schemes and reduce the amount of income available to finance the Short-time Working Fund. And although such a Fund would seem to solve many practical problems in the availability and administration of compensation for work shortages certain conceptual problems remain. For example, the use of such a Fund blurs some of the issues as to how we should categorize partial unemployment. Is it to be seen as a labour market regulation problem or is it a wider social security issue? If we categorize partial unemployment as being a labour market issue, explicit and implicit contract theory would suggest that firms should organize the regulation of partial unemployment since they want to retain their investment in skilled labour. If partial unemployment is viewed as a social security issue then the case can be made for state regulation and a sharing of the cost of compensation for partial unemployment.

Some conceptual purity is retained, however, by drawing the analogy with the classification of the existing statutory guarantee payment provisions which view partial unemployment as an aspect of employment protection relating to the *content* of the employment relationship. Other risks associated with protecting earnings, such as sick pay and maternity pay, have been 'privatized' in that they are administered by the employer, who receives reimbursement of the payments through the National Insurance system.[6] Partial unemployment could be compensated for in a similar way using a special Short-time Working Fund to finance the employers' reimbursements.

Thus, the definition of, and policy problems raised by, partial unemployment need to be carefully understood in any future responses by employers, trade unions and the state. One of the current political responses to work shortages is a strategy aimed at deregulating the labour market through a mix of flexibility in employment protection guarantees and flexibility in wage fixing. Chapter 1 outlined the reasons why such a policy is not an easy solution to apply to the problems raised by work shortages. The general debate on the regulation of the labour market, however, does have more far-reaching implications for the future attitude towards the regulation of partial unemployment. Particularly in political and economic circles the issue of partial unemployment, as identified in this book has become intertwined with the wider issues of adapting industrialized societies to the problems arising from lengthy economic depressions. The state has accepted a more active role in directing the labour market and there is more public scrutiny of legal, economic and fiscal measures designed to 'reorganize' working time. The problem with this debate is that partial unemployment has become conflated with general macroeconomic solutions to cyclical depressions and an important feature of partial unemployment is suppressed: this is the fact that partial unemployment can occur as a result of a wide variety of factors and *not* only general economic recessions. If employers are to be given the flexibility to respond to the particular problems faced by their industry or to unanticipated dislocations in production, and workers are to be given adequate protection in terms of job security and compensation, this particular aspect of partial unemployment must be explicitly recognized.

NOTES

1. See for example *Cresswell* v. *Board of Inland Revenue* [1984] IRLR 190.
2. See *Moon* v. *Homeworthy Furniture (Northern) Ltd.* [1977] ICR 117. See also the inability of individual employees to challenge business reorganizations under the unfair dismissal provisions, for example, *Hollister* v. *National Farmers' Union* [1979] ICR 542; Collins, H. 'Dismissal for Economic Reasons', 14 *Industrial Law Journal*, pp. 61–4 (1985). Note *Litster* v. *Forth Dry Dock Engineering* [1989] IRLR 161, noted by Szyszczak, E., 52 *Modern Law Review*, pp. 691–704 (1989).

3. Particularly in relation to the implementation of statutory sick pay employers have not encountered many administrative problems in introducing the scheme and in many instances the statutory scheme has prompted employers to introduce further occupational sick pay schemes; see Disney, R., *Statutory Sick Pay: An Evaluation*, IFS Working Paper Series No. 87/1, January 1987; Incomes Data Services, 'Sick Pay and SSP' *IDS Study 316* (June 1984).

4. Partington, T.M., 'Compensation for Short-time Working: New Government Proposals', 7 *Industrial Law Journal*, pp. 187–90 (1978).

5. Bourn, C.J., 'Statutory Exemptions for Collective Agreements', 8 *Industrial Law Journal*, pp. 85–9 (1979).

6. See Szyszczak, E., 'Employment Protection and Social Security', in Lewis, R., (ed) *Labour Law in Britain*, (Oxford, Basil Blackwell, 1986).

Appendix A

LEVELS AND VARIATION OF STATUTORY GUARANTEE PAYMENTS[1]

For any day before 1 February 1978 £6.00; Section 159(1) Schedule 15 para 6, Employment Protection (Consolidation) Act 1978.

For the period 1 February 1978 to 31 January 1979 £6.60 per day; The Employment Protection (Variation of Limits) Order 1977 (SI 1977 No. 2031).

For the period 1 February 1979 to 31 January 1980 £7.25 per day; The Employment Protection (Variation of Limits) Order 1978 (SI 1978 No. 1777).

For the period 1 February 1980 to 31 January 1981 £8.00 per day.[2] The Employment Protection (Variation of Limits) Order 1979 (SI 1979 No. 1722).

For the period 1 February 1981 to 31 January 1982 £8.75 per day; The Employment Protection (Variation of Limits) Order 1980, (SI 1980 No. 2019).

For the period 1 February 1982 to 31 January 1983 £9.15 per day; The Employment Protection (Variation of Limits) Order 1982 (SI 1982 No. 77).

For the period 1 February 1983 to 31 January 1984 £9.50 per day; The Employment Protection (Variation of Limits) (No. 2) Order 1982 (SI 1982 No. 1866).

For the period 1 February 1984 to 31 March 1985 £10.00 per day; The Employment Protection (Variation of Limits) Order 1983 (SI 1983 No. 1962).

For the period 1 April 1985 to 31 March 1986 £10.50 per day; The Employment Protection (Variation of Limits) Order 1984 (SI 1984 No. 2019).

For the period 1 April 1986 to 31 March 1987 £10.70 per day; The Employment Protection (Variation of Limits) Order 1985 (SI 1985 No. 2032).

For the period 1 April 1987 to 31 March 1988 £10.90 per day; The Employ-ment Protection (Variation of Limits) Order 1986 (SI 1986 No. 2283).

For the period 1 April 1988 to 31 March 1989 £11.30 per day; The Employ-ment Protection (Variation of Limits) Order 1987 (SI 1988/276).

For the period 1 April 1989 to 31 March 1990 £11.85 per day; The Employ-ment Protection (Variation of Limits) Order 1989 (SI 1989/526).

NOTES

1. Section 15 Employment Protection (Consolidation) Act 1978 gives the Secretary of State the power to vary the limits of guarantee pay (s.15(1)) and also the relevant entitlement periods (s.15(2)). The latter were amended by section 14 Employment Act 1980. The original fixed quarters beginning on 1 February, 1 May, 1 August and 1 November were substituted by a rolling three month period (in effect from 1 October 1980).

Section 148(2) Employment Protection (Consolidation) Act 1978 sets out a list of factors to be considered by the Secretary of State when reviewing the limits in section 15 EPCA 1978:

(a) the general level of earnings obtaining in Great Britain at the time of the review.

(b) the national economic situation as a whole; and

(c) other matters as he thinks relevant.

If the Secretary of State decides to vary the limits a draft order must be laid before Parliament and approved by Resolution of each House of Parliament. If the Secretary of State decides *not* to vary the limits he merely lays a report before Parliament, thus the matter cannot be debated. Section 148(6) allows the Secretary of State to conduct further reviews in addition to the annual review in order to assess whether the limits in s.15 EPCA should be varied. However, if a negative decision is reached there is no obligation to publish reasons.

2. Section 14(1) Employment Act 1980 does not have any effect on workless days falling before 1 October 1980 except in so far as they are relevant to determining the entitlement to guarantee pay.

Appendix B

GUARANTEE PAYMENTS EXEMPTION ORDERS

Section 18 Employment Protection (Consolidation) Act 1978 (Derivation section 28 Employment Protection Act 1975). Exemption Orders made in 1977 and 1978 have effect by virtue of section 159(1) Schedule 15 para 1 EP(C)A 1978. Those made subsequently were made and have effect under section 18 EP(C)A 1978.

No. 1	SI 1977/156	Federation of Civil Engineering Contractors, and TGWU, GMWU, UCATT (in operation 2 February 1977).
No. 2	SI 1977/157	Federation of Demolition Contractors Ltd., and GMWU, TGWU, UCATT (in operation 2 February 1977).
No. 3	SI 1977/158	Federation of Building Trades Employers, National Federation of Roofing Contractors, and UCATT, TGWU, GMWU, FTATU (in operation 2 February 1977).
No. 4	SI 1977/208	Wire and Wire Rope Employers Association, Institute of Iron and Steel Wire Manufacturers, and ASWDKW, NUGMW, TGWU (in operation 14 February 1977).
No. 5	SI 1977/902	British Footwear Manufacturers Federation, and NUFLAT (in operation 4 July 1977).
No. 6	SI 1977/1096	National Federation of Master Steeplejacks and Lightning Conductor Engineers, and UCATT (Steeplejack Section) (in operation 1 August 1977).
No. 7	SI 1977/1158	Two agreements (i) Process and General Workers: British Paper and Board Industry Federation, and SOGAT, TGWU; (ii) Skilled Craftsmen: BPBIF, and AUEW (Engineering Section), EETPU, TGWU (Power and Engineering Group), UCATT (in operation 15 August 1977).

No. 8   SI 1977/1322   Smiths Food Group (Division of Toms Food Ltd., a subsidiary of General Mills Inc. (USA)), and TGWU (covering four establishments) (in operation 5 September 1977).

No. 9   SI 1977/1349   Cut Sole Associates, British Leather Federation, and NUFLAT (in operation 8 September 1977).

No. 10   SI 1977/1522   Fireboard Packing Case Employers Association and GMWU, SOGAT (in operation 18 October 1977).

No. 11   SI 1977/1523   Henry Wiggin and Co. Ltd., and GMWU (in operation 21 October 1977).

No. 12   SI 1977/1583   Two Agreements (i) Labourers: Refractory Users Federation and GMWU, TGWU, UCATT (Builders' Section). (ii) Bricklayers and Masons: RUF and UCATT (Builders' Section) (in operation 1 November 1977).

No. 13   SI 1977/1601   Multiwall Sack Manufacturers Employers' Association and NUGMW, SOGAT, TGWU (in operation 4 November 1977).

No. 14   SI 1977/2032   Tudor Food Products (division of Tom Foods Ltd., Subsidiary of General Mills Inc. (USA)) and GMWU (in operation 11 January 1978).

No. 15   SI 1978/153   British Carton Association and GMWU, SOGAT (in operation 14 March 1978).

No. 16   SI 1978/429   Two agreements: (i) Henry Wiggin and Co. Ltd., and EETUP. (ii) H.W. & Co. Ltd., and AUEW (in operation 19 April 1978).

No. 17   SI 1978/737   Scheme of Conditions of Service of the National Joint Council for Workshops for the Blind: Association of County Councils, Association of Metropolitan Authorities, Scottish Councils, National Association of Industries for the Blind and Disabled and the National League of the Blind and Disabled (in operation 27 June 1978).

No. 18   SI 1978/826   Employers Federation of Card Clothing Manufacturers and Card Dressers Society, ASWDKW, CSMTS (in operation 13 July 1978).

No. 19   SI 1979/1403   Employer's side of NJCMVRRI (repres. Motor Agent's Assoc. Ltd., and Scottish Motor Trade Assoc. Ltd.,) and Trade Union side of NJCMVRRI (repres. by Vehicle Building and Automotive Group of TGWU (Engineering Section)), GMWU, EETPU, NUSMW, CHDE (in operation 14 December 1979).

No. 20   SI 1980/1715   Federation of Master Builders and TGWU (in operation 22 November 1980).

No. 21   SI 1981/6   Contractors Plant Association and TGWU (Construction and Crafts Section), GMWU, UCATT (in operation 23 February 1981).

No. 22   SI 1983/571   Substantive Agreement of the Joint Negotiating Council for the UK Confectionery Division of Rowntree Mackintosh plc., and GMBATU, TGWU, USDAW (in operation 13 April 1983).

No. 23   SI 1987/1757   The Wire and Wire Rope Employers' Association and Wire Workers Union, GMBATU, TGWU (in operation 12 November 1987).

Appendix C

EXEMPTED GUARANTEED WEEK AGREEMENTS

Examples of guaranteed week agreements granted an exemption under section 18 of the Employment Protection (Consolidation) Act 1978.

1977/1322   Smiths Food Group (Division of Toms Food Ltd; a subsidiary of General Mills Inc. (USA)) and the TGWU.

1980/1715   The Federation of Master Builders and the TGWU.

1981/6   Contractors Plant Association and the TGWU, GMWU and UCATT.

1987/1757   Wire and Wire Rope Employers' Association and the Wire Workers' Union, GMBATU and the TGWU.

(*See opposite*. The Statutory Instruments reproduced on pp. 177–199 are British Crown Copyright.)

1977 No. 1322

TERMS AND CONDITIONS OF EMPLOYMENT

The Guarantee Payments (Exemption) (No. 8) Order 1977

Made –	*30th July 1977*
Coming into Operation	*5th September 1977*

Whereas the four Agreements between the Smiths Food Group (a division of Toms Foods Ltd.) and the Transport and General Workers' Union relating respectively to the division's establishments at –

19 Copse Road, Fleetwood;
Caistor Road, Great Yarmouth;
224 Southampton Road, Paulsgrove, Portsmouth;
Stockport Road, Cheadle Heath, Stockport

are collective agreements each of which makes provision whereby employees to whom the said agreement relates have a right to guaranteed remuneration:

And whereas the parties to each of the said collective agreements (whose descriptions are set out in Schedule 1 to this Order) have all made application to the Secretary of State under section 28(1) of the Employment Protection Act 1975**(a)** ('the Act'):

And whereas the Secretary of State having regard to the provision of each of the agreements (which so far as are material are set out in Schedule 2 to this Order) is satisfied that section 22 of the Act should not apply to those employees:

And whereas each of the said agreements complies with section 28(4) of the Act:

Now, therefore, the Secretary of State in exercise of the powers conferred on him as the appropriate Minister under section 28(1) of the Act and of all other powers enabling him in that behalf, hereby makes the following Order: –

Citation and commencement

1. This Order may be cited as the Guarantee Payments (Exemption) (No. 8) Order 1977 and shall come into operation on 5th September 1977.

Interpretation

2. – (1) The Interpretation Act 1889**(b)** shall apply to the interpretation of this Order as it applies to the interpretation of an Act of Parliament.

(2) The 'exempted agreements' are the agreements referred to in the preamble above.

(a) 1975 c. 71.   (b) 1889 c. 63.

Exemption

3. Section 22 of the Act shall not apply to any person who is an employee to whom an exempted agreement relates.

Signed by order of the Secretary of State.
30th July 1977.

Harold Walker,
Minister of State,
Department of Employment

SCHEDULE 1

Parties to the Collective Agreements

1. *Representing Employers*:

    the Smiths Food Group, a division of Toms Foods Ltd., a subsidiary of General Mills Inc. (USA).

2. *Representing Employees*:

    the Transport and General Workers' Union.

SCHEDULE 2
Material Provisions of Exempted Agreements

A.   THE FLEETWOOD AGREEMENT
Short Time Working Agreement

STAGE 1

The Company will seek to avoid lay off, short time working or redundancy by allowing normal wastage to reduce production capacity.

The Company will inform the stewards at an establishment where this 'run down' is taking place and will provide them with such information as to anticipated time scale and size of run down as is reasonable in the circumstances.

The Company will expect the remaining employees to work flexibly so as to maintain a balanced work force. When this results in an employee being required to accept work of a lower grade (e.g. machine minder to work as a packer) the higher rate of pay will be maintained for up to six weeks and thereafter will be reduced to that appropriate to the lower grade. Selection of people for work at a lower grade will be on a basis of length of service in the higher grade.

STAGE 2

Should reduction in production capacity effected by Stage 1 be insufficient to meet the reduced production requirement, the Company will give notice of its intention to work a short week or operate a lay off. Selection for lay off being on a basis of length of service whilst maintaining a balanced workforce. Consideration being given to short time or lay off of part time employees before full time employees are affected.

To protect the earnings of employees affected by this stage the Company will pay a basic day's wages for up to a total of five days of short time or lay off cumulative in any calendar quarter (1st January to 31st March, 1st April to 30th June, 1st July to 30th September, 1st October to 31st December). Before implementing short time working or lay off at an establishment the Company will discuss the matter with the shop stewards at least one week before it is intended to operate the short week or lay off.

QUALIFICATIONS FOR AND CALCULATION OF PAYMENT UNDER STAGE 2

Payment in respect of short time, that is to say where a short working week of less than five days is to be operated, or lay off, that is to say when employees are laid off for a period in excess of five consecutive days' duration will be made to employees who would normally have been at work on the day or days in question provided that the employee has a minimum of four weeks' service at the time of the start of the period of short time working or lay off.

No payment will be due to an employee who refuses reasonable alternative work within their competence for the day or days in question, selection for alternative work being at the discretion of management.

Any person absent from the establishment during a period of short time working or lay off due to certified sickness, holiday or prior permission without pay shall be excluded from benefit under this agreement.

No payment will be due if the short time or lay off results from Industrial Action at any of the Group's establishments. A basic day's wages shall be eight hours wages inclusive of any shift premium. The wage rate being that which would have been paid had the employee been at work. In the case of part time employees working less than a normal eight hour shift a day's work shall be the hours that they are normally contracted to work on that day.

APPEAL

Any employee who feels that he/she has been treated unfairly under the terms of this agreement shall have the right of appeal in accordance with the Company's grievance procedure. In addition, the employee has, in every case, the right to present a case to an industrial tribunal that the Company has failed to make a payment, or part of a payment, to which the employee is entitled under this agreement.

B. THE GREAT YARMOUTH AGREEMENT

S<small>HORT</small> T<small>IME</small> W<small>ORKING</small> A<small>GREEMENT</small>

STAGE 1

The Company will seek to avoid lay off, short time working or redundancy by allowing normal wastage to reduce production capacity.

The Company will inform the stewards at an establishment where this 'run down' is taking place and will provide them with such information as to anticipated time scale and size of run down as is reasonable in the circumstances.

The Company will expect the remaining employees to work flexibly so as to maintain a balanced work force. When this results in an employee being required to accept work of a lower grade (e.g. machine minder to work as a packer) the higher rate of pay will be maintained for up to six weeks and thereafter will be reduced to that appropriate to the lower grade. Selection of people for work at a lower grade will be on a basis of length of service in the higher grade.

STAGE 2

Should reduction in production capacity effected by stage 1 be insufficient to meet the reduced production requirement, the Company will give notice of its intention to work a short week or operate a lay off. Selection for lay off being on a basis of length of service whilst maintaining a balanced workforce.

To protect the earnings of employees affected by this stage the Company will pay a basic day's wages for up to a total of five days of short time or lay off cumulative in any calendar quarter (1st January to 31st March, 1st April to 30th June, 1st July to 30th September, 1st October to 31st December). Before implementing short time working or lay off at Gt. Yarmouth the Company will discuss the matter with the shop stewards at least one week before it is intended to operate the short week or lay off.

QUALIFICATIONS FOR AND CALCULATION OF PAYMENT UNDER STAGE 2

Payment in respect of short time, that is to say where a short working week of less than five days is to be operated, or lay off, that is to say when employees are laid off for a period in excess of five consecutive days' duration will be made to employees who would normally have been at work on the day or days in question provided that the employee has a minimum of four weeks' service at the time of the start of the period of short time working or lay off.

No payment will be due to an employee who refuses reasonable alternative work within their competence for the day or days in question, selection for alternative work being at the discretion of management.

Any person absent from the establishment during a period of short time working or lay off due to certified sickness, holiday or prior permission without pay shall be excluded from this agreement.

No payment will be due if the short time or lay off results from Industrial Action at any of the Group's establishments. A basic day's wages shall be eight hours' wages inclusive of any shift premium. The wage rate being that which would have been paid had the employee been at work. In the case of part time employees working less than a normal eight hour shift a day's work shall be the hours that they are normally contracted to work on that day.

APPEAL

Any employee who feels that he/she has been treated unfairly under the terms of this agreement shall have the right of appeal in accordance with the Company's grievance procedure. In addition, the employee has, in every case, the right to present a case to an industrial tribunal that the Company has failed to make a payment, or part of a payment, to which the employee is entitled under this agreement.

C. THE PAULSGROVE AGREEMENT

SHORT TIME WORKING AGREEMENT

STAGE 1

The Company will seek to avoid lay off, short time working or redundancy by allowing normal wastage to reduce production capacity.

The Company will inform the stewards at an establishment where this 'run down' is taking place and will provide them with such information as to anticipated time scale and size of run down as is reasonable in the circumstances.

The Company will expect the remaining employees to work flexibly so as to maintain a balanced work force. When this results in an employee being required to accept work of a lower grade (e.g. machine minder to work as a packer) the higher rate of pay will be maintained for up to six weeks and thereafter will be reduced to that appropriate to the lower grade. Selection of people for work at a lower grade will be on a basis of length of service in the higher grade.

STAGE 2

Should the policy of 'run down' be inadequate to meet the reduced production requirements the Company will reduce the working week, or lay off, all or part of the part time labour force in the latter case selection will be on the basis of length of service.

The shop stewards being kept fully informed of the situation prior to any action being taken to implement cuts in accordance with this state.

STAGE 3

Should reduction in production capacity effected by stages 1 and 2 be insufficient to meet the reduced production requirement, the Company will give notice of its intention to work a short week or operate a lay off of its full time permanent employees.

To protect the earnings of employees affected by either stages 2 or 3 the Company will pay a basic day's wages for up to a total of five days of short time or lay off cumulative in any calendar quarter (1st January to 31st March, 1st April to 30th June, 1st July to 30th September, 1st October to 31st December). Before implementing short time working or lay off at any establishment the Company will discuss the matter with the shop stewards at least one week before it is intended to operate the short week or lay off.

QUALIFICATIONS FOR AND CALCULATION OF PAYMENT UNDER STAGES 2 AND 3

Payment in respect of short time, that is to say where a short working week of less than five days is to be operated, or lay off, that is to say when employees are laid off for a period in excess of five consecutive days' duration will be made to employees who would normally have been at work on the day or days in question provided that the employee has a minimum of four weeks' service at the time of the start of the period of short time working or lay off.

No payment will be due to an employee who refuses reasonable alternative work within their competence for the day or days in question, selection for alternative work being at the discretion of management.

Any person absent from the establishment during a period of short time working or lay off due to certified sickness, holiday or prior permission without pay shall be excluded from this agreement.

No payment will be due if the short time or lay off results from Industrial Action at any of the Group's establishments. A basic day's wages shall be eight hours wages inclusive of any shift premium. The wage rate being that which would have been paid had the employee been at work. In the case of part time employees working less than a normal eight hour shift a day's work shall be the hours that they are normally contracted to work on that day.

APPEAL

Any employee who feels that he/she has been treated unfairly under the terms of this agreement shall have the right of appeal in accordance with the Company's grievance procedure. In addition, the employee has, in every case, the right to present a case to an industrial tribunal that the Company has failed to make a payment, or part of a payment, to which the employee is entitled under this agreement.

D.   THE STOCKPORT AGREEMENT

SHORT TIME WORKING AGREEMENT

STAGE 1

The Company will seek to avoid lay off, short time working or redundancy by allowing normal wastage to reduce production capacity.

The Company will inform the stewards at an establishment where this 'run down' is taking place and will provide them with such information as to anticipated time scale and size of run down as is reasonable in the circumstances.

The Company will expect the remaining employees to work flexibly so as to maintain a balanced work force. When this results in an employee being required to accept work of a lower grade (e.g. machine minder to work as a packer) the higher rate of pay will be maintained for up to six weeks and thereafter will be reduced to that appropriate to the lower grade. Selection of people for work at a lower grade will be on a basis of length of service in the higher grade.

STAGE 2

Should reduction in production capacity effected by stage 1 be insufficient to meet the reduced production requirement, the Company will give notice of its intention to work a short week or operate a lay off. Selection for lay off being on a basis of length of service whilst maintaining a balanced workforce.

To protect the earnings of employees affected by this stage the Company will pay a basic day's wages for up to a total of five days of short time or lay off cumulative in any calendar quarter (1st January to 31st March, 1st April to 30th June, 1st July to 30th September, 1st October to 31st December). Before implementing short time working or lay off at an establishment the Company will discuss the matter with the shop stewards at least one week before it is intended to operate the short week or lay off.

QUALIFICATIONS FOR AND CALCULATION OF PAYMENT UNDER STAGE 2

Payment in respect of short time, that is to say where a short working week of less than five days is to be operated, or lay off, that is to say when employees are laid off for a period in excess of five consecutive days' duration will be made to employees who would normally have been at work on the day or days in question provided that the employee has a minimum of four weeks' service at the time of the start of the period of short time working or lay off.

No payment will be due to an employee who refuses reasonable alternative work within their competence for the day or days in question, selection for alternative work being at the discretion of management.

Any person absent from the establishment during a period of short time working or lay off due to certified sickness, holiday or prior permission without pay shall be excluded from this agreement.

No payment will be due if the short time or lay off results from Industrial Action at any of the Group's establishments. A basic day's wages shall be eight hours wages inclusive of any shift premium. The wage rate being that which would have been paid had the employee been at work. In the case of part time employees working less than a normal eight hour shift a day's work shall be the hours that they are normally contracted to work on that day.

APPEAL

Any employee who feels that he/she has been treated unfairly under the terms of this agreement shall have the right of appeal in accordance with the Company's grievance procedure. In addition, the employee has, in every case, the right to present a case to an industrial tribunal that the Company has failed to make a payment, or part of a payment, to which the employee is entitled under this agreement.

EXPLANATORY NOTE

(This Note is not part of the Order.)

This Order excludes from the operation of section 22 of the Employment Protection Act 1975 employees at four establishments of the Smiths Foods Group (a division of Toms Foods Ltd.) being employees to whom collective agreements with the Transport and General Workers' Union relate.

Copies of the Agreements are available for inspection between 10.0 a.m. and noon and between 2 p.m. and 5 p.m. (Monday to Friday) at the offices of the Department of Employment, 8 St. James's Square, London SW1Y 4JB.

1980 No. 1715

TERMS AND CONDITIONS OF EMPLOYMENT

The Guarantee Payments (Exemption) (No. 20) Order 1980

Made	*7th November 1980*
Coming into Operation	*22nd December 1980*

Whereas the Working Rule Agreement of the Building and Allied Trades Joint Industrial Council made between the parties described in Schedule 1 to this Order on 23rd April 1980 and set out in a document entitled 'CONSTITUTION and WORKING RULE AGREEMENT' is a collective agreement ('the collective agreement'):

And whereas the collective agreement makes provision whereby employees to whom that agreement relates have a right to guaranteed remuneration:

And whereas all the parties to the collective agreement made application to the Secretary of State under section 18(1) of the Employment Protection (Consolidation) Act 1978(**a**) ('the Act'):

And whereas the collective agreement complies with section 18(4) of the Act:

And whereas the Secretary of State, having regard to the provisions of the collective agreement (which so far as are material are set out in Schedule 2 to this Order), is satisfied that section 12 of the Act should not apply to those employees:

Now, therefore, the Secretary of State, in exercise of the powers conferred on him as the appropriate Minister under section 18(1) of the Act and of all other powers enabling him in that behalf, hereby makes the following Order: –

Citation and commencement

1. This Order may be cited as the Guarantee Payments (Exemption) (No. 20) Order 1980 and shall come into operation on 22nd December 1980.

Exemption

2. Section 12 of the Act shall not apply to any employee to whom the collective agreement relates.

Signed by order of the Secretary of State.
7th November 1980.

P. B. B. Mayhew,
Joint Parliamentary Under Secretary of State,
Department of Employment.

(a) 1978 c. 44

SCHEDULE 1

PARTIES TO THE COLLECTIVE AGREEMENT

1. *Representing employers:*

The Federation of Master Builders.

2. *Representing employees:*

The Transport and General Workers Union.

SCHEDULE 2

MATERIAL PROVISIONS OF THE COLLECTIVE AGREEMENT

WORKING RULE 9—Guaranteed Week

Each operative shall be guaranteed 40 hours employment in each pay week paid at the appropriate standard rate of wages calculated by five days at eight hours per day, provided always that he is available for work during the normal working hours of each day.

In any week in which a public holiday falls, the period of guarantee shall be reduced in proportion to the period of public holiday. In the event of inclement weather, the guaranteed payment shall be made provided always that the operative maintains himself on site for working; that he is willing and able to perform satisfactorily such alternative work that he may be reasonably given and that he complies with the instructions of the employer as to when during normal working hours work is to be carried out, interrupted or resumed.

If an operative fails to keep himself available for work at any time during the normal working hours, unless otherwise instructed, he shall be deemed not to have kept himself available for any portion of the day. Where inclement weather persists and the operative is unable to work for any part of the guaranteed pay week, then the employer may give notice to suspend the guarantee and require the operative to register for unemployment benefit. An operative shall not be entitled to guaranteed payment for any time during a pay week in which his work is interrupted by virtue of a trade dispute involving himself or other operatives on his particular site.

Should any dispute arise over the payment of the Guaranteed Week provisions which is not capable of solution through the Conciliation Procedure (outlined in Appendix 'A'), the operative shall have the right to present his complaint to an industrial tribunal in accordance with S.18(4)(*b*) of the Employment Protection (Consolidation) Act 1978.

APPENDIX 'A'
CONCILIATION PROCEDURE

Parties to this Agreement have agreed that BATJIC should provide a means of conciliation in any industrial relations problem that arises between an affiliated employer and the trade union. Conciliation procedures under this Agreement shall not come into effect until the internal company procedure has been exhausted. It is the intention of the parties that the Regional Joint Councils should have the responsibility of providing conciliation in their areas and matters should only be referred to the National Council for conciliation where the regions have been unable to reach a mutual finding. It is emphasised that whilst the procedures are in operation there should be no strike, lock-out or other coercive action by either of the parties to the dispute.

The following are rules by which a Conciliation Panel hearing shall be conducted, either at Regional or National level:

(*a*) When the internal procedure of the company is exhausted it shall be open to either party to make application for a Regional conciliation Panel hearing by applying to the appropriate joint secretary. In certain circumstances it may be appropriate for a joint reference.

(*b*) Meetings of the Conciliation Panel should be convened at a time, date and place agreed by the joint secretaries and the Terms of Reference notified to the members of the Panel.

(*c*) The Conciliation Panel should consist of not less than three members from each side, including the joint secretaries and the Chairman, who shall have an independent vote.

(*d*) Written evidence should be submitted which may then be supplemented verbally at the hearing. The complainant party shall give evidence first, following which there may be questions from the respondent party.

(*e*) The respondent party shall then submit evidence after which the complainant may ask questions.

(*f*) The Conciliation Panel members will then have the right to question both parties on the evidence given in order to make their decision but there shall be no right of the parties to rechallenge the evidence of the other party.

(*g*) When all the evidence has been obtained, the parties shall withdraw from the hearing and the Conciliation Panel will determine its findings; each side voting independently to achieve an agreed finding.

(*h*) The decision will be forwarded to the parties to the hearing in writing.

EXPLANATORY NOTE

(This Note is not part of the Order.)

This Order, which comes into operation on 22nd December 1980, excludes from the operation of section 12 of the Employment Protection (Consolidation) Act 1978 employees to whom the Working Rule Agreement of the Building and Allied Trades Joint Industrial Council made between the parties described in Schedule 1 to this Order on 23rd April 1980 relates.

Copies of the Agreement are available for inspection between 10 am and noon and between 2 pm and 5 pm on any weekday (except Saturdays) at the offices of the Department of Employment, Caxton House, Tothill Street, London SW1H 9NA.

1981 No. 6

TERMS AND CONDITIONS OF EMPLOYMENT

The Guarantee Payments (Exemption) (No. 21) Order 1981

Made	*6 January 1981*
Coming into Operation	*23rd February 1981*

Whereas the Plant Hire Working Rule Agreement made between the parties described in Schedule 1 to this Order on 31st October 1978 and amended on 1st May 1980 and on 30th June 1980 is a collective agreement ('the collective agreement'):

And whereas the collective agreement makes provision whereby employees to whom that agreement relates have a right to guaranteed remuneration:

And whereas all the parties to the collective agreement made application to the Secretary of State under section 18(1) of the Employment Protection (Consolidation) Act 1978(**a**) ('the Act'):

And whereas the collective agreement complies with section 18(4) of the Act:

And whereas the Secretary of State, having regard to the provisions of the collective agreement (which so far as are material are set out in Schedule 2 to this Order), is satisfied that section 12 of the Act should not apply to those employees:

Now, therefore, the Secretary of State, in exercise of the powers conferred on him as the appropriate Minister under section 18(1) of the Act and of all other powers enabling him in that behalf, hereby makes the following Order: –

Citation and commencement

1. This Order may be cited as the Guarantee Payments (Exemption) (No. 21) Order 1981 and shall come into operation on 23rd February 1981.

Exemption

2. Section 12 of the Act shall not apply to an employee to whom the collective agreement relates.

Signed by order of the Secretary of State.

6th January 1981.

P. B. B. Mayhew.
Joint Parliamentary Under Secretary of State,
Department of Employment.

(a) 1978 c. 44

SCHEDULE 1

1. *Representing employers:*

the Contractors' Plant Association.

2. *Representing employees:*

1. the Transport and General Workers' Union (Construction and Crafts Section);
2. the General and Municipal Workers' Union:
3. the Union of Construction and Allied Trades and Technicians.

SCHEDULE 2

Material Provisions of the Plant Hire Working Rule Agreement

14.   Shift Work

14.1 'Shift Men'

Men whose normal duties are such as to require them to hold themselves available for work during mealtimes and in consequence have no regular mealtime, shall be deemed 'shift men' and shall be responsible for taking over from and handing over to their counterpart at commencement and completion of duty. They shall be paid the number of hours they are on duty on the job at ordinary rate plus one-fifth of ordinary rate per hour shift differential. If in the normal cycle of operations for the particular job they are required to be on duty between 10 p.m. Saturday and 10 p.m. Sunday, they shall during these hours be paid at the rate of time and a half plus one-fifth of ordinary rate per hour shift differential, provided that the shift differential of one-fifth of ordinary rate per hour shall be deemed to be a conditions payment and shall not be enhanced when calculating overtime payments. If work in such hours is not within the normal cycle of operations for the particular job, no shift differential shall be paid, but the rate of payment shall be double the ordinary rate.

This does not apply to men working under Rules 12, 13 or 14.2

14.2 Eight-hour Rotary Shifts

On all work which is being carried out by three eight-hour shifts in the 24 hours, men shall meet and be paid for eight hours per shift at ordinary rates plus in the case of men completing the shift, a shift differential of one-eighth of ordinary rate per hour. The normal aggregate number of shifts in the week shall be 15, which shall generally be worked between 10 p.m. on Sunday and 2 p.m. on the following Saturday. Provided that, if the shift commencing on Sunday night is worked, it shall be the first shift in the week. Provided further that, if the aggregate number of shifts in the week exceeds 15:

(*a*) the 16th and 17th shifts shall be paid at the rate of time and a half plus the shift differential of one-eighth of ordinary rate per hour provided that the shift differential of one-eighth of ordinary rate per hour shall be deemed to be a conditions payment and shall not be enhanced when calculating overtime payments, and

(*b*) the 18th and subsequent shifts in the week shall be paid at double the ordinary rate but no shift differential shall be paid.

14.3 Rule 14.2 will also apply in cases where two eight-hour shifts are worked in the 24 hours except that the normal aggregate number of shifts in the week shall be 10. Provided that, if the aggregate number of shifts in the week exceeds 10:

(*a*) the 11th and 12th shifts shall be paid at the rate of time and a half plus the shift differential of one-eighth of ordinary rate per hour, provided that the shift differential of one-eighth of ordinary rate per hour shall be deemed to be a conditions payment and shall not be enhanced when calculating overtime payments, and

(*b*) the 13th and subsequent shifts in the week shall be paid at double the ordinary rate but no shift differential shall be paid.

This does not apply to men working under Rules 12, 13 or 14.1

14.4 For the purpose of Rule 4 – Guaranteed Bonus, the first eight working hours of the first five normal day shifts, or the first five normal night shifts, as appropriate, in any payweek shall constitute normal working hours.

15. Guaranteed Minimum

15.1 Availability

An operative in the employment of an employer shall be deemed to have kept himself available for work during the whole of the normal working hours of any day if he complies with the following conditions:

(*a*) that, unless otherwise instructed by the employer, he has presented himself for work on the site or at the depot at the starting time prescribed by the employer and complies with the employer's instructions in regard to the period (during normal working hours) for which he shall remain on the site or at the depot;

(*b*) that he is willing and able to perform satisfactorily on the site, at the depot of elsewhere the work for which he was engaged or suitable alternative work; and

(*c*) that, in all circumstances, particularly weather conditions, he complies satisfactorily with the instructions of the employer as to when, during normal working hours, work is to be carried out, interrupted, or resumed.

If a man, during the normal working hours of any day, fails to keep himself available for work as aforesaid, he shall be deemed not to have kept himself available for any portion of such day except such hours as he has actually worked.

15.2 Guaranteed Minimum

(*a*) In respect of any pay week during any part of which a man has performed actual work on the job and, being in the employer's employment, has kept himself available for work (as aforesaid), the man shall be entitled to receive payment of not less than the equivalent of 40 hours at ordinary rates (hereinafter referred to as the 'guaranteed minimum'). Provided always that should a man not be available for work (as aforesaid) during the normal working hours of any day in such payweek, or should his employment be terminated during such payweek, he shall be entitled only to such proportion of the guaranteed minimum as the time he was available for work (as aforesaid) and in the employer's employment bears to 40 hours.

(*b*) If, following immediately upon a payweek in which the man has performed actual work on the job, there occurs a payweek in which the man being in the employer's employment keeps himself available for work (as afore-said) but does not perform actual work on the job, the man shall be entitled in respect of that week to payment of the guaranteed minimum. Provided always that should a man not be available for work (as aforesaid) during the normal working hours of any day of such last-named payweek, or should his employment be terminated during such payweek, he shall be entitled only to such proportion of the guaranteed minimum as the time he was available for work (as aforesaid) and in the employer's employment bears to 40 hours.

(*c*) If, during the next succeeding payweek or weeks, the man does not work on the job, he shall not be entitled to any payment whether he keeps himself available for work or not, it being his duty to register for unemployment benefit.

(*d*) If, in any payweek collective industrial action of any kind, in contravention of this Agreement, is taken by operatives employed on the site or at the depot under this Agreement, the employer shall at all times use his best endeavours to provide continuity of work for those operatives who are not involved in such action and who remain available for work. In the event that, by reason of such action, the employer cannot provide such continuity of work, the guaranteed minimum shall be deemed to be suspended until such time as normal working is restored.

(*e*) If, in any payweek a site or depot shall be closed for any day or days pursuant to Rules 9, 11(*b*), or the Holidays with Pay Agreement, or for any day or days of holiday pursuant to any general or local custom or to any custom in the employer's business, then as regards any man not required to work on such day or days, he shall be entitled in respect of that payweek only to such proportion of the guaranteed minimum as the time he was available for work (as aforesaid) on the remaining days of such payweek and in the employer's employment bears to 40 hours. Provided that the employer shall be entitled to substitute any day (whether in the said week or the week immediately preceding or following) for any other day (save a Bank or other Public Holiday) hitherto observed as a holiday pursuant to such last mentioned custom.

(*f*) For the purpose of calculating the guaranteed minimum:

(1) Any increases or decreases of pay or plus rates or any new plus rates shall if they come into operation on any day other than the first day of a payweek be deemed to come into operation only on the first day of the payweek immediately following.

(2) No part of the following earnings shall be taken into account:

  (i) Sunday earnings.

  (ii) Earnings in respect of work done outside the normal working hours.

  (iii) Bonus earnings.

  (iv) Plus rates payable in respect of conditions under which work is done.

  (v) The total amount of any increases or decreases of pay or plus rates or any new plus rates which come into operation on any day other than the first day of a payweek.

(g) No payment of guaranteed minimum in respect of time not worked shall be made under this rule in the following cases:

  (i) Tidework.

  (ii) Work paid by the shift.

  (iii) Sunday work.

  (iv) Time outside the normal working hours.

15.3 Guaranteed Bonus

Payment of Guaranteed Bonus, in addition to the appropriate guaranteed minimum, is in accordance with Rule 4.

15.4 Disputes

Disputes arising under this Rule (15) or concerning minimum payment due under Rule 14 – Shift Work or Rule 19 – Tide Work may, at the option of the Claimant, be referred to ACAS and/or an Industrial Tribunal in the event of no decision by the Conciliation Board referred to in Rule 36(3)(*d*).

19.   Tide Work

19.1 Where work under tidal conditions is carried out during part only of the normal working hours, and men are employed on other work for the remainder of the normal working hours, ordinary rates, and guaranteed bonus in accordance with the provisions of Rule 4 (with the addition of any plus rate payable in respect of the conditions under which work is done, e.g. boot money), shall be paid during the normal working hours and thereafter payment shall be in accordance with Rule 11.

19.2 Where work under tidal conditions necessitates the men turning out for each tide and they are not employed on other work, they shall be paid a minimum for each tide of 6 hours' pay at ordinary rates, provided they do not work more than eight hours in the two tides. Work over 8 hours shall be paid for proportionately. Work done on Saturday after 4 p.m. and all Sunday shall be paid at the rate of double time. Men shall be guaranteed 8 hours at ordinary rates for time worked between 4 p.m. and midnight on Saturday and 16 hours at ordinary rates for two tides worked on Sunday.

For the purpose of Rule 4 – Guaranteed Bonus, the first eight working hours of each of the first five days worked in the normal cycle of operations in a payweek shall constitute normal working hours.

32. Statement of Particulars Under Contracts of Employment Act

The Plant Hire Working Rule Agreement, including Rule 36 and Appendix shall be incorporated into the operative's Contract of Employment by reference in the Statement of Particulars under the Employment Protection (Consolidation) Act 1978.

36. Procedure for the Avoidance of Disputes

36.1 These provisions are applicable to general plant hire operatives, drivers and mechanics who are employed by the member-firms of the Contractors' Plant Association covered by this Agreement. The parties to this Agreement accept that the object of this procedure shall be to provide suitable measures for the settlement of disputes at all levels and to maintain normal working during the process. Therefore, until all the provisions of this procedure have been exhausted there shall be no stoppage of work, either of a partial or general character, including a go-slow, a work-to-rule, a strike, a lock-out, or any other kind of restriction in output or departure from normal working.

36.2 Negotiations under this procedure may be instituted by either the employer or the employee concerned.

36.3 Any questions arising at site or depot level, including those involving the application or interpretation or other matters affecting this Agreement, shall be raised in accordance with the following provisions:

(a) An employee desiring to raise a question in which he is directly concerned shall, in the first instance, do so with his immediate supervisor or foreman in his employing firm.

(b) Should settlement not be reached under clause (a) above, the matter shall be discussed with the recognised representative(s) of the firm's employees and with the representative(s) of the firm's management, in the presence of both the employee and the supervisor or foreman concerned.

(c) Failing settlement under clause (b) above, the matter shall be reported to the local official of the Union, and may be referred to a meeting with the employer at a place and occasion suitable to both sides.

(d) If the matter still remains unresolved and the intention is to pursue it further it shall be referred for immediate consideration to the National Secretary of the Transport and General Workers' Union (Construction & Crafts Section) and the Secretary of the Contractors' Plant Association who, after such consultation as they may deem necessary, shall decide whether the dispute or question can be dealt with by administrative action or requires reference to the Conciliation Board and shall act accordingly.

36.4 The Conciliation Board referred to in Rule 36.3 above shall be constituted as follows:

(a) The Chairman of the CPA Council, or his nominee and not more than two other duly authorised representatives of the Association;

(b) The National Secretary of the TGWU (Construction & Crafts Section), or his nominee and not more than two other appropriate full-time officials representing the Unions signatory to the Agreement.

36.5 In the event of failure to agree under 36.4 above the signatory parties may by joint consent invite a mutually acceptable independent party to act as arbitrator.

36.6 Failing settlement through the Conciliation Board under the provision of Rule 36.4 and 36.5 above the procedure shall be regarded as exhausted on the question concerned.

EXPLANATORY NOTE

(This Note is not part of the Order)

This Order, which comes into operation on 23rd February 1981, excludes from the operation of section 12 of the Employment Protection (Consolidation) Act 1978 employees to whom the Plant Hire Working Rule Agreement, made between the parties described in Schedule 1 to this Order on 31st October 1978 and amended on 1st May 1980 and on 30th June 1980, relates.

Copies of the Agreement are available for inspection between 10 a.m. and noon and between 2 p.m. and 5 p.m. on any weekday (except Saturdays) at the offices of the Department of Employment, Caxton House, Tothill Street, London SW1H 9NA.

Appendix C

1987 No. 1757

TERMS AND CONDITIONS OF EMPLOYMENT

**The Guarantee Payments (Exemption) (No. 23)
Order 1987**

Made	*5th October 1987*
Coming into force	*12th November 1987*

Whereas the National Agreements for the Wire and Wire Rope Industries are collective agreements which make provision whereby employees to whom the said agreements relate have a right to guaranteed remuneration;

And whereas the parties to the said collective agreements (whose descriptions are set out in Schedule 1 to this Order) all made application to the Secretary of State under section 18 of the Employment Protection (Consolidation) Act 1978(a) ('the Act');

And whereas the Secretary of State, having regard to the provisions of the agreements (which so far as are material are set out in Schedule 2 to this Order) is satisfied that section 12 of the Act should not apply to those employees;

And whereas the said agreements comply with the provisions of section 18(4) of the Act;

Now, therefore, the Secretary of State in exercise of the powers conferred on him as the appropriate Minister under section 18(1) and 18(5) of the Act and of all other powers enabling him in that behalf, hereby makes the following Order:

Citation and commencement

1. This Order may be cited as the Guarantee Payments (Exemption) (No. 23) Order 1987 and shall come into force on 12th November 1987.

Interpretation

2. The 'exempted agreements' mean the National Agreements for the Wire and Wire Rope Industries.

Exemption

3. Section 12 of the Act shall not apply to any person who is an employee to whom the exempted agreements relate.

4. The Guarantee Payments (Exemption) (No. 4) Order 1977(b) is revoked.

(a) 1978 c. 44.   (b)S.I. 1977/208.

Signed by order of the Secretary of State.

Patrick Nicholls
Parliamentary Under Secretary of State,
5th October 1987   Department of Employment

SCHEDULE 1

PARTIES TO THE COLLECTIVE AGREEMENTS

1. *Representing Employers*   the Wire and Wire Rope Employers' Association (formerly the British Steel Wire Industries Association and the Institute of Iron and Steel Wire Manufacturers).

2. *Representing Employees*   the Wire Workers Union; the General Municipal Boilermakers and Allied Trades Union; the Transport and General Workers Union.

SCHEDULE 2

MATERIAL PROVISIONS OF THE EXEMPTED AGREEMENTS

A.   GUARANTEED PAYMENT AGREEMENT

1. This Agreement supersedes the Guaranteed Payment Agreement dated 25th April 1985. Throughout this Agreement the expression 'Minimum Datal Rate' includes any supplements payable under the Minimum Datal Rate Agreement currently in force.

2. It is agreed that in the event of short-time working or temporary lay off, each employee will be paid the J.I.C. minimum datal rate for each day up to a maximum of TEN days in any period of twenty-six consecutive weeks. The amount to be paid in respect of each day will be a fifth of the J.I.C. minimum datal rate per standard working week of thirty-nine hours.

3. The guarantee shall apply only provided that during the period of the guarantee, the employee has been continuously employed by the same employer for not less than FOUR weeks, is capable of, available for, and willing to perform according to his/or her capabilities, the work associated with his/or her usual occupation, or reasonable alternative work when his/or her normal work is not available. When he/or she undertakes such alternative employment within the company, payment shall be made at the rate applicable to that alternative employment or his/or her company datal rate, whichever is the greater.

4. The guarantee shall not apply

    (a) at any plant or unit of plant

        (i) when that plant or unit is laid idle through avoidable absenteeism or failure of any employee to take reasonable action to keep the plant in operation.

        (ii) when by custom and practice, or by mutual agreement between the employer and employees, it is decided that a shift, or part shift at the commencement or resumption of holiday periods shall be an unpaid holiday.

    (b) to any individual employee who has been summarily dismissed without notice or has been suspended for disciplinary reasons.

    (c) to any employee who refuses to accept reasonable alternative employment when his/or her normal work is not available.

5. The guarantee shall be suspended automatically in the event of dislocation of work as a result of strike action or irregular action short of strike action within any company which is a party to the agreements of the J.I.C. for the wire and wire rope industries.

6. The guarantee shall be reduced in the case of a holiday recognised by agreement or custom and practice in respect of the standard working week in which the holiday takes place in the same proportion as the normal working days of shifts are reduced in that standard working week.

7. Any difference arising in relation to this agreement which cannot otherwise be resolved shall be reported to the Joint Secretaries of the Joint Industrial Council and will be dealt with under the J.I.C. procedure for settling differences and disputes or, if the claimant is not a member of a trade union party to this Agreement, it may be referred to an industrial tribunal.

8. This Agreement may be cancelled by either party giving three months' notice in writing.

B.   AGREEMENT ON PROCEDURE FOR SETTLING DIFFERENCES AND DISPUTES

14.   (i) In the event of any questions arising in relation to wages and/or working conditions which cannot be resolved by domestic procedure, the matter shall, in the first instance, be dealt with between the management of the employer and the area official(s) of the Trade Union(s) concerned.

          Failing a settlement, status quo* shall apply until the following procedure has been exhausted.

    (ii) The parties to the dispute shall define the dispute and forward their written submissions as quickly as possible to the Joint Secretaries. Any problems of definition shall be referred to the Chairman of the Joint Industrial Council. Within 14 days of notification, the Joint Secretaries will notify to the parties the date of a meeting of a Dispute Panel.

*i.e., Work shall be continued on the terms and conditions of employment in force prior to the question being raised.

(iii) The Dispute Panel will comprise two representatives appointed by each of the Employer and Trade Union Panels of the Joint Industrial Council under the Chairmanship, in a non-voting capacity, of the Chairman of the Joint Industrial Council, or in his absence the Vice-Chairman.

(iv) The decision of the Dispute Panel will be binding on both parties. In the event of a Dispute Panel being unable to reach a decision, the matter shall be referred to arbitration arranged through A.C.A.S., the decision of which shall be binding on both parties.

(v) The parties to a dispute shall pay the expenses of their respective sides of any committee to which the Dispute is referred, and shall share equally any other expenses which arise from the reference.

EXPLANATORY NOTE

(This note is not part of the Order)

This Order excludes from the operation of section 12 of the Employment Protection (Consolidation) Act 1978 employees to whom the National Agreements of the Wire and Wire Rope Industries relate. It supersedes the Guarantee Payments (Exemption) (No. 4) Order 1977 which is revoked by this Order. The present Order has been made to take account of the revised National Agreements the material provisions of which are set out in Schedule 2. These differ from the provisions in Schedule 2 to the previous Order in that the standard working week has been reduced to 39 hours and the procedure for settling disputes has been simplified. In addition paragraph 4(a)(ii) of Schedule 2 to the previous Order (dealing with short-time working) has been omitted.

Copies of the Agreements are available for inspection between 10 am and noon and 2 pm and 5 pm on any week-day (except Saturdays) at the offices of the Department of Employment, Caxton House, Tothill Street, London SW1H 9NF.

Appendix D

PART I   FEDERAL LEGISLATION

Public Law 97-248   Sept. 3, 1982

Short-time Compensation

Section 194

(a) It is the purpose of this section to assist States which provide partial unemployment benefits to individuals whose work-weeks are reduced pursuant to an employer plan under which such reductions are made in lieu of temporary layoffs.

(b) (1) The Secretary of Labor (hereinafter in this section referred to as the 'Secretary') shall develop model legislative language which may be used by States in developing and enacting short-time compensation programs, and shall provide technical assistance to States to assist in developing, enacting, and implementing such short-time compensation program.

(2) The Secretary shall conduct a study or studies for purposes of evaluating the operation, costs, effect on the State insured rate of unemployment, and other effects of State short-time compensation programs developed pursuant to this section.

(3) This section shall be a three-year experimental provision, and the provisions of this section regarding guidelines shall terminate 3 years following the date of the enactment of this Act.

(4) States are encouraged to experiment in carrying out the purpose and intent of this section. However, to assure minimum uniformity, States are encouraged to consider requiring the provisions contained in subsections (c) and (d).

(c) For purposes of this section, the term 'short-time compensation program' means a program under which:

(1) individuals whose workweeks have been reduced pursuant to a qualified employer plan by at least 10 per centum will be eligible for unemployment compensation;

(2) the amount of unemployment compensation payable to any such

individual shall be a pro rata portion of the unemployment compensation which would be payable to the individual if the individual were totally unemployed;

(3) eligible employees may be eligible for short-time compensation or regular unemployment compensation, as needed; except that no employee shall be eligible for more than the maximum entitlement during any benefit year to which he or she would have been entitled for total unemployment, and no employee shall be eligible for short-time compensation for more than twenty-six weeks in any twelve-month period; and

(4) eligible employees will not be expected to meet the availability for work or work search test requirements while collecting short-time compensation benefits, but shall be available for their normal workweek.

(d) For purposes of subsection (c), the term 'qualified employer plan' means a plan of an employer or of an employers' association which association is party to a collective bargaining agreement (hereinafter referred to as 'employers' association') under which there is a reduction in the number of hours worked by employees rather than temporary layoffs if:

(1) the employer's or employers' association's short-time compensation plan is approved by the State agency;

(2) the employer or employers' association certifies to the State agency that the aggregate reduction in work hours pursuant to such plan is in lieu of temporary layoffs which would have affected at least 10 per centum of the employees in the unit or units to which the plan would apply and which would have resulted in an equivalent reduction of work hours;

(3) during the previous four months the work force in the affected unit or units has not been reduced by temporary layoffs of more than 10 per centum;

(4) the employer continues to provide health benefits, and retirement benefits under defined benefit pension plans (as defined in section 3(35) of the Employee Retirement Income Security Act of 1974, to employees whose workweek is reduced under such plan as though their workweek had not been reduced; and

(5) in the case of employees represented by an exclusive bargaining representative, that representative has consented to the plan.

The State agency shall review at least annually any qualified employer plan put into effect to assure that it continues to meet the requirements of this subsection and of any applicable State law.

(e) Short-time compensation shall be charged in a manner consistent with the State law.

(f) For purposes of this section, the term 'State' includes the District of Columbia, the Commonwealth of Puerto Rico, and the Virgin Islands.

(g) (1) The Secretary shall conduct a study or studies of State short-time compensation programs consulting with employee and employer representatives in developing criteria and guidelines to measure the following factors:

(A) the impact of the program upon the unemployment trust fund, and a comparison with the estimated impact on the fund of layoffs which would have occurred but for the existence of the program;

(B) the extent to which the program has protected and pre-served the jobs of workers, with special emphasis on newly hired employees, minorities, and women;

(C) the extent to which layoffs occur in the unit subsequent to initiation of the program and the impact of the program upon the entitlement to unemployment compensation of the employees;

(D) where feasible, the effect of varying methods of administration;

(E) the effect of short-time compensation on employers' State unemployment tax rates, including both users and nonusers of short-time compensation, on a State-by-State basis;

(F) the effect of various State laws and practices under those laws on the retirement and health benefits of employees who are on short-time compensation programs;

(G) a comparison of costs and benefits to employees, employers, and communities from use of short-time compensation and layoffs;

(H) the cost of administration of the short-time compensation program; and

(I) such other factors as may be appropriate.

(2) Not later than October 1, 1985, the Secretary shall submit to the Congress and to the President a final report on the implementation of this section. Such report shall contain an evaluation of short-time compensation programs and shall contain such recommendations as the Secretary deems advisable, including recommendations as to necessary changes in the statistical practices of the Department of Labor.

Bibliography

Advisory Conciliation and Arbitration Service, *Redundancy Arrangements: The 1986 ACAS Survey*, (London, ACAS Occasional Paper No. 37, 1987).
——, *Labour Flexibility in Britain: The 1987 ACAS Survey*, (London, 1988).
Anon, 'Last Hired, First Fired Layoffs and Title VII', 88 *Harvard Law Review*, pp. 1544–70 (1975).
——, 'Jobs for Some of the Boys', *The Economist*, p. 45 (14 January 1978).
Appleby, G. and Ellis, E., 'Formal Investigations: The Commission for Racial Equality and the Equal Opportunities Commission as Law Enforcement Agencies', *Public Law*, pp. 236–76 (1984).
Bakke, E.W., *Insurance or Dole? The Adjustment of Unemployment Insurance to Economic and Social Facts in Great Britain*, (New Haven, Yale University Press, 1935).
Baldwin, R. and Hawkins, K., 'Discretionary Justice: Davis Reconsidered', *Public Law*, pp. 570–99 (1984).
Baldwin, R. and Horne, D., 'Expectations in a Joyless Landscape', 49 *Modern Law Review*, pp. 685–711 (1986).
Baldwin, R. and Houghton, J., 'Circular Arguments: The Status and Legitimacy of Administrative Rules', *Public Law*, pp. 239–84 (1986).
Batt, F.R., *The Law of Master and Servant*, (London, Pitman, 1929).
Beach, C.M. and Balfour, F.S., 'Estimated Payroll Tax Incidence and Aggregate Demand for Labour in the United Kingdom', 50 *Economica*, pp. 35–48 (1983).
Benjamin, D.K. and Kochin, L.A., 'Searching for an Explanation of Unemployment in Inter-War Britain', 87 *Journal of Political Economy*, pp. 441–78 (1979).
Bernstein, I., *The Lean Years: A History of the American Workers 1920–33*, (Boston, Houghton Mifflin, 1960).
Best, F. and Mattesich, J., 'Short-time Compensation Systems in California and Europe', 103 *Monthly Labor Review*, No. 7, pp. 13–22 (1980).
Beveridge, W.H., *Unemployment: A Problem of Industry*, (London, Longmans, Green and Co., 1909).
Birks, P., *An Introduction to the Law of Restitution*, (Oxford, Oxford University Press (PB, 1989).
Blau, F. and Kahn, L., 'Causes and Consequences of Layoffs', 19 *Economic Inquiry*, pp. 270–96 (1981).
Blumrosen, R.G., 'Work Sharing, STC, and Affirmative Action', in MaCoy,

R. and Morand, M.J. (eds) *Short-time Compensation: A Formula for Work Sharing*, (New York, Pergamon Press, 1984).

Blumrosen, A.W. and Blumrosen, R.G., 'The Duty to Plan for Fair Employment Revisited: Work Sharing in Hard Times', 28 *Rutgers Law Review*, pp. 1082–1106 (1975).

Booth, A., 'Extra-statutory Redundancy Payments in Britain', 25 *British Journal of Industrial Relations*, pp. 400–18 (1987).

Bourn, C.J., 'Statutory Exemptions for Collective Agreements', 8 *Industrial Law Journal*, pp. 85–99 (1979).

——, *Redundancy: Law and Practice*, (London, Butterworths, 1983).

Brewster, C. and Teague, P., *European Social Policy: Its Impact on the UK*, (London, IPM, 1989).

Briggs, S., 'Allocating Available Work in a Union Environment: Layoffs vs. Work Sharing', 38 *Labor Law Journal*, pp. 650–7 (1987).

Brown, W. and Hepple, B., 'Foreword: The Monitoring of Labour Legislation', in Fosh, P. and Littler, C. (eds) *Industrial Relations and the Law in the 1980s*, (Aldershot, Gower, 1985).

Buchan, D., 'Storm Cloud Gathers over the Social Charter', *Financial Times*, 12 June 1989.

Buck, T., 'Unemployment Benefit: The "Full Extent Normal" Rule', *Journal of Social Welfare Law*, pp. 23–6 (1987).

——, 'Part-time Workers and Unemployment Benefit', 52 *Modern Law Review*, pp. 93–104 (1988).

Bullock, A., *The Life and Times of Ernest Bevin*; Vol. II, *Minister of Labour 1940–45*, (London, Heinemann, 1967).

Burstein, P., *Discrimination, Jobs, and Politics: The Struggle for Equal Employment Opportunity in the United States since the New Deal*, (Chicago, University of Chicago Press, 1985).

Callender, C., 'Gender Inequality and Social Policy: Women and the Redundancy Payments Scheme', 14 *Journal of Social Policy*, pp. 189–213 (1985).

——, 'Women and the Redundancy Process: A Case Study', in Lee, R.R. (ed) *Redundancy, Layoffs and Plant Closures*, (London, Croom Helm, 1987).

Carty, H., 'Dismissed Employees: The Search for a More Effective Range of Remedies', 52 *Modern Law Review*, pp. 449–68 (1989).

Clark, J. and Wedderburn, Lord, 'Modern Labour Law: Problems, Functions and Policies', in Wedderburn, Lord, Lewis, R. and Clark, J. (eds) *Labour Law and Industrial Relations: Building on Kahn-Freund*, (Oxford, Clarendon Press, 1983).

Clifton, R. and Tatton-Brown, C., *The Impact of Employment Legislation on Small Firms*, (Department of Employment Research Paper No. 6, July 1979).

Collins, H., 'Capitalist Discipline and Corporatist Law', 11 *Industrial Law Journal*, Part I pp. 78–92, and Part II pp. 170–7 (1982).

——, 'Dismissal for Economic Reasons' 14 *Industrial Law Journal*, pp. 61–4 (1985).

——, 'Market Power, Bureaucratic Power, and the Contract of Employment', 15 *Industrial Law Journal*, pp. 1–14 (1986).

——, 'Labour Law as a Vocation', 105 *Law Quarterly Review*, pp. 468–84 (1989).

Colloquium Sponsored Jointly by the Centre for Socio-Legal Studies, Oxford University, and The Frances Lewis Law Center School of Law, Washington and Lee University 'Discretion in Making Legal Decisions', *Washington and Lee Law Review*, pp. 1161–1311 (1986).

Cordova, E., 'From Full-time Wage Employment to Atypical Employment: A Major Shift in the Evolution of Labour Relations', 125 *International Labour Review*, pp. 641–57 (1986).

Cornfield, D.B., 'Ethnic Inequality in Layoff Chances: The Impact of Unionisation on Layoff Procedure', in Lee, R.R., *Redundancy, Layoffs and Plant Closures*, (London, Croom Helm, 1987).

Coyle, A., *Redundant Women*, (London, The Women's Press, 1984).

——, 'An Investigation into the Long Term Impact of Redundancy and Unemployment amongst Women', *EOC Research Bulletin*, No. 8, pp. 68–84 (1983-4).

Cross, M., *Workforce Reduction: An International Survey*, (London, Croom Helm, 1985).

Curtin, D., *Irish Employment Equality Law*, (Dublin, Round Hall Press, 1989).

Daintith, T., 'Public Law and Economic Policy', *Journal of Business Law*, pp. 9–22 (1974).

——, 'Regulation by Contract: The New Prerogative', 32 *Current Legal Problems*, pp. 41–59 (1979).

Daniel, W.W., 'Great Britain' in Cross, M. (ed) *Workforce Reduction: An International Survey*, (London, Croom Helm, 1985).

Daniel, W.W. and Stilgoe, E., 'The Impact of Employment Protection Laws', *Policy Studies*, Vol. XLIV, No. 577 (London, June 1978).

D'Apice, C. and Del Boca, A., 'The Impact of Social Policies on Income Distribution and the Labour Market in Italy', 14 *Journal of Social Policy*, pp. 385–401 (1985).

Davies, P. and Freedland, M., (eds) *Kahn-Freund's Labour and the Law*, 3rd edn, (London, Stevens, 1983).

——, *Labour Law: Text and Materials*, 2nd edn, (London, Weidenfeld and Nicolson, 1984).

Davis, K.C., *Discretionary Justice: A Preliminary Inquiry*, (Baton Rouge, Louisiana State University Press, 1969).

Deacon, A., 'Systems of Interwar Unemployment Relief', in Glynn, S. and Booth, A. (eds) *The Road to Full Employment*, (London, Allen and Unwin, 1987).

Deakin, S., 'Labour Law and the Developing Employment Relationship in the UK', 10 *Cambridge Journal of Economics*, pp. 225–46 (1986).

——, 'Towards a Social Europe: Social Policy and Reform Strategies after the Single European Act', 35 *Low Pay Review*, pp. 12–17 (1988/89 Winter).

Deakin, B.M. and Pratten, C.F., *Effects of the Temporary Employment Subsidy*, (Cambridge, Cambridge University Press, 1982).

Dennis, B.D., (ed) *Industrial Relations Research Association Series, Proceedings of the 38th Annual Meeting December 28–30 1985*, (New York, 1986).

Department of Employment, *Employment Protection Bill: Consultative Document*, (London, 1974).

——, *Compensation for Short-time Working: Consultative Document*, (London, 1978).

——, 'Temporary Short-time Working Compensation Scheme', 88 *Employment Gazette*, pp. 478–81 (1980).

——, 'Special Employment Measures', 90 *Employment Gazette*, pp. 470–72 (1982).

——, *Employment: The Challenge for the Nation*, Cmnd 9474, (London, HMSO, 1985).

——, *Consultative Paper on Wages Councils* (1985).

——, *Wages Councils: 1988 Consultation Document* (1988).

——, *Releasing Enterprise* Cm 512 (1988).

——, *Employment for the 1990s* Cm 540 (1988).

——, *Removing Barriers to Employment* Cm 655 (1989).

——, 'Industrial Tribunal Statistics', 97 *Employment Gazette*, pp. 257–61 (1989).

——, *Consultation Paper on Industrial Tribunals* (1989).

Department of Trade and Industry, *Burdens on Business: Report of a Scrutiny of Administrative and Legislative Requirements*, (London, HMSO, 1985).

D'Harmant, A.F. and Brunetta, R., 'The Cassa Integrazione Guadagni', 1 *Labour*, pp. 15–56 (1987).

Dickens, L., 'Falling through the Net: Employment Change and Worker Protection', 19 *Industrial Relations Journal*, pp. 139–53 (1988).

Dickens, L., Jones, M., Weekes, B. and Hart, M., *Dismissed: A Study of Unfair Dismissal and the Industrial Tribunal System*, (Oxford, Basil Blackwell, 1985).

Disney, R., 'Unemployment Insurance in Great Britain', in Creedy, J. (ed) *The Economics of Unemployment in Britain*, (London, Butterworths, 1981).

——, 'Theorising the Welfare State: The Case of Unemployment Insurance in Britain', 11 *Journal of Social Policy*, pp. 33–57 (1982).

——, *Statutory Sick Pay: An Evaluation*, Institute for Fiscal Studies Working Paper Series No. 87/1, (London, January 1989).

Disney, R. and Gospel, H., 'The Seniority Model of Trade Union Behaviour:

A (Partial) Defence', 27 *British Journal of Industrial Relations* No. 2, pp. 179–95 (1989).

Disney, R. and Szyszczak, E.M., 'Protective Legislation and Part-time Employment in Britain', 22 *British Journal of Industrial Relations*, pp. 78–100 (1984).

——, 'Part-time Work: Reply to Catherine Hakim', 18 *Industrial Law Journal*, pp. 223–8 (1989).

Dolding, L., 'The Wages Act 1986: An Exercise in Employment Abuse', 51 *Modern Law Review*, pp. 84–97 (1987).

Drake, C. and Bercusson, B., *The Employment Acts 1974–80: With Commentary*, (London, Sweet and Maxwell, 1981).

Earnshaw, J., *Sex Discrimination and Dismissal: A Review of Recent Case Law*, (University of Manchester, Department of Management Sciences, Occasional Paper No. 8505, 1985).

Elias, P., 'Unravelling the Concept of Dismissal', 7 *Industrial Law Journal*, Part I pp. 16–29, and Part II pp. 100–12 (1978).

——, 'The Structure of the Employment Contract', 35 *Current Legal Problems*, pp. 95–116 (1982).

Elias, P., Napier, B. and Wallington, P., *Labour Law: Cases and Materials*, (London, Butterworths, 1980).

Emerson, M., 'Regulation or Deregulation of the Labour Market', 32 *European Economic Review*, pp. 775–817 (1988).

Equal Opportunities Commission, *Formal Investigation Report: British Steel Corporation*, (Manchester, 1981).

Ewing, K.D. and Grubb, A., 'The Emergence of a New Labour Injunction?', 16 *Industrial Law Journal*, pp. 145–63 (1987).

Fallon, R.H. and Weiler, P.C., 'Firefighters v. Stotts: Conflicting Models of Racial Justice', 1 *Supreme Court Review*, pp. 1–68 (1984).

Fox, A., *Beyond Contract: Work, Power and Trust Relations*, (London, Faber and Faber Ltd., 1974).

Frank, F.W., *The New Industrial Law*, (London, The Thames Bank Publishing Co. Ltd., 1950).

Fraser, D., *The Evolution of the British Welfare State: A History of Social Policy since the Industrial Revolution*, (Basingstoke, Macmillan, 1973).

Fredman, S. and Lee, S., 'Natural Justice for Employees: The Unacceptable Faith of Proceduralism', 15 *Industrial Law Journal*, pp. 15–31 (1986).

Freedland, M.R., *The Contract of Employment*, (Oxford, Clarendon Press, 1976).

——, 'The Obligation to Work and to Pay for Work', 30 *Current Legal Problems*, pp. 175–87 (1977).

——, 'Leaflet Law: The Temporary Short-time Working Compensation Scheme', 9 *Industrial Law Journal*, pp. 254–8 (1980).

——, 'Labour Law and Leaflet Law: The Youth Training Scheme of 1983', 12 *Industrial Law Journal*, pp. 187–90 (1983).

——, Book Review: *Quasi Legislation, Legal Studies*, pp. 229–34 (1988).

Fryer, R.H., 'Redundancy and Public Policy', in Martin, R. and Fryer, R.H. (eds) *Redundancy and Paternalist Capitalism: A Study in the Sociology of Work* (London, Allen and Unwin, 1973).

Fulbrook, J., *Administrative Justice and the Unemployed*, (London, Mansell, 1978).

Fyfe, T.A., *Employers and Workmen under the Munitions of War Acts 1915–17*, 3rd edn. (London and Edinburgh, William Hodge and Co., 1918).

Ganz, G., *Government and Industry: The Provision of Financial Assistance to Industry*, (Abingdon, Oxon., Professional Books, 1977).

——, *Quasi-Legislation: Recent Developments in Secondary Legislation*, (London, Sweet and Maxwell, 1987).

Gersuny, C., 'Origins of Seniority Provisions in Collective Bargaining', 37 *Labor Law Journal*, pp. 518–24 (1982).

——, 'Erosion of Seniority Rights in the US Labor Force', 12 *Labor Studies Journal*, pp. 62–75 (1987).

Gilbert, B.B., *The Evolution of National Insurance in Great Britain*, (London, Batsford, 1966).

Gilson, M.B. and Riches, E.J., 'Employers' Additional Unemployment Benefit Schemes in Great Britain', 21 *International Labour Review*, pp. 348–94 (1930).

Grais, B., *Lay-off and Short-time in Selected OECD Countries*, (Paris, OECD, 1983).

Grunfeld, C., *The Law of Redundancy*, (London, Sweet and Maxwell, 3rd edn, 1989).

Hakim, C., 'Trends in the Flexible Workforce', 95 *Employment Gazette*, pp. 549–60 (November 1987).

——, 'Employment Rights: A Comparison of Part-time and Full-time Employees', 18 *Industrial Law Journal*, pp. 69–83 (1989).

Hamermesh, D.S. and Rees, A.R., *The Economics of Work and Pay*, (New York, Harper and Row, 4th edn, 1988).

Harris, J., *Unemployment and Politics: A Study in English Social Policy 1886–1914*, (Oxford, Clarendon Press, 1972).

Hart, R.A., *Shorter Working Time: A Dilemma for Collective Bargaining*, (Paris, OECD, 1984).

——, *Working Time and Employment*, (London, Allen and Unwin, 1987).

Hepple, B., 'A Right to Work?', 10 *Industrial Law Journal*, pp. 65–83 (1981).

——, 'Individual Labour Law', in Bain, G.S., *Industrial Relations in Great Britain*, (Oxford, Basil Blackwell, 1983).

——, 'Restructuring Employment Rights', 15 *Industrial Law Journal*, pp. 69–83 (1986).

——, 'The Crisis in EEC Labour Law', 16 *Industrial Law Journal*, pp. 69–83 (1986).

——, 'Labour Law and Social Security in Great Britain', in Rood, M., *et al.*

(eds) *Fifty Years of Labour Law and Social Security*, (Deventer, Kluwer, 1986).

Hepple, B. and Byre, A., 'EEC Labour Law in the United Kingdom – A New Approach', 18 *Industrial Law Journal*, pp. 129–43 (1989).

Hepple, B., Partington, T.M. and Simpson, B., 'The Employment Protection Act and Unemployment Benefit: Protection for Whom?', 6 *Industrial Law Journal*, pp. 54–8 (1977).

Hoerr, J., Glaberson, W.G., Moskowitz, D.B., Cahan, V., Pollock, M.A. and Tasini, J., 'Beyond Unions', *Business Week*, pp. 72–7 (8 July 1985).

Hogarth, T., 'Long Distance Weekly Commuting', 8 *Policy Studies*, pp. 27–43 (1987).

Holland, J. and Chandler, A., 'Implied Mobility Clauses', 17 *Industrial Law Journal*, pp. 253–6 (1988).

Hoover, H., *The Memoirs of Herbert Hoover*; Vol. 3, *The Great Depression*, (New York, Macmillan, 1952).

Incomes Data Services, 'Guaranteed Pay in a Changing Situation: A Study of Conditions', *IDS Report 24*, pp. 16–22 (June 1967).

——, 'The Guaranteed Week – Part 1', *IDS Study No. 20*, (London, January 1972).

——, 'The Guaranteed Week – Part 2', *IDS Study No. 22*, (London, February 1972).

——, 'The Guaranteed Week – Part 3', *IDS Study No. 81*, (London, August 1974).

——, 'Lay-offs and Short-time (1): What the Law Says', *IDS Brief 56* (March 1975).

——, 'Lay-offs (2) Guaranteed Week Agreements', *IDS Brief 57*, pp. 12–17, (London, March 1975).

——, 'The Guaranteed Week', *IDS Study 128*, (London, August 1976).

——, 'Guaranteed Week and Lay-off', *IDS Study 192*, (London, April 1979).

——, 'Short-time to Save Jobs', *IDS Study 241*, (London, May 1981).

——, *Lay-offs and Short-time*, (London, IDS Handbook Series No. 19, 1981).

——, 'The Guaranteed Week', *IDS Study 235*, (London, February 1981).

——, 'Redundancy Schemes', *IDS Study 250*, (London, September 1981).

——, 'Redundancy Terms', *IDS Study 280*, (London, December 1982).

——, 'Guaranteed Week and Lay-off', *IDS Study 297*, (London, September 1983).

——, 'Redundancy Terms', *IDS Study 327*, (London, December 1984).

——, 'Redundancy Terms', *IDS Study 369*, (London, September 1986).

——, 'Sick Pay and SSP', *IDS Study 316*, (London, June 1984).

——, 'Flexible Working', *IDS Study 407*, (London, April 1988).

——, 'Redundancy Terms', *IDS Study 422*, (London, December 1988).

Industrial Relations Services, 'Guaranteed Pay Agreements', *Industrial Relations Review and Report No. 23*, pp. 3–8 (January 1972).

——, 'France: Working Time Law Reform', *European Industrial Relations Review*, 97, pp. 16–20 (February 1982).

——, 'France: Bargaining on Reduced Working Time', *European Industrial Relations Review*, 105, pp. 21–3 (October 1982).

——, 'International Unemployment Benefits in 12 Countries', *European Industrial Relations Review*, pp. 12–19 (October 1982).

——, 'International Short-time and Lay-offs', *European Industrial Relations Review* No. 111, pp. 15–19 (April 1983).

——, 'Lay-off: Part 3 Redundancy Payments', *Industrial Relations Legal Information Bulletin 236* (July 1983).

——, 'Guaranteed Week Agreements 1: Pay and Eligibility', *Industrial Relations Review and Report 324*, pp. 2–7 (24 July 1984).

——, 'Guaranteed Week Agreements 2: Suspension of Guarantees', *Industrial Relations Review and Report 235*, pp. 2–9, (London, 7 August 1984).

——, 'Changing Terms of Employment Contracts', *Industrial Relations Legal Information Bulletin 340*, pp. 2–10 (3 November 1987) and Part 2 at *IRLIB 341*, pp. 2–9 (17 November 1987).

Jackman, R. and others, *A Job Guarantee for Long-term Unemployed People*, (London, Employment Institute, 1986).

Keevash, S., 'Wages Councils: An Examination of Trade Union and Conservative Government Misconceptions about the Effect of Statutory Wage Fixing', 14 *Industrial Law Journal*, pp. 217–32 (1985).

Klare, K., 'The Public/Private Distinction in Labour Law', 130 *University of Pennsylvania Law Review*, pp. 1358–1422 (1982).

Labour Research Department, *Europe 1992: What It Means to Trade Unionists*, (London, LRD, 1989).

Leadbeater, C. and Lloyd, J., *In Search of Work*, (Harmondsworth, Penguin, 1987).

Leighton, P., 'Observing Employment Contracts', 13 *Industrial Law Journal*, pp. 86–106 (1984).

Leighton, P. and Doyle, B., *The Making and Varying of Contracts of Employment*, (London, Department of Law Research Paper, The Polytechnic of North London, 1982).

——, 'Section 11, Sick Pay and the Demise of the "Officious Bystander"', 11 *Industrial Law Journal*, pp. 185–88 (1982).

Leighton, P. and Painter, R.W., 'Vulnerable Workers in the UK Labour Market: Some Challenges for Labour Law', 9 *Employee Relations* (Special Edition) (1987).

Lewis, P., 'Twenty Years of Statutory Redundancy Payments in Great Britain', Occasional Papers in Industrial Relations, Universities of Leeds and Nottingham (1985).

Lewis, R., 'Collective Labour Law', in Bain, G.S. (ed) *Industrial Relations in Britain*, (Oxford, Basil Blackwell, 1983).

Lewis, R. and Simpson, B., *Striking a Balance? Employment Law after the 1980 Act*, (Oxford, Martin Robertson, 1981).

Lloyd-Jones, C. and Chapman, V., *Small Employment Claims in the County Court – A Guide for Employees and Their Advisors*, (London, Tower Hamlets Law Centre and the Low Pay Unit, 1988).

Low Pay Unit, *Wages Councils: The Need for Minimum Wage Protection*, (London, 1985).

McAuslan, P., 'Administrative Law, Collective Consumption and Judicial Policy', 46 *Modern Law Review*, pp. 1–20 (1983).

McCrudden, C. (ed) *Women, Employment and European Equality Legislation*, (London, Eclipse, 1988).

McMullen, J., 'The Legality of Deductions from Strikers' Wages', 51 *Modern Law Review*, pp. 234–40 (1988).

MacNeil, K., 'Social Europe: The Potential and the Pitfalls', 35 *Low Pay Review*, pp. 18–22 (1988/9 Winter).

MaCoy, R. and Morand, M.J., *Short-time Compensation: A Formula for Work-Sharing*, (New York, Pergamon Press, 1984).

Meisel, H., 'The Pioneers: STC in the Federal Republic of Germany', in MaCoy, R. and Morand, M.J. *Short-time Compensation: A Formula for Work-Sharing*, (New York, Pergamon Press, 1984).

Mesa, J.M., *Short-time Working as an Alternative to Lay-off: The Case of Canada and California*, (Geneva, International Labour Organisation, 1982).

Metcalf, D., 'Labour Market Flexibility and Jobs: A Survey of Evidence from OECD Countries with Special Reference to Great Britain and Europe', Discussion Paper No. 254, (London, Centre for Labour Economics, LSE, 1986).

——, 'Employment Subsidies and Redundancy', in Blundell, R. and Walker, I. (eds) *Unemployment, Search and Labour Supply*, (Cambridge, Cambridge University Press, 1986).

Metcalf, D., Nickell, S. and Floros, N., 'Still Searching for an Explanation of Unemployment in Inter-War Britain', 90 *Journal of Political Economy*, pp. 386–99 (1982).

Metcalf, D. and Richards, J., 'Subsidised Worksharing, Redundancies and Employment Adjustment: A Study of the Temporary Short-time Working Compensation Scheme', Working Paper No. 22 (Short-time Working Project 1983–85, Canterbury, University of Kent, September 1985).

Morris, G., 'Deductions from Pay for Industrial Action', 16 *Industrial Law Journal*, pp. 185–88 (1987).

Napier, B.W., 'Aspects of the Wage–Work Bargain', 43 *Cambridge Law Journal*, pp. 337–48 (1984).

Neal, A.C., 'Recent Developments in Unfair Dismissal – Part II', 137 *New Law Journal*, pp. 669–71 (1987).

Nemirow, M., 'Short-time Compensation: Some Policy Considerations', in

MaCoy, R. and Morand, M.J. *Short-time Compensation: A Formula For Work-Sharing*, (New York, Pergamon Press, 1984).

O'Donovan, K. and Szyszczak, E., *Equality and Sex Discrimination Law*, (Oxford, Basil Blackwell, 1988).

OECD, *Flexibility in the Labour Market: The Current Debate*, (OECD, Paris, 1986).

Ogus, A.I., 'Unemployment Benefit for Workers on Short-time', 4 *Industrial Law Journal*, pp. 12–23 (1975).

Ogus, A. and Barendt, E., *The Law of Social Security*, (London, Butterworths, 3rd edn, 1988).

Okun, A.M., *Prices and Quantities: A Microeconomic Analysis*, (Oxford, Basil Blackwell, 1981).

Partington, T.M., 'Compensation for Short-time Working: New Government Proposals', 7 *Industrial Law Journal*, pp. 187–90 (1978).

Perlman, S., *A History of Trade Unionism in the US*, (New York, Macmillan, 1922).

Poggi, G., *The Development of the Modern State: A Sociological Introduction*, (London, Hutchinson, 1978).

Pollert, A., 'The "Flexible Firm": A Model in Search of Reality (or a Policy in Search of a Practice?)', *Warwick Papers in Industrial Relations* No. 19, (University of Warwick, SIBS, December 1987).

Prosser, T., 'Towards a Critical Public Law', 9 *Journal of Law and Society*, pp. 1–19 (1982).

Reich, C., 'The New Property', 73 *Yale Law Journal*, pp. 731–87 (1964).

Reid, F. and Meltz, N.M., 'Canada's STC: A Comparison with the California Version', in MaCoy, R. and Morand, M.J. *Short-Time Compensation: A Formula for Work Sharing*, (New York, Pergamon Press, 1984).

Richards, J., 'Explaining the Distribution of the Short-time Working Compensation Scheme', Working Paper No. 4 (revised), (Short-time Working Project 1983–5, Canterbury, University of Kent, September 1984).

——, 'The Use of the Unemployment Benefit System for Short-time Working in Great Britain', Working Paper No. 8, (Short-time Working Project 1983–5, Canterbury, University of Kent, August 1984).

Richards, J. and Carruth, A., 'Short-time Working and the Unemployment Benefit System in Great Britain', 48 *Oxford Bulletin of Economics and Statistics*, pp. 41–60 (1986).

Richards, J. and Szyszczak, E., 'Guarantee Pay and Unemployment Benefit: Criticisms and Evidence', Working Paper No. 18, (Short-time Working Project 1983–5, Canterbury, University of Kent, May 1985).

Rideout, R., *Reforming the Redundancy Payments Act*, (London, Institute of Personnel Management, 1969).

Robson, W.A., 'Industrial Law', 51 *Law Quarterly Review*, pp. 195–210 (1935).

Rubenstein, M., *A Practical Guide to the Employment Protection Act 1975*, (London, Institute of Personnel Management and Industrial Relations Review and Report, 1975).

Rubin, G.R., 'The Munitions Appeal Reports 1916–20: A Neglected Episode in Modern Legal History', 3 *The Juridical Review*, pp. 221–237 (1977).

——, *War, Law and Labour: The Munitions Acts, State Regulation and the Unions 1915–21*, (Oxford, Clarendon Press, 1987).

Sachs, E., *The Law of Employment: A Summary of the Rights of Employers and Employees*, (London, Pitman, 1947).

Sales, P., 'Contract and Restitution in the Employment Relationship: No Work, No Pay', 8 *Oxford Journal of Legal Studies*, pp. 301–11 (1988).

Samuels, H., *The Law Relating to Industry*, (London, Pitman, 1931).

Sedley, S., 'Pin Money: A Test Case on Discrimination against Part-time Workers', in Wallington, P. (ed) *Civil Liberties 1984*, (Oxford, Martin Robertson, 1984).

Selznick, P., *Law, Society and Industrial Justice*, (New York, Russell Sage Foundations, 1969).

Smith, G.F., ' "Part Work No Pay?": The Obligation to Pay Wages for Part Performance of Contracts of Employment', Working paper No. 39, Labour Studies Programme, Faculty of Economics and Commerce, University of Melbourne (1988).

Spiegelman, P., 'Court-ordered Hiring Quotas after *Stotts*: A Narrative on the Role of the Moralities of the Web and the Ladder in Employment Discrimination Doctrine', 20 *Harvard Civil Rights – Civil Liberties Law Review*, pp. 339–424 (1985).

Steiber, J., 'Most US Workers Still May Be Fired under the Employment at Will Doctrine', 107 *Monthly Labor Review*, pp. 34–8 (1984).

Summers, C.W. and Love, M.C., 'Work Sharing as an Alternative to Lay-offs by Seniority: Title VII Remedies in Recession', 124 *University of Pennsylvania Law Review*, pp. 893–941 (1976).

Szyszczak, E., 'Employment Protection and Social Security', in Lewis, R. (ed) *Labour Law in Britain*, (Oxford, Basil Blackwell, 1986).

——, 'Vulnerable Workers: A European Community Solution?', 9 *Employee Relations*, pp. 41–8 (1987).

——, 'Employment Protection on the Transfer of a Business', 52 *Modern Law Review*, pp. 691–703 (1989).

Taylor, R., 'EEC Job Subsidies', *New Society*, p. 256 (2 February 1978).

Tilly, C., 'Title VII, Seniority Discrimination, and the Incumbent Negro', 80 *Harvard Law Review*, pp. 1260–83 (1967).

Tillyard, F., *The Worker and the State: Wages, Hours, Safety and Health*, (London, Routledge, 1923).

Trade Union Research Unit, *The Guaranteed Week: A Study Commissioned by the General Federation of Trade Unions*, (Ruskin College, Oxford, 1973).

Trades Union Congress, *Maximising the Benefits, Minimising the Costs*, (London, TUC, 1988).

Turnbull, P., 'The Economic Theory of Trade Union Behaviour', 26 *British Journal of Industrial Relations*, pp. 99–118 (1988).

Turner, H.A., *Trade Union Growth, Structure and Policy: A Comparative Study of the Cotton Unions*, (London, Allen and Unwin, 1962).

United States Commission on Civil Rights, *Last Hired, First Fired*, (Washington, 1977).

United States Department of Labor, *Short-time Compensation: A Handbook of Basic Source Material*, (Washington, Unemployment Insurance Services Occasional Paper 87-2, 1987).

Vranken, M., 'Deregulating the Employment Relationship: Current Trends in Europe', 7 *Comparative Labor Law*, pp. 143–65 (1986).

Wedderburn, K.W. (Lord), *The Worker and the Law*, (Harmondsworth, Penguin Books, 3rd edn, 1986).

Whiteside, N., 'Welfare Legislation and the Unions during the First World War', 23 *Historical Journal*, pp. 857–74 (1980).

Winkler, J., 'Law, State and Economy: The Industry Acts in Context', 2 *British Journal of Law and Society*, pp. 103–28 (1975).

Wise, D.C., Bernstein, A. and Cuneo, A.Z., 'Part-time Workers: Rising Numbers, Rising Discord', *Business Week*, pp. 62–3 (1 April 1985).

Women's Legal Defence Fund, *Between Equals*, Issue 1, Summer 1989.

GOVERNMENT PUBLICATIONS

Cmnd 7225 (1947) Ministry of Labour and National Service Report for the Years 1939–46.

Cmnd 9609 (1955) National Insurance Act 1946. Benefit for Very Short Spells of Unemployment or Sickness.

Cmnd 3872 (1931) Royal Commission on Unemployment Insurance, First Report.

Cmnd 5157 (1972) Unemployment Statistics: Report of an Inter-Departmental Working Party.

Cmd 6130 (1974) DHSS Annual Report 1974.

Cmnd 7049 (1978) The Government's Expenditure Plans 1978–9 to 1981–2.

Cmnd 8667 (1982) The Social Security (Claims and Payments) Amendment No. 2 Regulations 1982 (SI 1982 No. 1344) and the Social Security (Unemployment, Sickness and Invalidity Benefit) Amendment No. 2 Regulations (SI 1982 No. 1345), Report of the Social Security Advisory Committee.

Cmnd 9474 (1985) Employment: The Challenge for the Nation.
Cmnd 9571 (1985) Lifting the Burden.
Cmnd 9794 (1986) Building Businesses, Not Barriers.
Cm 512 (1988) Releasing Enterprise.
Cm 540 (1988) Employment for the 1990s.
Cm 655 (1989) Removing Barriers to Employment.
Cm 664 (1989) Employment in the Ports: The Dock Labour Scheme.

Table of Statutes

Chronological Table of Statutory Instruments

1955/143 National Insurance (Unemployment and Sickness Benefit) Amendment Regulations 1955.

1975/564 Social Security. The Social Security (Unemployment, Sickness and Invalidity Benefit) Regulation 1975.

1976/323 Social Security. The Social Security (Unemployment, Sickness and Invalidity Benefit) Amendment Regulations 1976.

1977/674 Employment Protection (Recoupment of Unemployment Benefit and Supplementary Benefit) Regulations 1977.

1976/677 Social Security. The Social Security (Unemployment, Sickness and Invalidity Benefit) Amendment (No. 2) Regulations 1976.

1978/608 Social Security. The Social Security (Unemployment, Sickness and Invalidity Benefit) Amendment (No. 2) Regulations 1978.

1980/1608 Terms and Conditions of Employment. Industrial Tribunals. The Employment Protection (Recoupment of Unemployment Benefit and Supplementary Benefit) (Amendment) Regulations 1980.

1981/1794 The Transfer of Undertakings (Employment Protection) Regulations 1981.

1982/1344 Social Security. The Social Security (Claims and Payments) Amendment (No. 2) Regulations 1982.

1982/1345 Social Security. The Social Security (Unemployment, Sickness and Invalidity Benefit) Amendment No. 2 Regulations 1982.

1983/1598 Social Security (Unemployment Sickness and Invalidity Benefit) Regulations 1983.

1984/458 Social Security. Industrial Tribunals The Social Security Adjudication (Consequential Amendment) Regulations 1984.

1985/250 Redundancy Payments (Variation of Rebates) Order 1985.

1985/782 Terms and Conditions of Employment The Unfair Dismissal (Variation of Qualifying Period) Order 1985.

1989/526 Terms and Conditions of Employment The Employment Protection (Variations of Limits) Order 1989.

1989/527 Terms and Conditions of Employment The Unfair Dismissal (Increase of Compensation Limits) Order 1989.

1989/528 Terms and Conditions of Employment The Unfair Dismissal (Increase of Limits of Basic and Special Awards) Order 1989.

Table of European Community Legislation

Council Directive 75/129/EEC – on the approximation of the laws of the member states relating to collective redundancies. OJ L 48/29, 2 February 1975.

Council Directive 77/187/EEC – on the approximation of the laws of the member states relating to the safeguarding of employees' rights in the event of transfers of undertakings, businesses or parts of businesses. OJ L 61/26, 5 March 1977.

Council Directive 76/207/EEC – on the implementation of the principle of equal treatment for men and women as regards access to employment, vocational training and promotion and working conditions. OJ L 39/40, 14 February 1976.

Table of Cases

Index